Royal Betrayal

Michael Scott

First published in 2017 by Endeavour Press Ltd.

TABLE OF CONTENTS

Nottingham 11 June – The anti-baccarat crusade was earnestly begun and will extend rapidly all over the Kingdom. The landlord of the Albert Hotel was arrested and fined £10 yesterday, and his licence revoked for keeping his house open after regulation hours and permitting the obnoxious baccarat to be played therein. Five others who were indulging in this game so much loved by the Prince of Wales were fined £1 each.
The Morning Call, San Francisco, 12 June 1891.

To make an occupation of baccarat, to want it always as a distraction, to play it against a host's known disfavour, to play it so that a guest may think it worthwhile and not very risky to cheat, - all this is not only bad form, but is a distinct encouragement to a kind of society which makes of recreation the end of life instead of its relief, and which always ends, sooner or later, by rotting down. We can quite understand all that is said in defence of the Prince of Wales, and have on occasion said much of it ourselves. There is no position in the world so trying as that of an Heir-Apparent to a Throne, with no real work to perform, barred oat from his natural occupation, which is politics, and bored to suffocation by ceremonial duties which are not even stately, as reviews are, and which, we venture to say, no man on earth ever regarded with any feeling milder than weary toleration. The position is intolerable, has ruined every Hanoverian male heir since the Act of Settlement, and has in our own time sent an heir of the little Dutch Throne to Paris, and an heir of the great Austrian Throne to suicide,—but still, noblesse oblige, and there are compensations. A King should be on the serious side, and an avowed preference for the other irritates a people which gambles itself, and bets itself, and speculates itself, but all the same retains its admiration for a healthier and higher ideal, and does not want to be encouraged from above in its own weaknesses. Old Pepys was an old sinner, and no better, but he was an Englishman, and he could not abide the scene in Whitehall, which was very much what the average English mind, most unfairly, imagines the scene at Tranby Croft to have been like.
….They [the people] wanted a sharp rebuke to be given to "the gambling lot of rich folks" who, with the heir to the Throne in the midst

of them, could find no better way of passing the time than playing every night a game for which poor folks are punished every week.

The Spectator, London, 13 June 1891

A NOTE ON MONEY

Converting the value of money in 1890 to today's is a little more complicated than merely multiplying one with a percentage increase to find the other.

The best measure of the relative value over time depends on comparing the cost or value of a Commodity, Income or Wealth.[1]

For 'casual' amounts, such as Gordon-Cumming's winnings at cards, I have used the simple *Purchasing Power Calculator; the Commodity value calculation.* This is obtained by multiplying the sum in question by the percentage increase in the *RPI* from 1890 to today.

To compare the Income or Wealth value of Gordon-Cumming's annual income, for example, in 1890, I have used the economic power value of that income or wealth.

I have used, in the text, the value as given at the time, with today's in [square brackets].

FOREWORD

This is not the first book to be written about the royal baccarat scandal of 1890. But it is the first to be written by someone who has such close empathy with the main protagonist.

Like Sir William Gordon-Cumming, Mike Scott was commissioned into the Scots Guards. Both men saw action and Scott, who comes from a distinguished military family, was decorated for gallantry in the Falklands war. That makes him well suited to understand the sense of duty and self-sacrifice that would permit a soldier to lay down his reputation for the sake of his future Sovereign.

Why else would Gordon-Cumming have promised never to play cards again? Why would he have signed an undertaking that read more like a confession? He did so, as Scott tells us, because he was ordered to by the Prince of Wales. The consequences for Gordon-Cumming were devastating. The Prince of Wales merely gave up baccarat for whist.

That's not to say the soldier was necessarily innocent. Like a good judge, Scott weighs up the evidence for both sides. It was Gordon-Cumming's misfortune that the defamation claim he hoped would clear his name was tried before Lord Coleridge, who does not emerge from Scott's account as a very good judge at all. We have every right to question the jury's verdict.

The box in which that jury sat can still be seen in the lord chief justice's court, which is largely unchanged since it was opened by the Prince's mother less than a decade before he gave evidence. Another parallel with the 1890s is that we have a Prince of Wales who has spent the most productive years of his life waiting to become King. And now, as then, we have a Queen who is concerned for the future of the monarchy.

But there, I suspect, the similarities end. We no longer regard it as more disreputable for men to deprive their friends of money by sharp practice than for them to seduce their friends' wives. We expect more of our royal family than self-indulgence and debauchery. And we expect incriminating documents to leak.

As the first non-lawyer to take responsibility for complaints against barristers, Scott is a shrewd observer of the trial that stands at the heart of this book. But it is as a military man and a historian that he sets that story in context. He has researched the case diligently in his Regimental records and the Royal Archives.

This book gives us a fascinating glimpse of those golden years before the first world war when officers could buy promotion to the higher ranks and still have time enough to hunt tigers. It takes us back to a time when honour was something worth fighting for. For the military today, it still is.

Joshua Rozenberg

INTRODUCTION

This is the story of the great baccarat scandal of 1890 which rocked the throne of England. For two nights, at a house party at Tranby Croft, the residence of one of the richest men in England, a card game is played, instigated by the Prince of Wales. During the evening of the second day, one of the players, Lieutenant Colonel Sir William Gordon-Cumming Bt, is accused of cheating. This leads, inexorably, to a sensational court case to which the Prince of Wales is summoned as a witness. Queen Victoria is beside herself with worry and wrote, 'the Monarchy almost is in danger.' The Country itself is divided; some for the plaintiff, some for the defendants and provides grist to the mill of neo-Republicans, the Non-Conformist clergy and muck-raking Press, both sides of the Atlantic.

The tale has all the ingredients of a Victorian melodrama; vast amounts of money, illegal gambling, the royal family, mistresses, cover-up, deception, blackmail and motives for half-truths and deceit. Stakes at the card game are relatively low but the emotional stakes immense; shame, ruin and social outcast are inevitable for one side or the other.

The cast reads like the pages from a novel; the scandal-prone Prince of Wales, drifting through a life of mistresses, killing thousands of pheasants, gambling with his own special counters, over-eating and drinking. His friend, Gordon-Cumming, the swashbuckling decorated soldier in the Guards, from whom no man's wife is safe. Then the immensely rich ship-owning family, the Wilsons, who see the scandal ruining their climb through the social strata. The younger men in the party, too rich, too idle, and not enough to do and with little experience, are confronted with a situation rapidly becoming out of control. The two wily courtiers, Lord Coventry and General Owen Williams, close confidants of the Prince, who will stop at nothing to keep him out of the limelight and the courts. In the shadows, the now impecunious court-jester, Sykes, and the curious 'diplomat' Count Lutzow. Waiting in the wings is the orphaned American heiress, Florence, standing by her fiancé, Sir William. Colouring in the backcloth are the best barristers in the land, gossip-mongering journalists, ladies of quality and the lower classes of innumerable servants 'below stairs' and the riff-raff of the racecourses.

The saga ranges from the wind-swept remoteness of Gordonstoun in Scotland, big game hunting in Africa and India, to life in the Guards in London and action in the Zulu Wars and Egyptian Campaign of 1882. There is a suspicion that there are undercurrents with the fledgling Secret Service of the day. What, though, did life hold for the Prince of Wales? Harshly brought up by Prince Albert, he was forbidden any access to State papers, so had really little to do except open bazaars, attend dinners and take part in ceremonial occasions. No wonder that he sought diversion with other men's wives and the *grandes horizontales* of Paris. There is the celebrated court case, presided over by the Lord Chief Justice of England, no less, who issues tickets to his friends to attend the proceedings, and has a habit of falling asleep until prodded by his attractive young wife. The verdict is greeted with disbelief and astonishment and the book finishes with an analysis of whether cheating really took place, if so why, and if not, why was Gordon-Cumming so accused?

Previous versions of the story have concentrated mainly on the court case or exaggerated it into fictional drama. This true account, however, reveals little-known aspects of the case, and, for the first time, the Gordon-Cumming family papers are brought to light, including many of Sir William's diaries and letters. His record, gathering dust in Regimental Headquarters Scots Guards and undisturbed until now, exists in its most basic form. The detail, which one would expect concerning an officer in this situation, is missing: deliberately or by accident? It is suggested, in the Royal Archives, that there are more anxieties amongst the royal family than originally thought. After Queen Victoria's death, her youngest daughter, Princess Beatrice destroyed many of her mother's letters. The Queen's journals make no mention of the case at all. Was there something there that would have been an embarrassment? There is deliberate cover-up by the courtiers, which has been unchallenged until today. Did the Wilson family play a larger part than earlier thought? Did they have something on the Prince's eldest son, Eddy? Previously undiscovered, there are far from coincidental connections between Gordon-Cumming and the Intelligence community. What was he really up to and why didn't the Prince, his close confidant and friend, bail him out? Views of present-day descendants of those involved are revealed for the first time. The mystery remains to this day and readers are encouraged to reach their own conclusions. Was Gordon-Cumming a cheat or not? Or was he the scapegoat for something which is shrouded in even more mystery?

CHAPTER 1 - The Cheat

'In consideration of the promise, made by the gentlemen whose names are subscribed, to preserve silence with reference to an accusation which has been made in regard to my conduct at baccarat on the nights of Monday and Tuesday 8th and 9th September 1890, at Tranby Croft, I will on my part solemnly undertake never to play cards again as long as I live.'[2]

The rest of the paper was blank.

With a shaking hand, Lieutenant Colonel Sir William Gordon-Cumming Bt., Scots Guards, signed his name.

*

During the evening of 8th September 1890, a card game of baccarat was played after dinner at the luxurious residence, Tranby Croft, of the shipping industrialist, Arthur Wilson. The house-party guests, headed by the Prince of Wales, were staying for the Doncaster Races. Others included the Earl and Countess of Coventry and General Owen Williams, close friends of the Prince; the Wilson son, Jack; daughter and son-in-law, Edward Lycett Green, and a young officer from Sir William's Regiment. It had been a good day at the racecourse, followed by a sumptuous dinner at the house. Cigar smoke swirled and eddied, and brandy glasses were constantly refilled. As the evening progressed though, Jack Wilson convinced himself that Gordon-Cumming was cheating. Instead of confronting him, Jack disclosed his suspicions to others.

The following evening, when the game was played again, a close watch was kept on Sir William with the result that other players also thought they had seen him cheat. Or had they really?

Later, challenged by Lord Coventry, who had not seen him cheat but had merely been told that he had, Sir William indignantly and emphatically denied it. Appalled, he demanded to see His Royal Highness.

He received little sympathy. In the light of the accusations, the Prince insisted he sign the document. Gordon-Cumming, although realising that this was tantamount to accepting guilt, signed, in order, he thought, to preserve the secret and shield the Prince of Wales from public scandal and contempt. The alternative, he was told, if he did not, was exposure and disgrace at the racecourse the following day. Blackmail and coercion were words which came uneasily to mind.

In Gordon-Cumming's absence, the following conspirators signed the highly incriminating document:

Albert Edward P
Coventry
Owen Williams
Arthur Wilson
A C E Somerset
Edward Somerset
E Lycett Green
A Stanley Wilson
Berkeley Levett
R D Sassoon

The secret was safe and His Royal Highness's reputation secure. Or was it?

CHAPTER 2 - The Guards

Gordon-Cumming's youth was spent in nineteenth century Gordonstoun in Morayshire, the ancestral home of the Gordon-Cumming family. It was a dark forbidding place; eight hundred years old, grey and full of evil. Huge trees surrounded the house, and from enormous birds' nests, rooks blackened the sky at sunset. Beyond the shelter of the trees, the countryside was bare and bleak, a patchwork of turnip and corn fields, divided by straight roads dotted with windbreaks of close-grown fir trees braced against the storms direct from Scandinavia. A grass track, without a bend, ran for a mile and a quarter from the front door to the sea. There was said to be a secret tunnel from the house to the sea shore. Smugglers' steps were cut into the cave-riddled cliffs.[3]

In the Middle Ages the house had been the seat of the de Oggeston family. Sir Robert Gordon – son of the Earl of Sutherland and Jean Gordon, a former wife of Bothwell – remodelled and added to the place, settling there to establish the family of Gordon of Gordonstoun. Sir Robert, known as the Wizard, had allegedly sold his soul to the Devil while studying magic in Spain, and then cheated fate by throwing his shadow into the Devil's arms. He was reputed to be able to cross a local loch in a coach and four after only one night's frost.

Imposing stone steps, a foot deep, led up to the front door. Within, there was a vast flagged-stoned corridor on the ground floor. The dining-room and drawing-room on the first floor, and the billiard-room on the second, ran the whole length of the building. There were paintings, trophies and curiosities, claymores and animal heads. There were spears and arrows, and leather halters with which Arabs harnessed their slaves.

There was a schoolroom next to the dungeons. Climb down a few ragged steps, grope along a passage and you would look down into an oubliette. In the water-dungeon, a mouldering coffin lay across two beams to which victims were supposed to have clung as water rose. The room faced south onto the kitchen garden but the windows were high up near the ceiling and heavily barred. Sunlight never penetrated. On each side of the fireplace were mysterious cupboards, six feet deep. Outside, there was a shed where a gallows had once stood. Under a stone staircase was supposed to lie the skeleton of a daughter of the house, seduced by her own father, and, when pregnant, murdered by him.[4]

For generations, the Gordon family spent the summer here and the winters in the rather more benign Altyre, a mere seventeen miles away. Altyre was soft and well-fed, almost smug in its beauty. Beeches and limes shadowed the mossy lawns; rhododendrons carpeted the pine woods; where there was a clearing, lilac and laburnum sprang from heather and broom. Trees spread for miles in every direction and even the moors were not bleak but looked out over the mountains of seven counties. It was not a beautiful house but comfortable, sprawling, and friendly. Cummings had occupied it since the 13th century.[5]

By the mid-18th century, the Cummings of Altyre had become stalwarts of local society, taking their feudal and civic responsibilities seriously. George Cumming, for instance, was Provost of Forres 1757-59. He took part in the battle of Falkirk having his horse shot under him, and then having the ignominy of being trampled on by retreating cavalry. At the end of the war in 1763, he retired from the army to Altyre and had much influence over the estate. He was succeeded by his grand-nephew, Alexander Penrose Cumming, who had seven sons and nine daughters. The Gordon-Cumming baronetcy was created on 27 May 1804 for the then Alexander Cumming-Gordon, formerly Member of Parliament for Inverness Burghs.

Having the most lasting effect and influence over the young William Gordon-Cumming was his uncle, the charismatic Roualeyn, the Lion Hunter; a title he had acquired after a lifetime spent pursuing big game in Africa. Born in 1820, he was the second son of the second baronet. It is not difficult to see the two of them, the intrepid sportsman and the impressionable youth, sipping their whisky through the long nights at Gordonstoun; William enthralled by the tales of his swashbuckling uncle. To the bachelor Roualeyn, William would have seemed the son he never had. Little wonder that he spent much of his later life trying emulate the deeds and lifestyle of the Lion Hunter.

After an early life spent in the wilds of Morayshire, fishing, shooting and stalking, Roualeyn grew to love nature and the challenges of rugged outdoor living. In 1839, aged 19, seeking adventure, he sailed for India to join the 4th Madras Light Cavalry. The dull British Army was resting on its post-Napoleonic laurels and so he changed his allegiance to the East India Company. On the way, he stopped off at the Cape where he acquired the taste for the sort of hunting that was to last a lifetime. India turned out to be a disappointment and, in 1843, he joined the Cape Mounted Riflemen in South Africa under command of the charismatic Colonel Somerset. Again boredom set in, and leaving the Army, he took up hunting full time with the aim of penetrating far into the interior where no white man had gone before.[6] He was to tackle most animals, using his bare hands if necessary. He once plunged into a pool containing a wounded hippopotamus, cut notches into its flank with his knife and passed leather thongs through the loops thus formed. With the aid of his men he was able to drag it to the land. Much later, he came across a large rock snake. Never having seen one before, he was unsure how to deal with it. He did not want to shoot the snake and spoil the skin so he cut a stout stick about eight foot long and seized the snake by its tail to try to pull it out from the rocks. This failed, so with the help of one of his natives, he got a thong round its middle and they both pulled. At that moment the snake relaxed its coils and, turning its head, lunged at them with its mouth bared, its fangs narrowly missing Roualeyn's leg. It slithered away fast but they hit it a number of times and when they hung it up dead, it measured fourteen feet. On the whole, they lived well – on tongues, brains, narrow-bones, kidneys, rich soup and delicious venison. Locusts could also be eaten; they were caught in the cold of the early dawn before they could fly and, mashed up, they made an excellent sort of porridge for man, horse, ox and dog. Roualeyn was not called the Lion Hunter for nothing. In one incident, he and his men were camped for the night and suddenly there was a terrifying roar of a lion bursting on them. There were shouts of 'Lion! Lion!' and one of his men rushed into the camp, shouting that a lion had got Henric (one of the European staff). Roualeyn told the natives to stop running around as, if there was a pride, the lions would have them all. Everyone was brought into the cattle kraal and they waited nervously for daybreak, with their guns cocked. The dogs identified where the lion lay, some forty yards away, as it turned out, happily eating the man it had killed. It was devastating. Henric was one of Roualeyn's best men and when they inspected the scene, all that was left were remnants of his jacket and a lower part of his leg with the shoe still on the foot. They then hunted the lion with the dogs, found it and held it at bay. Roualeyn finished it off with a shot to its shoulder and a second through its head. Trophies of his kills were carefully preserved with alum and arsenic soap, a process often carried out under extremely adverse weather conditions. He had many adventures, including meeting the legendary Dr Livingstone,[7] but after five years away from Scotland, yearned for home. So, he set sail accompanied by his little Bushman, his Cape wagon and some thirty tons of carefully packed trophies. The collection was exhibited in London in 1851 at the Great Exhibition and in 1858, he went to live at Fort Augustus. In retirement, he set up a local museum and became somewhat of a tourist attraction himself.

In 1861, aged 13, William Gordon-Cumming went to Eton. He was in Mr Samuel Evans's House and his tutors were Mr George Dupuis and Mr Edward Stone. Every boy had a tutor in addition to a house master; the younger boys had an ordinary tutor, the older ones a more specialist one. The tutor saw his pupils at least once a week, and was responsible for their academic and, to some extent, other welfare. The regime at Eton had not changed much over the years. Gordon-Cumming was made a fag to a senior boy in the Sixth Form, in his House, who rowed in the Monarch, a ten-oared Upper Boat. He was lucky in that his fagmaster was relatively benign. Boys had to be in School for lessons at 7am in the summer and 7.30am in winter for an hour then back to their rooms for breakfast. They would 'mess' with a friend; in other words brew up breakfast and tea together or cook it for their fagmaster. At 9.15 there was Chapel for half an hour, followed by School until 1030am and then again from 11.15 to 12. The two hours after midday was called 'After Twelve' which they spent with their tutor. Lunch was at 2pm followed by School 2.45 to 3.30 and 5 to 6. Then they were free until 'Lock Up' which was at 8.45. Half-holidays were on Tuesdays, Thursdays and Saturdays when afternoons were free but their names had to be answered at 'Absence' roll call at 3pm in winter and 6pm in summer to ensure boys did not stray too far before 'Lock Up'. Sundays were freer but 'Sunday Questions' had to be completed then. On top of that, boys were expected to work in their rooms.[8]

However, for reasons which are unclear, Gordon-Cumming left after two years for Wellington. There are leaving books, signed by boys when they left, but his name does not appear. They do show, however, that he was not the only boy to leave at that sort of age, with several others leaving at 15 or 16. There are no records of why Gordon-Cumming left the school, but there could have been a number of reasons. There may have been financial problems but given his background, it is unlikely. In any case Wellington would not have been that much cheaper unless his father had acquired some sort of rebate through family military service. There is no evidence that this was so. His asthma and shaky hands[9] may have prevented him taking part fully in sports. More probably, he simply did not get on with the Eton system. The school during the 1860s was not necessarily as good as it could have been, and the Public Schools Commission, established in 1861, found many areas where the school was lacking, including the curriculum, largely Classical, accommodation and teaching standards. Many changes were made during the 1870s, but perhaps these came too late for Gordon-Cumming.[10] There was a rumour that the wife of his 'crammer' in Windsor was the first woman he ever 'perforated'.[11] There is no evidence for this or, indeed, why he needed a 'crammer' at Windsor but, given his later attraction for women, losing his virginity to an older, experienced, lady would not have been surprising. Was it, though, a reason for leaving Eton? He survived a further two years at Wellington, leaving in December 1865. His career, both scholastically and overall, hardly marked him out as one of their star pupils; in his final term he was overall, placed 12th out of 19 in the 5th form.[12]

A year later, his father died and he inherited the baronetcy aged 18. Too young to take over the estates which were, in any case, being properly managed; hardly intellectually qualified for the Foreign Office or the Bar, and temperamentally unsuited to the Church, there was only one thing for it; the Army. In December 1867, he purchased a commission in the Scots Fusilier Guards.[13]

What sort of army was he joining? In December 1868, Edward Cardwell was appointed Secretary of State for War. The series of reforms that he instituted started the changes from the army that had fought Napoleon, and had recently failed in the Crimea War, to something more modern.[14] The British Army was in a unique position because unlike its European rivals it had no common land borders to protect. The power of the Royal Navy meant that Britain could afford to have a small army manned by volunteers. The first line of defence, however, was always going to be the Royal Navy, which itself cost a great deal to maintain.

Then there was the question of the status of the Army. Apart from the expense, a large standing army was anathema to the British psyche. It smacked of dictatorship and memories of Cromwell were still embedded in the minds of Englishmen. They preferred the militia or citizen army. There were also wider social aspects. A soldier's life was a hard one. They were subject to brutal and humiliating punishment, often for quite minor offences even by Victorian standards, and living conditions were poor, as was pay and life expectancy. There was also a very real chance of death, or perhaps worse being crippled and confined, more often than not, to life as a beggar. All this resulted in the army only being able to recruit from the lowest section of society, and joining the army for many was a way out of an even more desperate life in the slums of industrial cities or back-breaking work in the field. Nevertheless, for many it became the family they never had. They were among their friends and fought well together. Men did not close the gates at Hougoumont or rally to the Colours at Inkerman because they were afraid of discipline; it was that discipline that kept them together. However, some were luckier than others. Nowadays one would say this man had won the lottery. The following article appeared in the Household Brigade Magazine of 1878:[15]

'A private[16] in the Scots Fusilier Guards, named Melville, has come into possession of a fortune amounting, it is said, to the sum of 1,400,000*l*[17] [£118 million]. The property was amassed by a relative in India, and has been in Chancery since 1813. The presumed heir to it was Melville's father, who is still resident in Scotland; but he did not think it worthwhile to spend money in the prosecution of his claim, and he assigned his right to his only son. Melville is a single man, twenty-six years of age, and before his enlistment he was employed in the whaling trade. In the Scots Fusilier Guards he was servant to Lord Charles Ker. By Lord Charles's advice, and with his Lordship's assistance, Melville employed a respectable solicitor to investigate the claim; and as it involved a journey to India, the terms agreed upon were a payment of 10 per cent upon the amount realised.

The result is that Melville's claim was substantiated, and that he is now the possessor of property to the amount above mentioned. He has purchased his discharge, as well as that of several of his most intimate friends in the regiment - a regiment which is unsurpassed in the British army for the steadiness of its men. We understand that he is now in Scotland, and intends going abroad to reside some time.'

Whilst the public enjoyed the spectacle of the army on parade and took pride in its exploits in the ever-expanding Empire, what it did not want was to see soldiers in its towns or cities or have to pay any more in taxes to support them. Kipling's *Tommy*, published in 1892, hits the very point. As a consequence the only time that reform of the army was taken seriously was when the Country was under threat. With the Prussian army crushing all before it, the case for reform grew. As invasion scares (which came and went throughout the Victorian period) arose, so did the cry for action to reform the army, but governments realised, as they do today, that if they were perceived to be doing something, normally by establishing a commission or inquiry, the heat would, hopefully, evaporate.

Between 1815 and 1914 Britain only once fought a European power; during the Crimean War of 1854-5. This did not, however, mean peace. There was hardly a year in which there was not some sort of action and soldiers being killed. From 1863 to 1872 there was the 3rd Maori War; in 1870 the Red River expedition in Canada: the Ashanti War in West Africa in 1873 and the Perak campaign in Malaya in 1875. Then followed the first Boer War of 1880, Burma operations in 1885 and the North West Frontier, Tirah, Samana and the Punjab Frontier of the late 1890s.[18]

It can be argued that the British Army became extremely efficient at fighting such wars. The record of the British in colonial campaigns was superior to that of any other European nation. With its ability to 'project power' the Royal Navy clearly gave it a great advantage. As a result the army became accustomed to, and skilled at what would now be called expeditionary warfare. Forces were organised and deployed without too much trouble. The practice of drawing men from other regiments was still common for forces going overseas, as they needed to bring their battalions up to strength, but this had more to do with the peculiarities and strength of the regimental system, particularly after the Cardwell Reforms, than anything else. Such forces were cobbled together for particular expeditions and often, especially after an early setback, troops were sent from other parts of the Empire to bolster them up. In some ways this showed the strength of the British system. Wherever in the world an incident occurred, there were always British, Colonial or Royal Naval forces available to provide support. The obvious example of this is India from where troops, mostly British but occasionally Indian, were sent to support operations in Africa and the Mediterranean.[19]

But all this was well above the head of a newly joined subaltern and, indeed, most of which was in the far distant future for the young Gordon-Cumming. As he had bought his commission, there was no requirement for him to attend Sandhurst[20] or, indeed, carry out any training at all prior to joining his Regiment. He had to learn his soldiering as he went along, mainly from his platoon sergeant. For a 20 year old it must have been daunting. Still serving were officers like Colonel Stephenson, who had served in the Crimea, including the battles of Alma, Balaklava, Inkerman and the siege of Sebastopol. He had the medal with four clasps, Knight of the Legion of Honour, 4th Class of the Medjidie and the Turkish Medal. He was on the expeditionary force to China 1857-1860, including being present at the capture of Canton, the storming and capture of the Taku Forts and subsequent advance on Pekin. Lieutenant Colonel Gipps was bayoneted in the hand at the Alma and shot through the neck at Inkerman. Lieutenant The Hon W Coke (later Earl of Leicester) was wounded in the trenches before Sebastopol and Mentioned in Despatches as was Lieutenant Colonel Baring, who was wounded at Inkerman and by grape-shot at Sebastopol. Lieutenant Colonel The Hon H Annesley was severely wounded in the right arm in the Kaffir War of 1851.[21]

However, he was with a group of young officers commissioned a couple of years before him; Elwes, Buller, Bridgeman, and those just the year before, Home Drummond-Moray, Palk, Villiers, Montgomery and Scarlett. His own vintage included Viscount Melgund and Scott.[22] Some of these names exist in the Regiment today. Particular conventions had to be learnt; only salute the Commanding Officer the first time you met him in the day and always call him, 'Sir', never 'Colonel.' All other officers, including the most senior major were called by Christian name except when on parade. Never abbreviate or use initials, so the CQMS (the administrative non-commissioned officer in a Company) was called the Company Quartermaster Sergeant – somewhat of a mouthful when said quickly. Hats and belts could be worn in the Officers' Mess, even at meals. This stemmed from the practice of wearing one's hat in the coffee houses and only removed when in peoples' private houses. Always stand up in the Officers' Mess when the Commanding Officer came in and never buy another officer a drink. Discipline was just as heavily imposed for officers as it was for soldiers and the terrifying ordeal of having to attend Adjutant's Orders for the least infringement was something to be avoided at all costs. Social life in London was, however, most enjoyable for young officers. There were always balls, dinners and house parties to attend, hosted by ladies anxious to marry off their debutante daughters, after having them 'presented' at Court. *The Journal of the Household Brigade* covered Athletic Sports, Aquatics (rowing not swimming), Cricket, Pigeon Shooting, Yachting, Polo (at Hurlingham and Windsor), Theatricals, Balls and Concerts, Moors, Manors and Forests (stalking and grouse shooting), the Coaching Club, the Turf and the Chase. Almost as an afterthought were Aldershot Manoeuvres where battalions were exercised under the critical eyes of the Major General and the Duke of Cambridge.

Gordon-Cumming joined the 1st Battalion Scots Fusilier Guards at Chelsea Barracks. The main commitment was to provide Guards for Public Duties; Buckingham Palace, St, James's Palace, the Tower Guard, Bank of England Picquet and Tylt Yard (present day Horse Guards, Whitehall) were the standard ones. For a young officer it was a matter of routine rather than hard work. There were administrative tasks within his Company like 'shirt smelling', 'blanket shaking', and kit and foot inspections. They would have to attend Company Commander's Orders, when soldiers were marched in for small offences, and expected to speak for their men. Occasionally, they would be taken for a member of a Court Martial or, more terrifyingly, be chosen to represent a soldier before the Court. There was plenty of drill on the Square in the mornings under the watchful eye of the Adjutant and Regimental Sergeant Major. Standards had to be impeccable. There was very little training for operations bar some 'musketry' on the ranges at Pirbright and the occasional Commanding Officer's field day, in a training area not far from London. In the summer, the Battalion went to Aldershot to train for a couple of weeks.

The Battalion was busiest from March to mid-July when Public Duties were at their height, including the Queen's Birthday Parade. For an officer on guard this entailed parading at Wellington or Chelsea Barracks at 10.30am, marching to Buckingham Palace where the Guard was changed and detachments marched off to their posts. From then on there was not a great deal for the officer to do; inspect a few sentries and reliefs, ensure the men's food was adequate, then adjourn to the Guards Club in Charles Street, Mayfair, between 4 and 7pm, leaving one officer in charge at the Officers' Mess at St. James's Palace. The head waiter at the Guards Club was a Frenchman, Paul Leroy, who had fought in the Franco-Prussian War. He was a mine of saucy gossip and racing tips. There was also a barber there, who made his own hair oil. Once a titled officer said, 'Bamford,[23] your hair lotion smells like the inside of a tart's bedroom.' The response was immediate, 'I'll have to take your word for that, milord.' Then dinner back at St. James's. There were five Foot Guards officers, often joined by the two Household Cavalry officers from their guard at Horseguards. Very occasionally, senior officers such as Gold Stick, Silver Stick or the Field Officer in Brigade Waiting might come to dinner. A Piper would play round the table afterwards. Dinner for those on Guard was, of course, paid for by the State but guests were privately funded. Pol Roger or Dagonet champagne was usually drunk. Then after dinner cards would be played – whist, nap, poker or baccarat. Stakes could be high. It was not unusual for £25 [£2000] to rest on the turn of a card. People had been known to win or lose £200 [£16,000] a night. However, the Captain of the Guard ensured that his young officers did not play for more than they could afford; the high players were usually civilian guests. In Gordon-Cumming's time, the Commanding Officer laid down a limit on stakes and decreed only whist and nap were allowed. Guests had to leave by 11pm and the officers returned to their Guards by midnight. The Captain then went on 'Grand Rounds', with a drummer in front with lantern, to inspect the sentries. The Lieutenant went round at 1am and the Ensign at 3am.[24]

After the Cardwell Reforms, regiments assumed much more of an identity rather than being merely, say, the 29th of Foot. 'County' regiments were born and with their identities came traditions and regimental ties amongst other specific accoutrements. The Guards, including the Household Cavalry, adopted the Royal racing colours for their tie; alternate dark blue and red. It is now almost as well known as the Old Etonian, MCC and Garrick tie. One convention was that officers were not allowed to wear it in London except for Regimental occasions such as Memorials or the Birthday Parade. It was always said that this 'rule' emanated from the Prince of Wales who did not like his Guards officers to be seen coming out of houses of ill-repute wearing the tie and therefore readily identifiable.

A Commanding Officer and his Second-in-Command would expect six month's leave a year, sometimes eight, although, obviously, not at the same time. As there had been little action since the Crimea, some officers used up their leave entitlement by volunteering for service in Ashanti, Zululand or the Indian Frontier, others took their leave fox hunting or big-game hunting. For the Subalterns, leave was much less. Nevertheless, Gordon-Cumming, from May 1871 a Lieutenant and Captain, did manage some shooting in the Sudan and India between 1874 and 1877.[25] It was not, however, the comfortable life of a modern tourist. In these remote and inhospitable regions there was constant danger from, obviously, wild animals but also from weather conditions and local banditry. Disease from filthy water, dysentery, malaria, yellow and enteric fever was ever present. Gordon-Cumming kept meticulous diaries, listing, mainly, his game results rather than, sadly, his thoughts and views. The following is an extract from an account, based on his 1876-77 diaries, of a shooting expedition to India.[26]

'Landing at Bombay on 10 November 1876, I left for Travancore the following day, and, after a week's tiring journey by rail, bullock-cart and canal, arrived at the Resident's bungalow, Peermade. I shot in the Cardamon Hills area with the President of Travancore for nearly a month. There was plenty of ibex, bison, and sambhur,[27] and one or two sightings of elephant. It was not a good time of year, though, for shooting; the height of the grass and density of the jungle make this country the most difficult to hunt in I have ever encountered. I then left for Delhi, via Trichinopoly, and Madras, and languished in the excessively dull town of Bombay for five days, awaiting the arrival of my main luggage. The hunting clothes I had at Travancore were hardly up to standard for such an important event as the Proclamation of the Queen as Empress of India![28]

At Delhi I met many old friends, some of whom had served in the Brigade of Guards, and spent a pleasant week there, as guest of the Governor of Madras. I reached Calcutta on the 19th of January, spending a few days en route at Lucknow, where I shot some black buck. I found, on my arrival at Calcutta, letters informing me that a shoot I had arranged on the Godavery had fallen through, partly owing to the bad weather, and partly to the guns I was to have joined, being stricken with fever. I consequently had to stay in Calcutta rather longer than I intended, getting a few days' pig-sticking and buffalo shooting on the Brahmaputra River.

Later, in Kotra, a tiger swam the river, and a second went back through the beaters. We went down to the nullah,[29] where we guessed it was lying low, and, as we approached, it bolted up the far bank, affording only a snap shot. On the next beat, a tiger emerged from a nullah opposite my stand, and went back towards the beaters. I fired with the Express,[30] causing it to change course, and, then hit it with the second barrel. I quickly mounted an elephant, and, almost immediately, came upon a tiger, which I reckoned was the one I had just shot at. I fired and rolled it into a nullah. Dismounting from the elephant (against the wishes of old Hirsa Singh, the head shikari,[31] who was behind me), I tried to flush it with firecrackers and stones. While I was doing this, G.[32] fired two shots from a tree close by, killing a tiger in the same ravine. We went down to look at it, when a cry was raised that a second tiger was lying dead nearby. This was the one I had hit with the Express; the one shot by G. was the tiger I had fired at from the elephant.

Hirsa Singh, the old shikari, had been in the Central India Horse for many years. He actually held rank of sergeant, but had for many years refused to do any regimental duty, alleging that it interfered with his calling as a shikari. Somehow, he got away with it. He had been present at the death of some five hundred tigers, and was about as cool and courageous a man as could be found in India. Someone once presented him with a muzzle-loading rifle, of which he was very proud. Surprisingly, he rather neglected it, and it was never certain whether it was loaded or not. He attempted on one occasion to fire it at a tiger which had charged the line of beaters, putting everyone but himself to flight, but it failed to go off. He subsequently explained that he had lately lent it for a month to a friend who must have fired it without letting him know.

We had some very good sport over the next few days, marred by the theft of L.'s kit overnight in addition to some of G.'s clothes. Luckily, mine were untouched. We shot bear and panther, and any amount of blackbuck. At Ramnugger on May 21st a bear, closely followed by a fine tiger, came towards my post. I hit the tiger with a shot from the Express under the eye, turning it to C., who killed it. I also wounded a large pig. Three more bears were seen but were not shot at. On the third beat, L. wounded a bear, which came and lay up near me. I followed and finished it off. On the last beat, I dropped a tigress with a ball in the head.

The following day we arrived at Narghur, where we were joined by Man Singh, the local Rajah, who, on the outbreak of the Mutiny, had started a little operation on his own account, without declaring for either side. He pointed out with some pride the marks of shot from his guns on the walls of the castle. These peccadilloes were forgiven when he delivered up to justice the famous rebel Tatya Tope.[33] On the third beat, G. shot a bear and C. a panther, and the Rajah wounded a bear from an elephant, which we followed up and killed. At Futtegurh, three bears passed a little above G., who fired at the hindmost. At this, they all turned back and charged him. G. ducked and they missed him, tumbling over the rocks into the nullah, where he shot one of them. Two more bears were seen, one of which was shot by C.'s orderly.

On May 26[th,] I returned to Gunah, then left that night for Indore, reaching Bombay on the 3rd of June, after a very hot and tedious march. Duty calls and I left for England and more adventures soon afterwards.'

Indeed, there were adventures but not until 1879 and then, perhaps, not quite what he bargained for.

CHAPTER 3 – Zulus

In the early hours of 1 March 1879, as the mists swirled round the Port of London, the Clyde, a British Cargo Steamer of 2,256 tons, slipped her moorings from T Pier, Royal Arsenal, Woolwich, bound for Durban, South Africa.[34] Under command of Captain A H Luckhurst, she was a 'ship taken up from trade' for service with the Army.[35] Following the disaster at Isandlwana in Zululand on 22 January and then the heroic defence of Rorke's Drift, an urgent demand had gone out to the Army for volunteers to reconstitute the 1st Battalion 24th of Foot (later The South Wales Borderers). The volunteers were guaranteed transfer to the 24th or return to their parent regiment at the conclusion of the Zulu campaign. In the ship were 549[36] such volunteers, under command of Colonel Henry Davies, Grenadier Guards. Among the officers was Captain Sir William Gordon-Cumming Bt., Scots Guards. He was not, though, the only representative of the Brigade of Guards. There were three officers from the Grenadiers, one from the Coldstream and another from the Scots Guards. There were also a Colour Sergeant and six Sergeants.

In addition to crew and the reinforcements, she carried remount horses, four Gatling guns37 with 36,000 machine gun rounds, and one and a half million rounds of Martini-Henry rifle ammunition. Amongst a large quantity of other stores were 200 tons of gunpowder, tentage, bedding, sword blades, and 12,000 lbs of biscuit, 250 gallons of rum, 10,000 lbs of sugar and 3,000 lbs of salt beef, together with thousands of spades, shovels, and pickaxes.[38]

The voyage was uncomfortable. Conditions were cramped; men slept in hammocks. Fitness training was difficult and while a certain amount of shooting practice was able to take place at targets floating in the sea, life was very boring.

Then, at 4.35am on 3 April the lights went out and there was an enormous crashing and grating sound and the ship came to a shuddering halt. Men were thrown from their hammocks, baggage was flung across the decks, and tables and lockers overturned. The ship had gone aground, hitting a submerged reef. Officers were immediately called to emergency stations and, as soon as it was light, an island could be seen about two or three miles away on the starboard beam. It was Dyer Island, about 80 miles south-east of Cape Town.[39] The ship was clearly locked fast fore and aft. Assembly was sounded and the men fell in by Companies in good order. There was no panic. Sentries were posted over the lifeboats and the spirit room.

By 5.25am two lifeboats were ready. Breakfast was then prepared for troops. The preserved meat containers, tea, and biscuit were brought onto the upper deck and water transferred into carriers. The remaining Companies made ready.

At 6.20am the sick, under Surgeon-Major Ward, and as many men of D Company as the boats would hold, having had breakfast, and filled their water-bottles with tea or water, and biscuits in their haversacks, left for the shore under Captain Brander, 24th Regiment, and Lieutenant Carey, 98th Regiment.[40] Each boat took preserved meat and water with them.

When they landed, appearing from the interior, came an ox-drawn wagon, driven by a well-built Boer, dressed in homespun clothing and a large slouch hat. This turned out to be the local farmer, Albert Van der Byl. He was remarkably helpful and advised on safer parts of the beach to disembark and one of his men, who knew the waters well, rowed out to the ship. By now there was two or three feet of water in the holds and by 7.30am it had risen to eight foot.

The first wave of boats returned and started ferrying men between the ship and shore until about 11am when all the troops had landed except 4 officers and 84 men, who were left on board as a working party. The chief officer, Mr. Abbott, then left in the smallest boat for Simon's Bay, about 70 miles away to report to the senior naval officer, leaving five boats behind. The working party began to make a raft and a non-commissioned-officer and five men were dispatched to Dyer Island to find a larger boat. Earlier, Albert Van der Byl had marked the safest place to land with flags. He also offered to supply the troops with fresh meat. He had sent a telegram to Simon's Bay, via Caledon, about 45 miles away.

The rum and porter in forward and aft holds was destroyed, and hatches over the wine nailed down. The raft was now ready, and Van der Byl's large Dutch boat came alongside. Skippered by a local, Francis

Anthony, this was extremely useful for both disembarking and embarking on the following day.

A memo was received on board from Lieutenant Carey, now ashore, reporting that he had found a good camp site with fresh water and plenty of wood about two miles from the landing-place.

The raft, loaded with preserved meat and biscuit, towed by a boat, made for the shore. It was joined by another, halfway. Unfortunately, before it could get there, the ship was sinking so fast that the boats had to cast it off and come to the assistance of those still on board, consequently nearly all the biscuit was lost. The working party had tried to save some of the officers' baggage and the horses. Two of the latter were thrown overboard and safely made it to the shore.

At 12.15pm, the tide having risen, there was about 12 foot of water in the hold and the ship slowly slipped into deeper water. As the ship was now sinking fast in about 40 foot of water, as many men as possible were dispatched in the boats that were alongside. Colonel Davies remained on board with Captain Cotton and 27 non-commissioned-officers and men, besides some of the crew. At 12.45pm Captain Luckhurst let go the anchor. Sheep-pens, hencoops, hatches, and ladders were thrown overboard, and a small raft was constructed by Captain Cotton and the soldiers.

As Captain Luckhurst shouted, 'The ship might sink at any moment,' the raft, with four men, was sent off and lifejackets distributed to the rest. Everyone was ordered into the rigging. The situation was now critical; the ship was sinking fast, and none of the boats were near at hand. The officers in charge of the boats could not have realised the danger, the circumstances had altered so quickly since they left the ship. Despite the imminent danger the men remained as calm as if on parade.

Three boats had left with the horses. Those still on board the sinking ship shouted, fired pistols, and waved to the men in the boats, who, after a short time became aware of the danger and rowed back fast as possible. At 1.30pm, having seen the last soldier into the boats, Captain Cotton and Colonel Davies left the ship.

With a full boat, Colonel Davies was rowed to the shore. Captain Cotton's boat, with very few men in it, remained alongside. They returned on board and threw the other horses overboard, which were safely towed ashore. With the assistance of Lieutenant Colville,

Grenadier Guards, they saved two more boat loads of baggage. Colonel Davies then walked to the camp site where he found that Captain Brander and Lieutenant Carey had constructed kitchens, and were preparing shelters for the men. They had chosen an admirable spot; plenty of wood and water, and a certain amount of brushwood and grass, which kept the dust down. The bivouac was well sheltered. When Colonel Davies returned to the landing-place, he found the other two horses and 2400 rounds of Martini-Henry ammunition just being landed. The boats went back to the ship, but when they got there Captain Luckhurst told Lieutenant Colville, who was in charge, that it was not safe to go on board.

Every man was fed before 3pm either on fresh beef or preserved meat, biscuit and tea. At 5.45pm, the boats were hauled up above high-water mark, and the men sent to the camp site. Colonel Davies waited for Captain Luckhurst, who landed at dusk. He said he expected the ship to go down immediately. By 8.30pm all the men had eaten supper and everyone was under cover for the night, rifles and valises having been stowed in the shelters. It was very cold and, of course, many of the men were soaked through. That evening, a bullock waggon, lent by Van der Byl, arrived and brought most of the baggage from the landing site.

At daylight next day, Friday 4 April, it was apparent that the ship had sunk during the night, with the sea about half-way up the lower masts. Soon afterwards, Her Majesty's Steamship *Tamar* came into sight and by 10am the *Tamar's* boats came ashore. By 8pm that evening every man and all baggage and stores which had been saved (except the preserved meat and tea left on shore with Captain Luckhurst, who had to remain) were safely embarked on board the *Tamar*, not only without any loss of life, but also with no injury. After the men had boarded the *Tamar*, they were taken to Simon's Bay, where they remained until 7 April when the *Tamar* sailed to Natal.

Had the weather not been so favourable, it might have been a very different story. As it was, some 450 men were landed over five hours, some three miles from the ship, through rough surf. It would not have escaped anyone's memory that when the *Birkenhead* was lost, not far away, many from the ship were attacked by sharks.[41]

Colonel Davies, rightly, praised his Adjutant, Captain the Hon. R. Cotton, Scots Guards, and wrote how much he owed Lieutenant the Hon.

C. Colville, Grenadier Guards, for the admirable way in which he took charge of the boats, and to Captain Brander, 24th Regiment, and Lieutenant Carey, 98th Regiment, for the great judgment they showed in selecting a landing-place and camp site, and the rapid construction of shelter. Formally, written in an official report, this was designated "Mentioned in Despatches".[42] He also singled out Mr Albert Van der Byl for the enormous help had given and hoped that he would receive some formal recognition for his services. (Sadly, there is no evidence that he did).

Although Gordon-Cumming was not mentioned in the formal report, there was no doubt that he had played, together with the other officers, a significant part in the rescue operation. More than most, his upbringing in the unforgiving Scottish environment and the harsh surroundings of rivers and mountains, would have inured him against the hardships of field soldiering. In the hands of his father's ghillies and stalkers, he would have learnt fieldcraft, survival techniques and the self-confidence that would be so important in his later life.

After recovering in Simon's Bay from the shipwreck ordeal, Gordon-Cumming and his companions were taken to Natal in the *Tamar* and disembarked at Durban on 11 April 1879. Still hoping to be attached to the 24th of Foot, he set out for where the action was, in the company of Lieutenants Carey and Malet on 16 April.[43] It would not have been easy for them arriving in a Regiment whose B Company of the 2nd Battalion, had been awarded eleven VCs. At least they could say they had survived a shipwreck.

Arriving at Howick a week later they met up with Chelmsford's Staff. Morale was at a low ebb. By April, General Lord Chelmsford, Commander-in-Chief South Africa, was broken and dispirited. He had suffered the indignity of defeat at Isandlwana at the hands of the Zulus and very nearly lost Rorke's Drift. On top of that, he learned that he was to be replaced by General Sir Garnet Wolseley. Chelmsford had served with distinction in the Crimea, Abyssinia and the Indian Mutiny and, having dealt with the Xhosa in South Africa the year before, hopelessly underestimated the Zulus. British tactics had developed little from those of the Crimea and serried ranks in line were no match for the undulating flow and outflanking Impis of the Zulu. The enemy were not going to take up defensive positions convenient for the British to attack them; the only solution was massive force to obliterate their kraals and homesteads, lay waste to their livelihood of cattle farming and force a truce. The British government could not contemplate a further disaster and therefore sent reinforcements to South Africa in significant numbers; Chelmsford received all he asked for, and more. He was determined to rescue at least some of his reputation by defeating the Zulus before Wolseley could arrive and take over.

Gordon-Cumming, in the meantime, travelled via Colenso, crossed the Tugela River and arrived at Ladysmith on 29 April where he found his old friend, Needham. Pushing on, they toured Isandlwana and Rorke's Drift on 7 and 8 May. On 9 May he returned to Dunbar, where he knew two companies of the 24th had arrived, clearly hoping to be given a command. However, to his great disappointment, although flattering, he received a letter requiring him to report to General Newdigate's newly formed 2nd Division where he was to be Aide-de-Camp to the General.

On 1 June, Lieutenant Carey, Gordon-Cumming's old friend from the days with the *Clyde* and the shipwreck, arrived at the Headquarters with the staggering news of the killing of the Prince Imperial by the Zulus. The Army went into shock.

Napoleon Eugene Louis Jean Joseph, the Prince Imperial of France, was born in Paris on 16 March 1856. He was the son of Napoleon III, Emperor of France, the third son of Louis Bonaparte, King of Holland in the time of his brother, the great Emperor. When he was fourteen, the Franco-Prussian war broke out and, on 19 July 1870, dressed in the uniform of a *sous-lieutenant*, he rode out with his father who was to take personal command of the French forces. On 2 August, he had his first experience of battle at the skirmish of Saarbruchen. The war, however, was short-lived and Napoleon surrendered to the Prussians on 2 September. The Emperor was taken prisoner-of-war and Empress Eugenie and Louis sought sanctuary in England. Napoleon was soon released by the Prussians and joined his wife and son at Chislehurst in Kent where they were befriended by Queen Victoria. This is not surprising given the great success of the royal visit to Paris in 1855 when all vestiges of Francophobia, effectively, dissolved. Added to this were Victoria's very firm views on the sanctity of the European monarchies whose crowned, or nearly crowned, heads were, in many cases, her relations. In 1872, to his great delight, Louis became an officer cadet at the Royal Military Academy, Woolwich. Woolwich then trained officers for the Royal Artillery and Royal Engineers, while Sandhurst trained the cavalry and infantry. The first Emperor himself had started life in the artillery, so what could be more appropriate for his great-nephew? With no actual commission in the British Army, despite his education at Woolwich, he could not command troops nor fill a post on the Staff. The Establishment had made a serious problem for itself; what was he actually going to do? The Anglo-Zulu War contained the required spice of danger with, for him, no international complications. Perhaps some nice little sinecure could be arranged, tucked away in Chelmsford's Headquarters, well out of harm's way? With the tacit approval of Queen Victoria, the Duke of Cambridge, the Commander-in-Chief, overcame Disraeli's refusal to allow the Prince to go, with the understanding that the boy was to be there in a private capacity with no official standing. The Duke wrote to Sir Bartle Freer, the High Commissioner in South Africa:-

"I am anxious to make you acquainted with the Prince Imperial, who is about to proceed to Natal by tomorrow's packet to see as much as he can of the coming campaign in Zululand in the capacity of a spectator. He was anxious to serve in our army having been a cadet at Woolwich, but the government did not think that this could be sanctioned; but no objection is made to his going out on his own account, and I am permitted to introduce him to you and to Lord Chelmsford in the hope, and with my personal request, that you will give him every help in your power to enable him to see what he can. I have written to Chelmsford in the same effect. He is a charming young man, full of spirit and energy, speaking English admirably, and the more you see of him, the more you will like him. He has many young friends in the artillery, and so I doubt not, with your and Chelmsford's kind assistance, will get through well enough."

One could almost see the self-protective umbrellas being raised.

The Prince reached Durban on 31 March 1879 and was placed under Colonel Harrison, the Assistant Quarter-Master General who, as such, was responsible for the administration of the Command. Far from being tucked away as the Commander-in-Chief wished, Louis was allowed out on patrol.[44] It was on one such patrol that he was attacked and killed by the Zulus. Carey was, ostensibly, in command of the patrol and was court-martialled ten days later.

Appalled, Gordon-Cumming left camp on 2 June with two squadrons of the 17th Lancers to the scene to search for bodies. They found the Prince with assegai wounds in the chest and right eye. They picked up two carbines and found another body stripped naked. When the body of the Prince was discovered, Surgeon Major Scott, who accompanied the search party, reported: -

"To the best of my belief the body had not been moved before I got there. I think he died where I found him. He was laying on his back, with the left arm across him, in the position of self-defence. I counted 18 assegai wounds, all in front. It is true there were 2 wounds found in his back, but from their nature, I am satisfied that they were the terminations of wounds inflicted in front. Any of 5 of the wounds would have proved mortal. There were no bullet wounds on the body."

A funeral procession was conducted at 5pm.

With fresh troops, Chelmsford now had two cavalry regiments, five batteries of artillery and twelve infantry battalions, amounting to 1,000 regular cavalry, 9,000 regular infantry and a further 7,000 men with 24 guns. On 3 June, the main thrust of the invasion began its slow advance on Ulundi. On 28 June Chelmsford's force was only 17 miles from Ulundi when he learned that Wolseley had arrived in Cape Town. Wolseley cabled Chelmsford not to undertake any serious actions before his arrival but the message arrived late enough for Chelmsford safely to ignore it. He had no intention of letting Wolseley stop him from making a last effort to restore his reputation. Wolseley sent a second message on 30 June:

"Concentrate your force immediately and keep it concentrated. Undertake no serious operations with detached bodies of troops. Acknowledge receipt of this message at once and flash back your latest moves. I am astonished at not hearing from you." [45]

An increasingly frustrated Wolseley, desperate to take over, was prevented by bad weather from landing at Port Durnford and had to take the slower route by land. At the very time Wolseley was riding north from Durban, Chelmsford was preparing to engage the enemy. He had beaten Wolseley to it.

On 3 July, Wolseley's 30 June telegram reached Chelmsford, and with only five miles between him and glory, it was ignored. That evening Chelmsford issued his orders. The British, at last having learned the lesson from Isandlwana, had no intention of advancing in line or column on the porous ranks of Zulus; instead they would start at first light in a hollow square with mounted troops covering their flanks and rear. This was, in a sense, a reversion to old style tactics but it worked. The leading element was made up of five companies of infantry, with four further companies on both flanks. They were supported by Gatling guns in the centre, and light field guns on the flanks. The rear was protected by another four companies and two squadrons of cavalry.

This phalanx of over 5,000 men began to cross the plain. Suddenly, an entire Zulu regiment rose out of the grass to their front, followed by regiment after regiment rising up all around them. The Zulu Army, around 12,000 to 15,000 strong, were in a horseshoe shape encircling the north, east and southern sides of the British square. At 9 am, four ranks of British infantry, with the front two kneeling, opened fire at 2,000 yards into the advancing Zulus. As they closed, the Zulus had to face massed rifle fire, machine-gun rounds from the Gatling guns and point-blank grapeshot from the light guns. Their casualties were mounting as Chelmsford ordered the cavalry to charge the now fleeing Zulus. Gordon-Cumming's friends, Phipps and Milne were shot close to him, but his diary does not reveal whether the wounds were fatal. The pursuit continued until not a live Zulu remained on the plain, with the cavalry slaughtering the wounded, in revenge for Isandlwana.

Zulu military power was finally broken. Chelmsford ordered the royal kraal of Ulundi to be burnt and handed over command to Wolseley on 15 July. British ascendancy was again complete in South Africa. Chelmsford's reputation was partially restored; he received a GCB, but never served in the field again. He died, playing billiards in his club, in 1905.

On 26 July Gordon-Cumming was ordered home[46] with a medal, and clasp, and a Mention in Despatches, 'Captain Sir W Gordon-Cumming, my extra ADC, ...worked hard and [was] present during the action'.[47] He was entrusted with the sad, but important, task of conveying the condolences of the Army to Empress Eugenie on the death of her son, the Prince Imperial. It must have been a harrowing undertaking. After the first paroxysm of grief was over, she neither wept nor spoke, but listened with feverish despair while Gordon-Cumming related all the circumstances of her son's death, not withholding a single painful detail.

On 28 July 1880, Gordon-Cumming was promoted Captain and Lieutenant Colonel. That December, he again managed to obtain leave to shoot in India. Interestingly, one of the party was his old friend Owen Williams, who is to appear later so significantly in his life. Others were Rutledge and De Grey, whose life he was alleged to have saved but, maybe characteristically, he makes no mention in his diary.[48] By the end of May 1881 he was back in England.

CHAPTER 4 - Egypt

From 1878, serious disturbances had been occurring in Egypt as a result of the inadequacy of the Khedive, Tewfik Pasha.[49] A coup was instigated by the War Minister, Arabi Pasha, who had the support of the Army and much of the population. Britain suggested to France that, owing to their common interests, they should intervene. A Joint Note was, consequently, sent in January 1882, recognising the Khedive. Nothing happened, so the French agreed to a demonstration by an Anglo-French fleet off Alexandria. However, all this did was to make matters worse and the Egyptians started to erect defences around the harbour and town. The English admiral, Seymour, was infuriated but his demands for the work to cease were ignored. At this point, the French withdrew and would have nothing more to do with it. Seymour then bombarded the town, reducing it to ruins, and forcing Arabi to withdraw to a position covering the road and railway to Cairo. However, without a landing force, there was little more that Seymour could do. A token force was assembled in Cyprus in July and landed subsequently at Alexandria. Very little happened so it was decided to send an expeditionary force of two divisions from home. The force, which consisted of two infantry divisions, a cavalry division and an Indian Contingent, was under the command of the redoubtable General Sir Garnet Wolseley who, initially, directed the fleet to gain control of the Suez Canal. Gordon-Cumming was in the 1st Battalion Scots Guards which was part of the Guards Brigade in the 1st Division which sailed from Tilbury on 30 July, with a strength of thirty-one officers and seven hundred and sixty-five other ranks. The Battalion had embarked at Westminster Bridge in three steam launches which then took them to Albert Docks where they boarded the *Orient*. The Commanding Officer was Colonel G W 'Curly' Knox and the Adjutant The Hon N de C Dalrymple (-Hamilton), second son of the 10th Earl of Stair, an old Scots Guards family.[50] They were seen off by the Prince and Princess of Wales. The Prince's brother, the Duke of Connaught, Colonel of the Regiment, as Commander of the Guards Brigade of 2nd Grenadiers, 2nd Coldstream, and 1st Scots Guards, sailed with them. The Queen wrote in her *Journal*, 'Constantly thinking of darling Arthur's departure. I had a telegram from him before he left, & or mine, with a message to the Guards.' The ship was roomy and comfortable, even with electric light in the saloon. Iced drink was available, with lime juice being particularly popular. Stopping at Malta, they were allowed to go ashore and the officers dined at the Club, an old house with high ceilinged rooms. The soldiers availed themselves of the more exciting delights of the ladies of Valetta. They left the Grand Harbour for Alexandria on 9 August but after a demonstration before Aboukir, sailed on for the Suez Canal. They arrived in the morning and after some delay entered the Canal, but the Suez Canal Company refused to produce any pilots. The *Catalonia* with the 50th Foot on board, a Cunard Line ship which had never been in the Canal before, ran aground. The next morning, however, the *Nevada*, in front of the Scots Guards, steered past, followed closely by their ship. The *Batavia*, another Cunard ship, however, with the Grenadiers on board, got stuck attempting the same manoeuvre.

The Brigade of Guards landed at Ismailia on 22 August with a view to advancing on Cairo by the Sweet Water Canal which joins the Suez Canal at Ismailia, and passes through Tel-el-Kebir and the railway junction of Zagazig on its way to Cairo. They bivouacked beside the canal and, although in the open, were well shaded by trees. There were no mosquitoes but much sand and dust. They wore goggles and a rudimentary sort of face veil. White pith helmets, which had now been stained brown with tea and a lighter jacket, albeit still red (khaki was not around until the Suakin campaign in 1885) had been issued. A small element from the other Brigade had pushed on ahead but met a superior force of Egyptians at Tel-el-Mahuta. On the 24th the Guards were summarily ordered forward in support. A twelve-mile march in the heat of the day was exhausting but the water trucks kept up with them and constantly filled water-bottles. On arrival, they found the enemy had withdrawn, ultimately, to the lines of Tel-el-Kebir. This position was extensive, covering a breadth of some 6000 yards over a wide area of open sand. Wolseley decided on a dawn attack with a preliminary night approach march; in those days a novel operation for a force of this size. The attack went in at 5am on 13 September with the Highland Brigade leading. By the time the Scots Guards reached the enemy's defences, the battle was, effectively, over.

Lieutenant Balfour takes up the story.[51] 'We struck tents a 6pm [on the 12th] just as the sun had gone down so that Arabi might not see our movements. At 7pm we paraded and after some delay began to march. Owing to the necessity of keeping the Brigade together and the darkness of the night we had to keep going Half-Right, Half-Left, Fours Right, Left Turn, Step Short, and so on; and how in the world we got there I can't imagine. But nothing was ever better timed. As the day began to break we halted and lay down, and the order was given for the Grenadiers and Coldstream to extend; Scots Guards reserve. The order had hardly been given when we heard Crack! Crack! Crack! Crack! Crackle! and the horizon was lit up with flashes just like summer lightning, with a continuous crackle like the rumpling of several *Times* newspapers. We were kneeling and sitting down when it began, and about the third crack came Boom! and a shell over our heads. It was very amusing how everyone promptly lay down. My own personal feelings were not what I should have expected. For the first time since this somewhat dull and intensely boring (up to the last week) campaign [began] I felt a sense of pleasurable excitement as the shots began to crackle, as I was afraid he [the enemy] was going to bolt. The shells I thought I should have felt inclined to bob my head at, but never any feeling of the kind - probably because I knew that once a shell is over one's head one is all right. They burst from one hundred to three hundred yards in rear of us, close to where the doctors were at first.

We then deployed into line in rear of the Coldstream and sat and smoked and listened to the whizzing and crackling, and watched bullets knocking up the earth in front and behind. One fell about three yards in front of me, among the Left Flank company but did no harm. I fancy there must have been more than one noticed going over our heads but I did not hear many. Jock's horse was hit and four of our men were badly hurt: one had a bullet straight through his helmet which just scraped his head. Nine Grenadiers and Bertie wounded, some rather badly; one sergeant killed; eight Coldstream and Sterling wounded, Sterling had a narrow escape. The bullet struck his field-glasses, which were hanging on his belt, smashed them, passed from them to his revolver the other side, ran along it and just wounded his hand, though the shock knocked him down. Beyond this and occasionally advancing or moving to a flank, we never did anything during the fifty minutes the action lasted, and then marched straight into the place. The Brigade advanced just as I expected in my letter to Julian and was in reserve on the left flank of Arabi's work. But the Egyptians made such a poor showing no support was required by the first line. Had it been otherwise, as at the Alma (when the Light Brigade (sic) in front fell back), the Brigade would have come up and, I have no doubt, mopped them up as effectually as the Highlanders did.'

Losses to the Battalion were only four men wounded, one of whom later died, although fifteen died of enteric fever (a plague which to cause many casualties in the later Boer wars). The rout of the Egyptian army was complete and the Scots Guards entered Cairo – the first infantry troops to do so - on 15 September with bayonets fixed and their pipes playing. They returned to London in November. Slightly to their embarrassment, for they had seen really little action, they were awarded the Battle Honours of 'Egypt 1882' and 'Tel-el-Kebir', the former carried on their Colours. For Gordon-Cumming, he could add another bronze star, with clasp, to his medal ribbons.

*

1884 started well for Gordon-Cumming. He was asked to stay at Sandringham with the Prince and Princess of Wales for the New Year. It was a grand party of the *glitterati* of the Marlborough Set. Together with Prince Eddy, there were the Duke and Duchess of Manchester, the Lord Charly Beresfords, the Alingtons, the Marquess of Hartington, the Keppels and the customary private secretaries and equerries. In his diary, there is a memo with on the reverse, what looks like a score: J.W. +50 2 - 11 22. Was it from a card game?[52]

On 4 January he returned to London and dined at the Gaiety the following evening with Lady De Clifford. The Regiment was plodding on with Public Duties and, as he was now Captain and Lieutenant Colonel, it clearly did not need him, so he left for Calais on 8 January. Travelling via Basle, Milan, Venice and Trieste he met up with Owen Williams for a little shooting in Corfu. However, the lure of bigger game was too much to resist and he headed for Bombay, stopping off in Somalia for some buck and sand-grouse. He was back, tiger shooting, in Hyderabad and Secunderabad by the end of February. Leave came to an end and he returned to England via Aden, Suez, Geneva and Strasbourg by the end of June.

Life, even in the London Season must have started to pall and, therefore, to his great excitement, on 16 September, he received a telegram recalling him to join the newly raised Camel Corps for service in Sudan.

In the aftermath of the 1882 campaign, the Egyptian Army needed thorough overhaul and reconstruction with British officers. This took time and, taking advantage of the vacuum, Mohammed Ahmed, an Egyptian government official and former slave-trader, declared himself to be the Mahdi and raised a strong force of fanatical Dervishes in the Upper Sudan. In October 1883 an Egyptian force, under British officers, was destroyed by the Mahdi near El Obeid and another in early 1884 by a follower of the Mahdi's at Suakin. Egyptian garrisons were consequently withdrawn from Upper Sudan with the aim of concentrating a force around Suakin. General Gordon was dispatched to Khartoum to supervise the withdrawal and General Graham to Suakin to organise its tactical area of operations. The British Government, however, vacillated and, leaving only a small garrison at Suakin, dithered over relieving Gordon when he found his loyal Egyptian troops impossible to evacuate; the old story of too little too late. Wolseley decided to move a relief force, in boats, up the Nile but, to gain time, he directed a column to move across the desert from Korti to Khartoum. This column was organised into a Camel Corps of Guards, Cavalry and Marines. Each Foot Guards battalion was to provide two officers and forty-three men. Gordon-Cumming and three other officers inveigled themselves into the two Scots Guards detachments.

On 24 September, after a mad scramble to get their field kit together, the seven detachments, under the command of Colonel 'Star' Boscawen, Coldstream Guards, with Lieutenant Charlie Crutchley of the Scots Guards as Adjutant, paraded at Wellington Barracks and were inspected by the Commander-in-Chief, the Duke of Cambridge. They were dressed in light-grey tunics, bandolier over the shoulder, blue puttees, brown laced boots, spurs, white helmets (later stained with tea), and carried no kit apart from a haversack and a water-bottle. They were issued with goggles, blue serge jerseys and fisherman's caps. Gordon-Cumming's diary entry of 26 September lists the names of all the soldiers in his detachment. They then travelled to Portsmouth and embarked on the P&O *Deccan*. The Heavy (Cavalry) Camel Regiment was also on board under command of Colonel Reggie Talbot of the 1st Life Guards. They were issued with the new Martini-Henry rifle but it later transpired that sand jammed the round in the breech and the long bayonet bent under pressure. Not what one wants to have, facing the blood-curdling Dervishes. Nevertheless, they tried out the new rifle with targets rigged on the yardarm and bottles in the sea.

They landed at Alexandria on 7 October and after a week's camp were sent up river to Wadi Halfa by train and steamer to meet their new charges. Throughout the ages the British soldier has been remarkably adaptable and a new challenge is something to be taken on, conquered and, more often than not, enjoyed. (An underlying lack of fear and a concern not to be shown up in front of comrades always helps, as anyone who has ever seen a soldier launch himself off a mountain on skis for the first time, will testify.) Imagine the thoughts, then, of soldiers, leaving their bearskins and tunics and the Forecourt of Buckingham Palace for operations with camels in the Sudanese desert. Typically, in a very short time, the men discovered how to handle these extraordinary creatures. Edward Gleichen describes the confrontation.

'The men were highly delighted with their first mount, and proceeded to trot and canter their steeds all over the plain, although a camel's anatomy is not constructed for the purpose of cantering; many were the croppers they came, especially when getting up, but it only made them the keener. Mounting a frisky camel is exciting work for a beginner, and nearly always results in a cropper. The mode of procedure should be thus: having made your camel to kneel by clearing your throat loudly at him and tugging at his rope, shorten your rein till you bring his head round to his shoulder, put your foot in the stirrup and throw your leg over. With his head jammed like that he cannot rise, and must wait till you give him his head. Unless you do as directed, he will get up before your leg is over; if this happens, stand in the stirrup till he is up, and then throw your leg over, otherwise you will infallibly meet with a hideous catastrophe. We found that with the rifle in the bucket it was impossible to get one's leg over, so always made the men pass the sling of the rifle over their left wrists before getting on. After a time we found it easier to stand alongside and give a big heave of the right leg over the saddle without touching the near stirrup at all. So much for mounting; dismounting is, of course, the same reversed.

I might add that being run away with on your camel at a hard trot - as several times happened to me - is a most alarming experience, for you feel so utterly helpless. You haul away at his rope-rein till his head comes right back to your pommel but his body still goes on! The only way to stop him is to haul him round in large circles until he stops from sheer exhaustion.

On the stony places I really pitied the podgy soft-looking feet of the camels, but they knocked their toes against the sharp stones with the greatest unconcern. I also once had practical experience that their feet are not soft by a violent kick I received from the hind-leg of a camel, who thought himself insulted by my examining his head-stall in the dark. A camel's hind-legs will reach anywhere - over his head, round his chest and on to his hump; even when lying down an evilly-disposed animal will shoot out his legs and bring you to a sitting posture. His neck is of the same pliancy. He will chew the root of his tail, nip you in the calf, or lay the top of his head on his hump. He also bellows and roars at you, whatever you are doing - saddling him, feeding him, mounting him, unsaddling him. To the uninitiated, a camel going for one with his mouth open and gurgling horribly is a terrifying spectacle; but do not mind him, it is only his way.

He hardly ever bites, but when he does you feel it for some time; as a matter of fact, we only once had a man laid up from a bite in the hand, but he had to go into hospital for it. I heard of one or two men having a leg broken from a kick at various times, but it was the exception and not the rule, for a camel is really a very docile animal, and learns to behave himself in the most trying positions with equanimity, though I fear it is only the result of want of brains.

Regarding his wonderful powers of endurance, I was told of journeys made across country from Dongola to Alexandria (950 miles) in eight days; of his marvellous powers of going for forty days running; of trotting 200 miles without a halt; of his going fifteen days without water, &c. My experience is that he gets a sore back after four days or less, does not go comfortably for more than five consecutive days; and as for trotting, it was only by a vigorous application of the *kurbash* that I could succeed in making mine go that pace for more than fifty yards at a time. I own that, though my first impression of a camel's powers were thus bad, and I do not now believe in those wonderful tales told me by wily natives, yet the beast rose wonderfully in my estimation some time afterwards, when we were in the thick of real business in the Bayuda Desert, on seeing the patient way in which our poor camels walked on and on, with no food or water whatever inside them, till they dropped dead in their tracks.'[53]

The force pushed along the east bank of the river from Halfa, and halted opposite Dongola. On 19 November Wolseley paid them a visit. His camel came trotting up and suddenly swerved unseating his illustrious rider, who came down hard on his shoulder. It is always fun for soldiers to see their senior officers discomforted but mirth soon turned to sympathy when they realised he was quite badly hurt. Anyhow, he remounted and rode on.[54] It was there they met the redoubtable Kitchener, then a Major in the Intelligence Department. He had been sent ahead with some troops, mostly Bashibozuks, belonging to the Mudir of Dongola, and was busily collecting information about the enemy. He was a tall spare man with a pointed beard and very piercing grey eyes. He was dressed in a khaki jacket and trousers, which had shrunk in the wash. He stayed with them until they reached Gakdul and then left to negotiate with the tribes for camels and supplies, thus, to his infuriation, missing the subsequent fighting.

On 14 December they arrived at Korti, the village at the bend of the Nile from where they were to start the march across the Beyuda Desert. They were joined there by the rest of the Guards Camel Regiment and a detachment, a hundred strong, of Royal Marines, who were to form the fourth company. Troops trickled in day by day, and by the end of the year the desert and river Columns were ready to start. Gordon-Cumming was an avid letter writer and would mark, in the margin of his diary, the initials of those to whom he wrote; 'HRH', obviously the Prince of Wales and 'Lady GC', presumably his mother, for instance. A laconic entry in his diary of Christmas Day reads, "25 Dec Tomlinson of my Coy [Company] died at 9 am of enteric & was buried in ev. Bonfire and singing."

On 30 December the force moved off across the desert, making good going, and, without incident, reaching the Gakdul Wells a hundred miles away on 3 January. Despite Gordon's cheery message from Khartoum that he, 'Could hold out for years,' every man knew time was critical to his rescue.

With the wonderful benefit of hindsight, there were those who thought they could have made much better time by marching on foot and merely use the camels for transporting supplies. The ground was hard going and not the soft sand that had to be crossed, mounted on camels. As it was, they wasted a week at Gakdul, waiting for camels to bring up stores and having to send their riding camels back to Korti to bring up supplies. Had they kept them to carry their kit and gone on foot they would have reached Metemmeh before the Mahdi and had no fighting at Abu Klea, although, clearly, there would have been some action before reaching Khartoum. They then might have rescued Gordon. Opponents of this theory maintain that the Mahdi could have easily taken Khartoum a week earlier anyway.

Having improved the essential water supply there, the force started its dash across the desert to the Nile on 14 January. Barring the way to the next vital water source at Abu Klea, were 5,000 Dervishes. The British immediately formed square to receive the Dervish charge which was beaten off and the Wells reached that evening. Overall, nine officers and sixty-five men were killed and a further nine officers and eighty-five men wounded. Gordon-Cumming and his men sustained only a few wounded but it was a significant battle, proving the Dervish was not invincible. One of the more colourful characters to be killed was Colonel Burnaby of the Blues.[55] Initially, he was positioned on the left of the British square. The forward skirmishers, withdrawing back into the square, were being hotly chased by the Dervishes who caught and killed two of them. Burnaby rode out to help the others in. He was armed only with a sword, having left his double-barrelled shotgun with his soldier scrvant in the square. His own horse had been killed under him that morning so he was on one borrowed from the 19th Hussars. He rode straight at a mounted Dervish who was pursuing a skirmisher. As he did so the Dervish changed direction and charged Burnaby, but was dropped by a shot from a soldier named Paporte. An Arab then thrust an eight-foot spear at Burnaby which he parried with his sword. A second Dervish ran his spear into Burnaby's shoulder from behind, but he was bayonetted by a British soldier. When Burnaby's attention was momentarily distracted, the first Dervish sank his spear into Burnaby's throat, severing the jugular. At this point Gordon-Cumming ran out to help. Three Arabs went for him. 'One of these, I bowled over with a bullet through the stomach with my revolver. Before starting on the desert march I had my sword ground as sharp as a razor. When the second man neared me, I cut his head clean off with one blow. Number three dodged, and, as I was following him, he was shot dead by a bullet fired from the square.'[56]

Moving on by day and night, the column, again, found the enemy blocking access to the next water point at Metemmeh. Immediate defensive measures were taken but the Dervishes managed to inflict a number of casualties. The following day the Nile was reached and contact was made with some of Gordon's steamers from Khartoum.

Realising that a large enemy force was approaching from Khartoum, the British pulled back to Gubat and attempted to reach Khartoum by river. Within sight of the town on 28 January, they learned that it had fallen two days earlier and Gordon had been killed. This was, effectively, the end of operations for Gordon-Cumming and his men. Later, the Regiment was involved in the Suakin campaign but Gordon-Cumming had, by then, returned home, decorated with the Egypt 1882 campaign medal with Tel-el-Kebir and Abu Klea clasps and the Khedive Bronze Star.

Now was the time he became of interest to the Secret Service.

CHAPTER 5 - Agents of the Crown

In Great Britain, throughout the centuries intelligence gathering, management of spies and agents, and interrogation was largely at the whim of the reigning monarch and, later, Parliament where the Foreign Office was loosely responsible and sought funding for, its, usually clandestine, operations. By the 19th century, it had become more formalised and several departments of the War Office were given responsibility for the different aspects of intelligence related work, particularly with maps. Centralisation was first carried out in 1873 when the Intelligence Branch was established, which became the Directorate of Military Intelligence in 1888. Nevertheless, it remained for a number of years the world of the enthusiastic amateur, some of whom were outstanding and extremely courageous. Royal Engineer officers, like Kitchener, were good at this on a more 'open' level; they were trained map makers, were good at sketching landscape features and had an eye for ground and the potential 'going' of any possible routes and approaches through obstacles. Others, because of their personality, like Burnaby, were adept at blending in with, and infiltrating the locals. They were not put off by the moral aspects of bribery and had the skill of 'turning' previously hostile tribesmen.

The world of secret intelligence was about as far away from the privileged lifestyle of the average Guards officer as it was possible to imagine. Few people knew, such was the clandestine nature of his work, that William Gordon-Cumming was involved, if not in deep cover, then certainly on the fringes of that world. Unsurprisingly, there is no evidence as to exactly when he was recruited but it must have been on his return from Egypt. Subjected to boring London Duties after the excitement of real soldiering, he would have been highly susceptible to approach from the shadowy men 'across the river.' Gordon-Cumming was not just the arrogant, womanising, swashbuckling decorated Guards officer of repute. There was rather more to him than that. Importantly, the Prince of Wales was also well aware of Gordon-Cumming's activities having gossiped with him late into the night. They were involved in a close and secretive relationship. But first the background of the very professional spy, Tulloch, whose path Gordon-Cumming undoubtedly crossed.

Tulloch was born in 1838 and commissioned in the Royal Scots in 1855, so he was 10 years older than Gordon-Cumming and 12 years his senior, however, there are some intriguing coincidences. Tulloch was undoubtedly a spy. His autobiography, to the infuriation of the security service, exposed his activities in detail.[57] He acquired his first taste for information and intelligence gathering in 1874. The Carlists, in Spain, were besieging Bilbao which was holding out for the Government.[58] Tulloch had discovered there was no British attaché with the Spanish Government troops but as he had considerable leave owing to him, he persuaded his superiors that he could temporarily fill the post. (Interestingly, at the same time, Burnaby was with the Carlist forces reporting for *The Times*.) Not only could he report back to the Intelligence Department but could also pick up useful information on mountain warfare in the Pyrenees. He inveigled himself into the Headquarters of the Spanish commander-in-chief, Marshal Serrano, Duc de la Torre, and was in a good position to write a detailed report on what he had seen. His report was shown to the Duke of Cambridge, who was so impressed that Tulloch was sent to the Staff College as an instructor in surveying, a euphemism for spying. His career was made.

A highly sensitive estimate of the Belgian defence capability and survey of the physical and man-made obstacles followed.[59] "We look on the report you sent in, in 1875, on Belgium, as a sort of text-book," Tulloch was gratifyingly told a number of years later. Lieutenant General Sir Garnet Wolseley, then the Quartermaster-General, had stressed the necessity of intelligence operations and described his ideal agent: 'whoever conducts the work should be of middle age, have a clear insight into human nature, with a logical turn of mind, nothing sanguine about him but of a generally calm and distrustful disposition.'[60] He must have been thinking of Tulloch. So, unsurprisingly, Wolseley made Tulloch his Head of Intelligence in the Egyptian Campaign in 1882.

However, one of Tulloch's most important operations was at Alexandria in the Nile Delta.[61] The head of the Intelligence Department,[62] Major General Sir Patrick MacDougall, a frail-looking intellectual sort of soldier, more the student of war than the hero of the battlefield, accompanied by Tulloch and a colonel, whom Tulloch calls 'B', made his way to Egypt via Marseille 'for his health'. The three officers disguised neither their presence nor their identities and, though they were not entirely honest about their motives, nor were the Egyptians so naïve as to believe their visit was entirely innocent. MacDougall wrote up the visit in a confidential report, noting with Victorian understatement that, 'arriving in Cairo as I did shortly after the purchase of the Suez Canal shares, I was led to conclude from the markedly polite but at the same time reserved manner of the Egyptian military authorities that the presence in Egypt of one of the principal officers of the English Head Quarters Staff was regarded with suspicion.' Tulloch assessed, in the light of the Suez Canal construction, the line of advance on Cairo was via the Canal to Lake Timseh and operate from there rather than Alexandria. How right he was.

At the beginning of 1882, as the British became increasingly concerned about the security of the Suez Canal, Tulloch offered his services to Wolseley, reminding him of the plan of attack he had written earlier and volunteered to 'combine business and pleasure' in a snipe-shooting holiday to Egypt. His offer was accepted and he sailed for Port Said, arriving at the end of January.[63] The mission was politically delicate as Gladstone, Liberal prime minister since 1880, had set himself firmly against intervention in Egypt, but Wolseley was determined the army should be ready for all eventualities. Basing himself in Shepheard's Hotel – clearly on expenses - Tulloch carried out reconnaissance to Tel el Kebir. Astonishingly, wearing civilian clothes, he also managed to inspect Arabi's troops (he described Arabi as, 'An ignorant fanatic, with some crude ideas about liberty.') Warming to his task, he addressed the assembled officers in grandiloquent terms, describing them all as brothers-in-arms with the British. It was politely pointed out to him that this was not possible as they were Mohammedans and he, English. He riposted that the real difference was that they had two wives and he, one. His loss, he said,[64] to much amusement. However, his intelligence assessments were invaluable in the impending operation. Tulloch's reports contained recommendations as to how to operate quickly in the event of hostilities. Both sabotage and special operations were considered. 'It is said that it would take no great amount of bucksheesh [sic] to have the principal magazine, that at Tourra, exploded,' he writes coolly to Colonel East on 17 February from Shepheard's. From Alexandria, in a letter dated 5 March, he describes in detail the state of the coastal defences. For the destruction of one of the batteries, Fort Meiks, he suggests, 'a boat landing might be effected just west of the fort within 100 yards and the assailants might scramble in to the place on the flank where the wall has fallen down.' Following the bombardment of Alexandria on 11 July 1882, a 40,000 strong British Expeditionary Force under Wolseley's command landed in Egypt. Appropriately enough, Tulloch led the successful landing party. As a result of the action, he was promoted Lieutenant-Colonel and recommended for the Victoria Cross. Instead, and given the nature of his work, Tulloch was awarded the CMG for extraordinarily important non-military service in a foreign country.

Tulloch's memoirs, published in 1903, sparked immediate controversy. The Times Literary Supplement reviewer strongly criticized its author for revealing his intelligence work, 'future agents of the department will not find their work any easier if their predecessors are not habitually reticent to the last degree as to every detail of their employment,' he scolded.

Tulloch had unquestionably broken the security service code of conduct. His chapter on the Egypt Campaign covered a detail lacking in other contemporary memoirs; the undercover missions behind enemy lines, counter-espionage operations, press disinformation techniques, and the use of bribery and spies. Yet it was Tulloch's intelligence reports from Egypt, circulated to the French and British cabinets in June 1882, which perhaps had the greatest impact. With prophetic accuracy, he assessed Egypt's defence arrangements and predicted a swift occupation with the minimum of casualties. Undoubtedly his analysis helped ministers to convince Gladstone to execute one of the great reversals of nineteenth-century politics.

Where did Gordon-Cumming fit into all this? Tulloch is not mentioned in any of Gordon-Cumming's letters or diaries and the latter is not listed in Tulloch's autobiography. This does not mean that that they did not meet or that they were not under the same intelligence department direction for particular operations. In this opaque world one would not expect it. Indeed, the old lawyer's saying, 'absence of evidence is not evidence of absence' is apt. Tulloch was specifically ordered to carry out tasks of a clandestine nature; others might not be, but would be under remit to report back to the Department on conclusion of a journey or expedition. The Prince of Wales relished this sort of activity and, because he was not allowed access to 'ordinary' State Papers, loved to be given tit-bits of cloak and dagger exploits by his friends.

Gordon-Cumming was an avid letter writer and the Prince was one of his major correspondents. Did Gordon-Cumming disclose, privately, intelligence that the Prince would not have acquired elsewhere? For example, he most certainly wrote to him about the Sudan expedition of 1884 and his views on how the campaign was conducted.[65] A draft of a letter from 'Near Metemeh' dated 23 January 1885 from Gordon-Cumming to the Prince of Wales about fighting there exists in the National Library of Scotland. Royal Archives, understandably, reveal no such thing.

In the mists of family folk-lore, it was rumoured that Gordon-Cumming had served in some capacity in the 1874 Carlist War in Spain. As he had only been commissioned in 1867, it is unlikely he would have been officially released from his Regiment or had the amount of leave required to undertake such an operation. But why the rumour? Is it based on the knowledge that Tulloch was, indeed, involved? Were they already connected in some way? There is no mention of it in his diaries for that year.

Later, Gordon-Cumming was ostensibly shooting in Sudan and India and his diaries reveal little other than places he had been and the amount of game he had shot. However, one of Tulloch's most important operations, as we have seen, was in Alexandria[66] and it is conceivable that there was some sort of liaison between the two of them in Cairo; Tulloch on a deliberate assignation and Gordon-Cumming 'on his way' to Sudan and India. The relevance to what happened later, in this part of the world, involving both of them cannot be completely ignored.

In 1878, Gordon-Cumming toured Canada and the United States. His diary records a banker's draft available to him in Halifax, Nova Scotia and then setting out for the Rocky Mountains to shoot. However, on 18 August he appears to have left Chicago for Denver where he met General Sherman at the American Hotel on the 20th. The purpose of this meeting is not clear and although there is a later letter to Gordon-Cumming from the General in the National Library of Scotland, it is relatively innocuous. Sherman had published his two-volume memoirs in 1875 which were critically well received and it may have been that Gordon-Cumming simply wanted to meet the great man. It is unlikely, though, that he would have been able to do so without some form of influential introduction. From whom? Sherman was an acknowledged strategist and exponent of 'total war'. Liddell Hart called him, 'the first modern general'. It is conceivable that far-sighted individuals in the War Office recognising this, needed inside briefing from the great man. Who better than Gordon-Cumming, who had the self-confidence of operational experience under his belt and would be, therefore, more appealing to Sherman than a civil servant or diplomat? Tulloch had been in Canada and New York earlier, in 1870 in a 'staff appointment' although quite what is unexplained. His biography[67] merely covers very much tourist activities and what he calls 'instructional work'. There seems to be no link between the two officers' visits but when British eyes were very much turned to Europe and the Middle East, Canada and America appear to be curious places to be sent. Gordon-Cumming did return to the States and Mexico in 1888 but for what purpose is unknown. Sadly, his diary is very light on detail. Perhaps deliberately?

In an earlier chapter, Gordon-Cumming's campaigning in Egypt has been described but not the link to Tulloch. In 1881 Gordon-Cumming had returned from India, travelling through Suez and Alexandria on 17 May. Had he written any reports on the situation there? Was there a liaison between him and Tulloch? The coincidence of them being in the same place at the same time is unavoidable.

From 1877 to 1893, Gordon-Cumming kept up considerable correspondence with Sir Montagu Gerard, the legendary soldier of North West India and Afghanistan campaigns. Gerard served on the staff of the Cavalry Division in the Egyptian campaign of 1882. He was at the battle of Tel el Kebir, and the surrender of Arabi Pasha. However, in 1881 and 1885 he was sent on a secret mission to Persia. Unsurprisingly, the letters do not reveal anything of this but, again, why the connection between Gerard and Gordon-Cumming during this time? In 1884, before the Sudan expedition, Gordon-Cumming's diaries cover a trip to India but, oddly, there is also a reference to staying in Corfu. It is difficult to imagine any shooting attraction for Gordon-Cumming there, so why? We know that part of Tulloch's remit, on his way to Egypt with MacDougall, had been to assess whether ports in Crete and Cyprus would be feasible bases for the Royal Navy (for various reasons, he concluded they would not). In Minorca lay the important harbour of Fort St Philip at Mahon which had proved so vital in the Napoleonic Wars for control of the Mediterranean. Was Gordon-Cumming tasked to see whether there were any further options in Corfu? He was back in the Mediterranean in 1890.

In 1889, by now a Major, he went to Russia from August to October. Even with his seniority, this could not possibly have been while on leave. He had to have been deliberately sent there and would have been heavily briefed. As a firm friend of the Prince of Wales, he would have been made welcome at the Czar's Court and may have even been briefed by the Prince himself, probably not in any cloak and dagger way, but encouraged to see what was going on and pick up nuances and indiscreet gossip. On 20 February, Gordon-Cumming left London for Paris, then to Monte Carlo and Cannes where he attended a dinner party which included the Prince of Wales. The Prince would have known exactly what Gordon-Cumming was doing and it may have well been then that he took him 'on one side'. As a Baronet, Gordon-Cumming would have had a gold-plated *entrée* into the Russian court, together with the Prince's very obvious and impressive patronage. The Intelligence Department may have taken it further. Returning to London, he did not leave for Moscow until 11 August, travelling via Berlin and St Petersburg. In his diary from 15 to 18 August, he has collected a number of visiting cards:

Mr Alexandre Koch

George W Wurts, US Charge d'Affaires

N Voyeikow ADC General to the Czar

Constantin ThDumba, Secretary to the Austro-Hungarian Ambassador

Aziz Bey, a Lieutenant of Cavalry and Regiment d'Entegroul

Mr de Glinka-Maurine ADC General to the Czar

Aaron Ward, US Navy Legation

A Riesenkampf

Count Nicolas Fersen

Of these, George Wurts, the American, appears in his diaries on a number of separate occasions. Why and what for?

On 18 August he was presented to the Czar and Czarina and, the following day, attended military manoeuvres at which the Czar was present. Gordon-Cumming wrote a number of letters to people in England, including the Prince of Wales, during his travels round Russia. He appeared to be free to go where he wanted and ended his tour in the Crimea, visiting the battlefields, unsurprisingly, of the Alma, Balaklava and Inkerman where his Regiment had so distinguished itself. He returned to Paris via the Bosporous. There were then more travels from March to May in 1890. Again he went via the Suez Canal – interestingly playing Baccarat at the Turf Club in Cairo – then on to Zanzibar and Colombo in Ceylon (Sri Lanka). He returned via Montenegro, Venice, Verona, Nurnburg and Heidelberg, staying at the Prinz Carl Hotel. In Innsbruck he attended the opera, *Aida*, in the company of Lady Louisa Legge, a daughter of the 4th Earl of Dartmouth. One of his many conquests? With his seniority, it would be safe to say that all this took place while he was on leave and there is no suggestion of any clandestine activity on his part.

Was he a spy? Possibly not in the pure sense but it is more than likely that he was instructed to report back to the Intelligence Department on return from travels, which were not as innocent as they might first appear, and his very loose connection to Tulloch could be more than just coincidence. His son, Michael, maintained that he told him he had been an agent.

In 1890, the *Sporting Times* called Gordon-Cumming, 'Possibly the handsomest man in London, and certainly the rudest.'[68] With his money, war record and friendship with the Prince of Wales, he had a swaggering self-confidence. Did he also have a secret that few others knew; that he had been a spy? His good looks, persistence, brazenness and rakish style made him irresistible to women and, somewhat more reluctantly, deference from men. He aspired to 'perforate' - his own word - large numbers of 'the sex', including Lillie Langtry, Sarah Bernhardt, Lady Randolph Churchill, and Daisy Brooke. He once said to Leonie, Lady Churchill's sister, when his advances were rebuffed, 'Silly little fool! All the young wives try me.'[69] The 'fast set' relished racy tales of his audacity and insolent wit. He gloried in the sobriquet of the most arrogant man in London.[70] Did he think this made him immune to the rules which governed others?

A man who met him for the first time, mentioned his name was Gillette with the G soft as in gentleman. Gordon-Cumming replied, 'I thought it was hard, as in beggar.' It was not even certain that 'beggar' was the word he used. A doctor, showing off that he had been summoned to treat an ill member of the Royal Family at Buckingham Palace, said, 'Did you see my brougham [coach] at the Palace gates?' 'No, really?' Gordon-Cumming replied, 'Is one of the servants ill?' On meeting Lord Hartington, the Postmaster General, he shouted, 'Harty-Tarty! When are you going to make Louisa an honest woman?'[71] (Louisa, Duchess of Manchester was Hartington's long term mistress, whom he did eventually marry, making her the famous Double-Duchess as he, by then, had become Duke of Devonshire.)

Years later, Gordon-Cumming's daughter, Elma, met Dame Nellie Melba in Australia. The great diva spoke so affectionately of him that Elma wondered if she had been one of his conquests. In reply to a letter from Elma, proudly telling him of this meeting, he wrote, 'I recollect Melba perfectly when she was *au mieux* with Philippe d'Orleans. She was common and very colonial.'[72] Later, the great Dame told Elma, 'Your father is a pig.'[73]

In August, he received an invitation from the Wilsons to join their house party for Doncaster Races. Daisy Brooke and the Prince of Wales were to be there. It was not a party to turn down.

But, first, more about His Royal Highness, the other major player in this saga.

CHAPTER 6 - The Prince

With practised ease, the nubile Nellie Clifden undressed and slipped into bed with the waiting Prince. Losing one's virginity is a significant, and memorable, step for most people; for the heir to the throne, with all its added dangers, it was even more momentous.

In September 1861, aged 19, the Prince of Wales was sent to join the 1st Battalion Grenadier Guards stationed at the Curragh in Ireland. Although dressed as a Lieutenant Colonel on the Staff, he had no role within the Regiment and, unsurprisingly, was not up to commanding very much, let alone a parade. Although not permitted to 'socialise' with officers of his own age, this did not bar a couple of them, dismayed by his ignorance of what went on under the petticoats, from recruiting Nellie from the pack of prostitutes lurking outside the barracks. Euphemistically labelled an 'actress' by later historians, she was nothing of the sort. Above average in prettiness and cleanliness though, she slept with the Prince on three separate occasions. Happily, she wrote no memoirs, nether resorted to blackmail nor infected the Prince with anything untoward, although it was suggested that they kept in touch and he saw her later at Cambridge. Today she would doubtless have earned a fortune selling her story to the tabloid press.

The Prince's parents, Queen Victoria and Prince Albert were first cousins. Albert was the younger son of Duke Ernest of Saxe-Coburg-Gotha and Ernest's sister, the Duchess of Kent, was Queen Victoria's mother. The family was almost wholly German. It is hardly surprising, therefore, that the Prince of Wales was to be brought up in the educational discipline of the Enlightenment[74] where a child's tuition was the greatest benefit a parent could bestow.[75] Prince Albert, despite many of his liberal qualities, was a controller. Effectively a workaholic, he could not resist interfering with everything from his wife's state papers to the minutiae of court etiquette. Aided by Baron von Stockmar.[76] Prince Albert's Teutonic prejudices and faults were magnified. He was determined to map out, in detail, the plan for his son's education and upbringing, the rigidity and harshness of which had a devastating effect on the Prince of Wales. He was to be brought up in accordance with the strictest of moral principles and to be surrounded by people of irreproachable quality. Under one such tutor, the dry and humourless Frederick Gibbs, there was a timetable from 8am to 7pm of six hourly lessons, six days a week. In between lessons riding, gym and drill took place.[77] The Prince rebelled against this. He was rude, aggressive and had fits of temper. He threw things about and called Gibbs names. The system, though, was misguided and psychologically cruel. The Queen was obsessed with the fear of the young and the contamination that association with others of his own age might bring to the Prince. Prince Albert, in his turn had an abhorrence of the English Public School. When a school was founded in honour of the Duke of Wellington, Albert hoped it was not going to resemble Eton or Harrow.[78] In later life, the Prince of Wales bitterly regretted the lack of companionship and friends in his early life. He craved the comradeship the Army would have provided and for sympathetic affection. This was a classic error by his parents leading to the boy's hasty judgements and intolerance. When the few, carefully selected, Etonians were invited to tea, Prince Albert was invariably present, dampening down any youthful behaviour.

What frightened the Queen was that the Prince of Wales had, of course, precedence over her beloved Albert. If she died, probably in childbirth, she would be succeeded by her backward and frivolous son. He seemed incapable of learning from his father who, however, never gave up trying to alter his perspective. He even tried to rope in Vicky, the Prince of Wales's elder sister and whom Prince Albert adored, to help. Try as he might, they became opposites. Prince Albert couldn't stomach smoking, the Prince smoked endless large cigars. To Prince Albert wine was a mere tonic, to the Prince it was something to be relished. The Prince loved women whereas Albert was frightened of them. The Prince of Wales's judgement was based on experience with people and watching them; Albert's was from books and theory. Like everyone, the Prince of Wales needed encouragement and occasional praise; he received nothing but reproach for failing to achieve expectations which were beyond him.

In August 1855 the Prince of Wales had probably the happiest time of his childhood. Together with Vicky, his parents took him on a state visit to Paris. No English monarch had set foot in the city since Henry VI. It was a wild success; the Emperor, Napoleon III, outrageously flirted with the Queen, something she had never experienced before. Prince Albert had to admit the shows and ceremonial were brilliant and their children fell under the French spell, not least that of the pretty Empress. There was an extraordinary moment when the Royal Family were taken to Les Invalides. A guard of honour of veterans of Wagram, Borodino, Waterloo and Inkerman were drawn up, flanking a coffin of Napoleon Bonaparte, yet to be interred in his tomb. As she leant on the arm of Napoleon's nephew, the Queen was overwhelmed by the significance of this act of unity between the two great nations who had been such enemies. The Prince of Wales, wearing the kilt, which fascinated the French, knelt at the coffin and old veterans wiped away their tears of emotion.[79] The visit proved not to be mere symbolism. After the defeat of the French by the Prussians in 1871, Queen Victoria provided sanctuary for the French royal family and, years later, as Edward VII, the Prince cemented the *entente cordiale*. It was his first taste of what would bring him lifelong happiness.

The Prince, though, continued to be a concern to his parents. Albert had been made Prince Consort and therefore came before the Prince of Wales in precedence. Did they worry that, if the Queen died, certain people would conspire against the foreign prince and oust him in favour of the Prince of Wales?[80] He was, though, allowed a short visit to Germany, with some carefully selected companions. His immaturity and lack of self-confidence was clear for all to see – though he did manage to kiss a girl – but the Queen regarded the visit important, after all he was a German as well as an English prince.[81] He was not allowed to join the Army – too risky for an heir to the throne - but his younger brother, Alfred, was able to join the Navy. The unfairness was not lost on him.

On 25 January 1858, the Prince's beloved sister, seventeen year old Vicky, married the Crown Prince of Prussia, Fritz. For years the Queen had bullied and reprimanded Vicky yet, once she had left England, she wrote affectionate letters to her, and her anger and distaste could now be fully directed onto the Prince of Wales. Victoria simply could not bring herself to love her son. Albert was the only person for her but, even so, she quarrelled endlessly with him.

The next stage in the Prince's rigorous education was to set him up at White Lodge in Richmond Park. This was not to allow him any freedom of his own, to learn and develop by experience, but to have him supervised in his curriculum even more closely. There were three equerries allocated to take it turns to look after him. One, deliberately, had not been to a Public School and two had VCs from the Crimean War,[82] including Major Lindsay of the Scots Fusilier Guards who saved the Colours at Inkerman and later became Lord Wantage (the first VC ever awarded). His 'Governor' was Colonel Robert Bruce, brother of the Lord Elgin who brought back the Marbles from the Parthenon. He was an irascible Grenadier who treated the Prince like an idle Guardsman. The detailed instructions from Prince Albert to this staff covered exactly how they were to behave with the Prince of Wales; he was not allowed any banter, no laughing at people or things, certainly no practical jokes, no card games, billiards or idle gossip. He was to be encouraged to cultivate his mind. His meals were prescribed by one of the worst doctors in England – seltzer water was allowed to be drunk at midday and one glass of diluted claret at night.[83] The Queen told him she disliked his Coburg nose (one might think with her German pride, it might have been the opposite), and his receding chin and large lips. While she was at it, she criticised his shooting shoes, the way he did his hair and the length of his overcoats.[84]

He went up to Oxford in October 1859. Escape at last and rooms with fellow undergraduates? Not a bit of it; he was incarcerated with the martinet Colonel Bruce in a private house in the town. Prince Albert saw Oxford as a place of refuge for study and improvement of the mind, not for growing up, having fun with contemporaries and sowing wild oats. The Prince's fellow undergraduates had to stand when he entered a lecture hall and not sit until he did; written lectures were delivered to his house. If this purgatory was not enough, Queen Victoria would write his report at the end of each holiday. She commented on his idleness, inattention, self-indulgence and admonished him for lying on a sofa or armchair. The trouble was that the Queen regarded only her relations suitable for friendship yet, at Oxford, there were some wonderfully raffish bad sorts of the Bullingdon Club who ate mackerel fried in gin for breakfast, washed down with a bottle of claret, and another who kept a pack of hounds and would appear in the Cathedral in his hunting boots.[85] The Prince of Wales would have learnt so much from them, *in how not to behave*, which was as important as to how to behave properly. How could he know what was wrong if he was only brought up in a stiflingly repressive regime? People also learnt by watching the mistakes of others. Prince Albert just could not see that.

In 1860, he was allowed to visit, formally, Canada and the United States. Both countries received him warmly and enthusiastically but, typically, the tour was deadened by the leadership of the austere and humourless Duke of Newcastle, reeling from divorcing his wife for running off with a Belgian courier and the elopement of his daughter with the alcoholic, violent and insane son of the Marquess of Londonderry.[86] The now General Bruce was in close attendance to relay Prince Albert's admonishments and provide drafts of mind-numbingly boring replies to speeches of welcome. In America, the Queen wrote to President Buchanan, that the Prince of Wales was to be addressed as Baron Renfrew because he had left her Dominions.[87] Quite what difference that made no one was really sure: the Americans, mystified, of course, called him the Prince of Wales. One enthusiast was warned off at a ball by the courtiers for trying to persuade the Prince to dance with his daughter. This was, presumably, before the dance floor collapsed (after the workmen repaired it, they discovered a carpenter nailed under the floor).[88]

He returned for a brief spell at Oxford, followed by Cambridge. Aged 19, he had been given permission by Prince Albert to smoke and took full advantage of it to smoke acrid cigars, to the Queen's disgust. She loathed the habit and it is surprising that Albert's ruling prevailed. Perhaps he realised he would have little control over this when the Prince was out of sight. A tiny glimmer of happiness also appeared in the Prince's life with the arrival of two men who were to remain firm friends for the rest of his life: Charles Carrington, one of the Etonians he had met before, and Nathaniel Rothschild of the immensely rich banking family.[89]

It was only after this, that he left for Ireland and the charms of the delightful Nellie...

When he heard about it from the notorious gossip, Viscount Torrington, Prince Albert was absolutely appalled. Did the news of the Prince's 'fall' really affect Albert's already failing health? Of course the Queen echoed his disgust and declared that her son had broken her beloved husband's heart. Prince Albert could see all the problems looming; illegitimate child, blackmail, gossip, social stigma and national disgrace. All that he tried to do for the Prince, in his eyes, had come crashing down. He was also a very sick man. On 14 December, Prince Albert died. At the time, it was widely diagnosed as typhoid but modern analysis suggests Crohn's Disease, unknown to science at the time.[90] He was 42 and the Queen never forgave the Prince of Wales for what she perceived as his part in hastening Albert's death.

Albert's death was a turning point in the Prince's life, though not as good as it should have been. No longer did the Prince have Albert mapping out his life and exerting his authority and restrictions over him but he still had his mother's refusal to acknowledge that he had grown up and should, gradually, be educated in the affairs of state. The Queen retired to a world of grief and seclusion, determined to maintain her beloved husband's policies to the complete exclusion of the heir to the throne. Mourning actually rather suited her; she could withdraw from tedious public events, refuse boring social engagements and retire into a small circle of favourite ladies-in-waiting who did exactly what she wanted. She never stopped blaming the Prince for causing Albert's death by his indiscretions at the Curragh. She continued to moan about his behaviour and criticise him. For his part, he was remarkably dutiful and obedient; astonishing given the thoroughly unpleasant way he had been brought up and treated.

If an heir to anything, be it a successful business, large estate or fortune, is not allowed to be trained for the eventual accession, what is he to do? Some reject the legacy and go their own way, some waste their time and money, others try to forge their own line for the takeover in due course. There are also those who develop an abiding interest in something completely different. For the Prince, his options were limited now he was not allowed any training for kingship. He was barely permitted minor royal activities; planting trees, opening bazaars, launching ships and heading charities. He certainly wasn't allowed to represent the Queen at anything major. He filled his life with shooting, gambling, racing and women. What else was he to do?

Clearly, the Prince's marriage was vital. But how to choose from the array of chinless Hohenzollerns or Palatinate princesses? Princess Alexandrina of Prussia, Princess Anne of Hesse-Darmstadt, niece of the Grand Duke of Hesse and of the Empress of Russia, Princess Augusta of Holstein-Glucksburg, Duchess Wilhelmina of Wurtemberg, Princess

Mary of Saxe-Altenburg or Princess Catherine of Oldenburg, sister of the Grand Duchess Nicholas of Russia?[91] Eventually, Princess Alexandra, daughter of Prince Christian of Denmark, was selected by the Queen and her closest cronies. There were a number of objections and, indeed, it would have been difficult to please the Queen with any contender. She could barely see the Prince as King, let alone someone else becoming Queen. Luckily the Prince, who had been brought into the selection system relatively late, approved and Alexandra and he were married on 10 March 1863. It is likely that the Princess knew of her future husband's not entirely chaste earlier life but would have had no conception of how unchaste her marriage was to be. Nevertheless, it became apparent that they were both very fond of each other and Alexandra, in her way, was wholly supportive of the Prince and he was very affectionate towards her.

The marriage was what Society had been waiting for. For too long it had suffered the dreariness of the Court; Albert cared nothing for the frivolity of balls, dinners and the theatre. Queen Victoria was socially invisible, so it was with delight that the beautiful Princess and her fun-loving husband were welcomed on Society's stage. In their turn, they thoroughly enjoyed themselves, perhaps the Prince more than his wife. While the Edwardian era technically did not start until the Prince became King in 1901, it was effective from this point. In March he liked to visit the French Riviera, without the Princess, fitting Paris in before or afterwards. The early summer was taken up with the London Season. After Ascot came Goodwood, followed by Cowes Week, then a short time in a German or Austrian spa and the south of France. October was spent in Scotland shooting and stalking, with Christmas invariably at Sandringham. Spare weekends, such as they were, found the Prince, not always accompanied by the Princess, staying at one of the great houses of the United Kingdom; with the Buccleuchs, the Devonshires, the Westminsters or the Portlands. The tireless Prince, who would happily smoke, drink and gossip to two in the morning would be up at seven for whatever was programmed for the day. Neither did it stop him enjoying the lower levels of entertainment in London music halls or the more exotic of the Parisian courtesans. He was jovial and easy to entertain and any woman was glad to sit next to him. He enjoyed female company and was exhilarated by conversation with intelligent women. Women who were also enjoying their new found freedom. The new silhouette required much thinner underwear than before, and it was in this period that underclothing took on the sensual connotations of the word '*lingerie*'. Sumptuous, overtly sexy and colourful underwear began to shift away from the boudoirs of courtesans and into the bedchambers of respectable women. Whereas Victorian underclothing had been functional, the sole *raison d'etre* of Edwardian underwear was to attract and tantalize men. It was the age of frou-frou, that exciting sound of chiffon and taffeta petticoats that whispered as a woman walked.[92] Although tantalising to someone like the Prince, it is a misjudgement to think that it was only because he wanted to go to bed with them, although that thought was never too far from his mind. For someone with such a harsh and isolated upbringing he was very good with the ordinary person; he found it easy to talk to ghillies, servants, soldiers and shopkeepers. While the Prince was particular about conventions over things like uniform and dress, he blurred the edges of social mobility in a way that others could never do. He was a boon to the self-made man's entry into Society and gave a second chance to some of Society's earlier rejects. His liking for Americans gave socially ambitious parents hope for their daughters and impoverished English aristocrats a saving of their estates by trans-Atlantic marriages. (More than 300 American women married into peers' or baronets' families between 1870 and 1914).[93] Previously disdained Jews, like the Rothschilds, Sassoons, Lawsons and Cassels became socially acceptable as friends of the Prince. A number of them, such as Maurice Hirsch, undoubtedly lent him vast amounts of money which were seldom repaid.[94] He enjoyed playing cards and it was rumoured that stakes were very high. Of course, he played with some very rich people but also those who could not really afford the stakes and resented the pressure. People did win and lose a lot of money gambling but it was, usually, of their own accord. Strait laced, pinch-lipped Puritans found the Prince an easy target for their strictures.

With such a wide ranging mix of acquaintances, relationships were bound to ebb and flow. The Prince, on the one hand was intensely loyal to his friends, but, on the other, could devastatingly drop them. When the Prince was Colonel of the 10th Hussars, not unnaturally, he became friends with the Commanding Officer, Lieutenant Colonel Valentine Baker. Baker was cashiered in 1875 and sent to prison for indecently assaulting a Miss Dickenson on a train. The case caused outrage and there were statements in the House of Commons expressing utter disgust at this scandalous behaviour. The newspapers screamed for a sentence of hard labour for such an atrocious crime. Baker, of course, lost many friends but not the Prince. The latter claimed the evidence was inconclusive and the punishment too severe. On Baker's release, the Prince helped him obtain a military post in Turkey. In another case, in 1885, the wife of a Member of Parliament told her husband that she had been the mistress of Sir Charles Dilke MP for three years. There were considerable undercurrents to the case but it became impossible for the innocent Dilke to refute the assertions. In the face of public anger, the Prince stood by his old friend and insisted he be re-admitted to Court.[95] It was an interesting friendship, given Dilke's republican views but, as a member of the Cabinet, he sneaked inside information to the Prince, which he loved. Others, who had incurred the displeasure of the Queen, found a refuge in the Marlborough Set; notably Louise von Alten, famously known as the Double-Duchess.[96] Queen Victoria thought her a flirt and far too 'fast'. She was probably right. The Prince, however, much admired her and admitted visiting her after she had become the Duchess of Manchester. It is not known whether she really slept with him but, given her reputation, it seems likely she would have encouraged him. She was certainly carrying on with the Marquis of Hartington, heir to the Duke of Devonshire (she married him in 1892, hence her 'Double'). This was an open secret and when the Prince stayed with the Manchesters, the Queen was horrified and tried to warn him off but to no avail; her was very loyal to Louise.

There was, curiously, the other side to him. Susan was the daughter of the Duke of Newcastle, who had led the Prince's trip to Canada and the United States. She ran off with the mad Lord Adolphus Vane-Tempest, son of Lord Londonderry. He died in 1864 and the Prince began a relationship with her in 1867 and, in 1871, she became pregnant. Was he the father? He told her to consult his doctor but she delayed doing so and, fed up, the Prince refused to have anything more to do with her apart from telling her to leave London to have the child. There was an inefficient effort by one of her friends to extort money from the Prince without success. A baby was born but no records exist. Susan died four years later. Scandal, for the time being, was narrowly avoided.[97] It seems that, while he was prepared to dabble on the fringe of scandal committed by others and, to be fair, support them, where it affected him directly, he was cold, heartless and calculating. This latter trait would appear significantly later.

The Prince's lifestyle made him highly vulnerable to blackmail. In 1864, he was threatened by a man called Green, who alleged the Prince had had intercourse with his wife three years earlier. There was little doubt that there had been some sort of honey-trap and the Greens were paid off and sent to New Zealand.[98] More seriously was the blackmail attempt by a rascal called Beneni.[99] He was the brother of the most famous Parisian courtesan of the time, Giulia Barucci. The Prince, among a number of luminaries, had enjoyed her favours since 1867. Allegedly, when meeting the Prince of Wales for the first time, she was told to behave with decorum. Upon being introduced, she promptly let her dress fall to the ground, revealing some beautifully exotic underwear. When she was reprimanded, she exclaimed, 'What, did you not tell me to behave properly to His Royal Highness? I showed him the best I have, and it was free!'[100] When she died, Beneni, to his great joy, found a cache of compromising letters including some extremely indiscreet ones from the Prince. Wasting no time, he demanded between twelve and fifteen hundred pounds for their return. The Prince and his advisers were determined not to pay and enrolled the services of one Mr J Kanne, who was described as the Queen's 'courier'. Kanne was just the man for an operation of this kind. Purporting to be a collector, he visited Beneni and subsequently, after airing a number of options with the Prince, went for the hard bargain. He drove the price down to £240 [£20,000] for the lot. Close examination revealed that they were not forgeries, which would have been damaging in themselves, but the genuine article. The Prince had had a narrow escape.[101]

By the early 1870s, the Monarchy was at its lowest level of popularity. The Queen had locked herself away in neurotic seclusion after Albert's death ten years previously. She refused to open Parliament in February 1870 on the grounds that the London traffic gave her a headache. She resisted the Prince's suggestions that she should be seen more in public and did her image no good by importing John Brown, her Scottish ghillie, into the inner circle of the Court. Brown was a bully and a drunkard and deeply unpopular with everyone bar the Queen.[102] The more scurrilous newspapers and pamphleteers had a field day. However, there was an underlying malaise. The British were, on the whole, a conservative lot and resisted change and revolution but there was a worrying Republican movement about, clearly anti the Monarchy and Government. *Reynold's News* was the leading critic amongst the newspapers; the Prince's speeches were ridiculed, the extravagance of the Court was questioned. *What Does She Do With It?* was the title of an anonymous pamphlet querying the Queen's expenditure. It was actually written by George Otto Trevelyan, the Chief Secretary to Ireland in the 1880s, but better known as a literary historian. His bestselling *American Revolution* was written without ever having set foot in America.[103] The Prince was spotted gambling in Homburg, Germany, when it was illegal in England; what a joy to the Republicans when it claimed the Prince was frittering away money earned by the hardworking population of the Country, money to which he was most certainly not entitled.[104] It was later rumoured, with no real evidence, that he was £600,000 [£57 million] in debt.[105]

There was increased pressure from the Country to reform the House of Commons. Huge meetings took place and there was a general feeling of the increasing respectability of the skilled working class. The Reform League, agitating for universal suffrage, became much more active and organized demonstrations of hundreds of thousands of people in Manchester, Glasgow and other towns. Though these movements did not use revolutionary language, nevertheless the threat was there. The crisis came when a demonstration in Hyde Park in May 1867 was banned by the Government. Thousands of troops and policemen were mobilised, but the crowds were so huge that the Government did not dare to intervene. The Home Secretary was forced to resign. Faced with the possibility of further popular revolt, the Government rapidly trebled the number eligible to vote. This, effectively, enfranchised most men who lived in urban areas and ultimately assisted the rise of the radical wing of the Liberal Party and helped Gladstone to victory.

In Europe, the Franco-Prussian War of 1870–1871 resulted in the defeat of France, and the overthrow of Emperor Napoleon III and the Second Empire. The Queen's loyalty to her numerous German relations made her unpopular at home and she clashed with the Prince whose sympathies, not unsurprisingly, lay with the French.[106] After Napoleon's capture by the Prussians in the Battle of Sedan, Parisian Deputies established the first Government of the Third Republic, headed by a President. This Government negotiated peace settlements with the newly proclaimed German Empire, resulting in the Treaty of Frankfurt, signed on 10 May 1871. To pressurise the Prussians into leave France, the Government passed a variety of controversial financial laws to pay reparations. In Paris, resentment rose and from April to May 1871, the workers revolted and established the Paris Commune, which maintained a radical left-wing regime for two months until its bloody suppression by the Government. Heads rested uneasily in the United Kingdom. Would this radicalism spread over here? There were predictions that when the Queen died, the monarchy would die with her.[107]

Unfortunately, amid all the difficulties swirling around the Prince at this time, came one of the most tricky he had to face; the Mordaunt affair.[108] No Prince of Wales had appeared before a Court in the land since the 15th Century. This was now to change with the Prince summoned to attend, as a witness, in the divorce court. Harriet Moncrieffe, barely eighteen, married Sir Charles Mordaunt in 1866. A ravishing beauty, she produced a premature son three years later. Sadly, the child was threatened with blindness. As a consequence, Harriet lost her sanity and confessed to her husband that he was not the father. It was Lord Cole, she said. She also admitted having affairs with other men, including the Prince of Wales. Apoplectic with anger, Mordaunt searched his wife's desk, discovering a diary and letters from, amongst others, the Prince. That April, she was served with divorce papers. Her parents swore she was deranged and the confessions inadmissible, and entered a plea of insanity. Sir Charles's lawyers regarded it as merely a ruse. Had she really admitted to adultery or was the confession a consequence of her madness? By February 1870, at the start of the trial, there was no doubt that she really was mad but had she been so when she confessed? She was certainly in no fit state to stand trial. There was considerable evidence to prove her insanity going back a long way, but Sir Charles's counsel maintained it was all an act. The Prince of Wales was really a very minor player in all this; the letters, which he had written, had somehow found their way into the newspapers[109] and, to the crowd's disappointment, were thoroughly innocuous and really only referred to his shooting parties, travel with his family and some ponies he had given her. They were printed in full in some American newspapers. The more sanctimonious could not resist commenting. *'SCANDAL IN HIGH LIFE – The papers have been full of the case before the English courts, touching the Prince of Wales and Lady Mordaunt, which we have not particularly alluded to from a disinclination to pander to that vitiate taste that gloats over the horrible and indecent. The conclusion arrived at was that Lady Mordaunt was deranged, but whether this was justified by the evidence, or a subterfuge to cover up the disgrace of a noble family we do not know. The evidence of Sir Charles Mordaunt is interesting as indicating the general feeling in regard to the character of the Prince of Wales. Sir Charles testified that before his marriage to Lady Mordaunt he knew of her intimacy with the Prince, and that after the marriage he warned her against continuing the acquaintance. "I told her," said he, "that I had heard in various quarters certain circumstances connected with his previous character that caused me to wish her to break off with him." Notwithstanding this wish, Lady Mordaunt continued to receive the Prince without the knowledge of her husband, until the time she made the voluntary confession that a criminal intimacy had been existing between them. Sir Charles also testified to the discovery of a batch of letters and a valentine from the Prince to his wife. The court loyally refused to permit the letters to be read.[110]*

Nevertheless, the fact that he had written to her and, indeed, visited her when her husband was away, made for salacious gossip. However innocent, it had the smack of an affair. While, of course, not on trial himself, that is what it looked like to the Country. The difficulty was to explain away his visits to a beautiful young woman in the absence of her husband. He was probably lucky not to be cited as a co-respondent. The Prince's reputation with women generally was not helpful. Of course, Queen Victoria was aghast at his appearing in Court and implored him not to attend. She firmly believed in his innocence but, understandably, realised the legal risks and felt his standing as a witness in a thoroughly unpleasant divorce, was damaging to the Monarchy and she was, arguably, right. However, noted for his straightforwardness and transparency, the Prince stood up well to questioning in Court and was believed. *Reynold's Newspaper,* though, went to town and declared him unfit and unworthy to rule over the country. On the other hand, *The Law Journal* came out in his support and held the view that, while Princes were not above the Law, they were entitled to its protection and privileges. Whatever the rights and wrongs of the case, it made the Prince deeply unpopular; he was hissed at Ascot and booed in the theatre. While people move on and, in time, these things are merely yesterday's news, this was not so for the Prince's advisers and courtiers. They were again tested with the Aylesford matrimonial scandal involving the rackety Marlborough family and Blandford's threat to call the Prince of Wales out to a duel. They would not forget and they would do anything to prevent the Prince ever appearing in Court again – if they could. (Colonel Owen Williams, who appears later in the story as a guest at Tranby Croft, was an equerry of the Prince's on his Indian trip, and brother of Lady Aylesford.)

There were 'professional' courtesans like Catherine Walters, known as Skittles, who were clever, discreet and knew the rules. As well as being a friend of the Prince of Wales she was Hartington's mistress and he set her up in great comfort in Mayfair.[111] There were the, mostly, wildly exaggerated stories, usually made up herself, surrounding the infamous Lily Langtry who had even been presented to the Queen. There were others who, perhaps, were not quite so sure of the boundaries. Patsy Cornwallis's son was allegedly fathered by the Prince and made much of it in his later life. The Princesse de Sagan's son was also rumoured to be a royal bastard but without foundation.[112] An interesting link with the Wilson family is that their eldest child, Susannah (Tottie) married, first, John Graham Menzies (Freddie). Their second son was Major General Sir Stewart Graham Menzies, the famous 'M' of the Security Service, born in January 1890. Apparently he used to wave at a portrait of Edward VII and, not entirely jokingly, refer to him as his father.[113] There is, of course, no proof of any of these myths but, nevertheless, because of his lifestyle, people happily believed these stories of the Prince.

Prince Albert Victor, known as 'Eddy' was the Prince of Wales's eldest son. He showed little interest in intellectual pursuits or reading though he did become involved in undergraduate life at Cambridge. In August 1884, he spent some time at Heidelberg University studying German. Leaving Cambridge in 1885, he was commissioned into the 10th Hussars. The chain-smoking Eddy was gormless and lackadaisical and liked to think of himself as a bit of a dandy.[114] When stationed in York with his Regiment, he became a good friend of Jack Wilson of

Tranby Croft. In July 1889, the Metropolitan Police discovered a male brothel in Cleveland Street, Bloomsbury. On investigation, the male prostitutes and pimps revealed the names of their clients, who included Lord Arthur Somerset, a son of the Duke of Beaufort, and an equerry to the Prince of Wales. At the time, men convicted of homosexual acts, faced two years' imprisonment with hard labour. The Cleveland Street scandal implicated numbers of the aristocracy and, it was rumoured, a member of the Royal Family. One of the rent boys was a waiter from the Marlborough Club;[115] uncomfortably close to the Prince's friends. The prostitutes, however, had not named Prince Eddy, and it is suggested that Somerset's solicitor, Arthur Newton, fabricated and spread the rumours to take the heat off his client.[116] The Prince of Wales refused to believe it and apparently said that it was no more true than if they had accused the Archbishop of Canterbury. (This was an unfortunate analogy as, unknown to the Prince, the Archbishop's wife was a lesbian and his three sons were homosexuals).[117]

The Prince of Wales interfered with the investigation; no customers of the brothel were ever prosecuted and nothing against Prince Eddy was revealed. Although there was no conclusive evidence of his involvement, or that he ever used a homosexual club or brothel, the rumours led some commentators to speculate that he did indeed visit Cleveland Street, and that he was possibly bisexual, probably homosexual. There was a *canard* going the rounds that Somerset fled to France to avoid prosecution when the full story, implicating Prince Eddy, would come out. Put into context, however, Eddy was also, ludicrously, thought to be involved in the Jack the Ripper case at the same time: much salacious gossip for the scandal sheets. Just as plans for both his marriage to Mary of Teck and his appointment as Viceroy of Ireland were under discussion, Prince Eddy fell ill with influenza in the pandemic of 1889–92. He developed pneumonia and died at Sandringham on 14 January 1892, less than a week after his 28th birthday. The Prince of Wales was devastated.

By the mid-1880s, the Prince's favourite mistress was Daisy Brooke. She was a daughter of Colonel the Hon Charles Maynard and his second wife Blanche FitzRoy. Charles Maynard was the eldest son and heir apparent of the 3rd Viscount Maynard. Blanche FitzRoy was a descendant of Charles II through his mistresses Nell Gwyn and Barbara Villiers. The fabulously rich Daisy married Lord Brooke, the eldest son of the 4th Earl of Warwick, in 1881. Lord Brooke succeeded to the Earldom in 1893, and the family moved into Warwick Castle.

After her marriage, Daisy began an affair with Lord Charles Beresford, an old friend of the Prince of Wales, who had commanded the royal yacht. He was the father of Daisy's second child. Daisy was later outraged to discover Mina, Lady Beresford, was pregnant by her husband who declared his affair with Daisy was, therefore, over. Furious, she wrote him a virulent letter demanding he leave his wife. Unfortunately, in her husband's absence, Mina opened the letter. Apoplectic with anger, she promptly handed over the letter to George Lewis, the society solicitor who was, later, to brief defendants' Counsel in the Tranby Croft case, for safe-keeping. Daisy then fell on the goodwill of the Prince of Wales, imploring him to help. He had known her in the past and, captivated by her tiny waist, blue eyes and curvaceous figure,[118] could not fail to come to her aid. He demanded the solicitor give up the letter. The latter properly refused but, improperly, allowed the Prince to read it. So he now tried to bully Mina into giving it up. She also refused but instructed the solicitor to write to Daisy warning her to stay away from London for the Season; if she complied, the letter would be returned. As a reward to the Prince of Wales, Daisy now happily ditched Beresford and became his mistress. The Prince of Wales made the situation worse by hinting to Mina that the position she and her husband held in Society would be endangered if the letter was not handed over. Beresford was incandescent with this blackmailing interference in a private matter by the Prince, calling him a 'blackguard' and very nearly coming to blows. The Prince, who should never have been involved, ostracised the Beresfords for a number of years, while Daisy occupied the premier place in the Prince's affections. Beautiful and an amusing conversationalist, her biggest flaw was that she couldn't keep a secret; rule number one in the successful courtesan's life, hence her sobriquet, Babbling Brooke. It was another instance, though, of the Prince's bad judgment and his complete failure to see how people would react to this sort of scandal.

From time to time, the Prince's friends lent him their houses for private assignations with his mistresses. One such friend was Bill Gordon-Cumming. On 6 September 1890, the Prince of Wales, returning unexpectedly early from a trip abroad, went round to Gordon-Cumming's house, 2 Harriet Street, where he looked forward to having a tryst with Daisy Brooke. To his consternation, not only was Daisy there, but so was Gordon-Cumming, *in flagrante*. He retired in confusion and embarrassment. The duplicity of Daisy and Gordon-Cumming weighed heavily on his mind and jealousy set in. His friendship for Gordon-Cumming now turned to barely concealed enmity.

This augured badly for the imminent stay at Tranby Croft to where they had all been invited. But who were the Wilsons, the fabulously rich owners of Tranby Croft?

CHAPTER 7 - The Shipping Magnate

The champagne bottle smashed against the gleaming green-painted hull, and the latest pride of the Wilson Line slid into the Humber, to the cheers of the dockyard workers. With a red funnel, and proudly flying the triangular white flag, emblazoned with a red circle, the 500 ton *Scandinavian* could carry forty first class and twelve second class passengers. It was 1852 and she was the largest ship to join the Line. Top-hatted, frock-coated merchants, puffing on cigars and fingering their watch chains, looked on with considerable satisfaction. The liner was registered to the 19-year old Charles Henry Wilson, brother of Arthur Stanley Wilson, later owner of Tranby Croft. By the end of the decade, the brothers would have increased the firm's capital to £70,000 [£129 million].[119]

In the early part of the nineteenth century, Hull was the centre of trade in that part of the world. It was a busy port complex of international shipping and the docks teemed with boats servicing those moored in the river. David Wilson was a lighterman. He would carry goods, in his small boat, from the wharves to ships in the Humber and return with their cargo. Although dependant on tides and weather, he, nevertheless, could make a reasonable living. He was hard-working and had a good eye for the main chance. He ensured that his sole surviving son, Thomas, was properly educated so that, in time, he would be able to understand and integrate with the merchants with whom David established an increasing authority and confidence. After an apprenticeship in the counting house of a successful merchant friend of his father's, Thomas, with the help of a useful dowry on marriage, was able to set up his own operation in 1817. Starting with what he knew best, he dealt in iron ore but, increasingly, became interested in shipping. Why pay someone else to carry your goods when you could do it yourself? Going into partnership with another trader, their first boat was a 51 ton sea-going vessel which carried coal, then a second was a 100 tonner. By now, they needed outside investment to expand. This came from a 'gentleman' of Newcastle, and a Hull druggist and importer of leeches.

Then came their chance. During the Napoleonic wars, Sweden had remained neutral and therefore mail could be sent by packet boat from Harwich to Gothenburg, by-passing the French trade blockade of the United Kingdom. With the arrival of peace, in 1834 this operation was cancelled and normal mail runs to the Continent were re-instituted. British sea-going merchant interest in Sweden waned. Wilson and his co-director decided, however, there was a commercial gap and ran a packet service between Hull and Gothenburg using a brig and two schooners. It was not a regular run but merely relied on demand. However, this was inadequate and people insisted on a proper timetable and mail consistently delivered by steamship. Steamships were relatively new but Thomas Wilson had had some experience and was prepared to take it on. With the death of his partner, he was on his own but still retained the loyalty of his financial backers.

At first, things went well but, given the unreliability of these new steamships, criticisms started to mount. In 1842, the Swedish Post Office cancelled their contract. The wily Wilson, though, had hedged his bets and still ran four sailing ships dealing, primarily, in Swedish iron ore. Wilson's backer withdrew his support but, by now, he had been joined by a number of his sons in the firm and was in a good financial position with a capital of £20,000 [£29 million]. More docks had been built in Hull and business was booming. Thomas and his boys knew, though, the value of the steamship and, in 1850, launched a powerful paddle steamer. Thomas Wilson Sons and Company negotiated a fresh deal with the Swedes and provided a fast and efficient service although they realised that a screw-driven vessel was the thing of the future. Railways started to become effective and there was an express link between Hull and London. These, of course, were the days of Isambard Kingdom Brunel. In 1860 for instance, a businessman could leave Gothenburg on a Friday at 1pm and be in London by 10pm on Sunday.

In 1869, the patriarch, Thomas, died leaving the thriving business in the hands of his sons. The Wilson business was expanding and, by 1880, with daughters marrying sons of merchants, the family had 12 agents in England and 49 abroad including America, St. Petersburg and India. All, though, had not been entirely smooth; the Crimean War, the Chinese Wars and Indian Mutiny had tested the courage and resourcefulness of the Wilsons, amongst others.

In 1863, Arthur Stanley Wilson had married Mary, the daughter of a relatively wealthy family, but was now very rich in his own right. They set up house in a residential part of Hull but, happily for Arthur, a workaholic, it was in the commercial centre and close to the docks. Children; Susannah (Tottie), Ethel, Arthur Stanley (always called Jack), Edward, Thomas, Muriel (Thetis) and Clive were born over the next few years. Arthur and his brother, Charles, continued to work extremely hard and within the next twenty years transformed their father's legacy into a shipping line of international importance and themselves into a pair of the richest men in the land. Mary had considerable social ambitions and why not? The world was changing and society was becoming used to men who had made money themselves and not just inherited it. The boys were sent to Eton, a significant step up the prestige ladder then, as it is now. Mary now needed a house to which society would come, certainly not in the centre of Hull.

In the meantime, Arthur's brother, Charles, had married a lady from the Duke of Wellington's family and launched a political career which was to end, in 1906, with a peerage. Although Arthur had no political pretensions and disliked public speaking, he had no wish to float along in his brother's wake even if Mary had let him. In 1873, he acquired 34 acres of land at Tranby Croft at Anlaby, near Hull in the East Riding of Yorkshire. Even before the house was built, the gardens were laid out with a lily pond, rock garden and banks of rhododendrons. The house itself was a sixty room, three storey mansion in Italianate style with a solid tower which added dignity to an otherwise plain structure. It had stabling for twenty horses and garaging for three large coaches. At the time of the completion of the house, the local hunt, the Holderness, was in dire financial straits and needed a wealthy Master. Who better than Arthur? Encouraged by Mary, this was another step into local society and, on becoming sheriff in 1888, the seal of acceptance was for all to see. The Wilsons had made it.

Tranby Croft might have been sneered at as being the house of a nouveau riche self-made man. However, life was changing rapidly in the vibrant industrialised country that England had become. The aristocracy's money was dissipating and therefore the likes of the Wilsons, with eligible daughters, were becoming very attractive. Invitations to lavish house parties were not to be turned down. Arthur even added another wing to the house to accommodate a billiard room, bringing the number of rooms up to a hundred.

A house such as this, with a family that was upwardly mobile, needed a considerable number of servants. Servants and family, in a sense, preserved their own privacy and each could get on with their lives to their own satisfaction. Corridors and back stairs led to the kitchens, sculleries, tap rooms and servants' quarters that went unseen by the inhabitants of the main house. Not all the servants lived in; a number were employed from the local village. Those that did, had rooms at the top of the house, with male and female carefully segregated. The hierarchy of the servants' hall was strictly maintained. The housekeeper presided but would take breakfast and tea in her own room served by the still room maid. There she could entertain the maids of the ladies staying in the house and, occasionally, give the butler a glass of sherry. The staff were divided into day and night shifts. The male staff were under the control of the butler and had little to do with the female servants who were under the housekeeper, cook or laundry mistress. The first job of the day shift was to prepare breakfast. It started early, as Arthur wanted to be on his way to the office, and went on until the last member of the household had eaten. Not for the faint hearted, breakfast consisted of porridge, eggs, cooked meat, bacon and devilled kidneys with thick slices of bread and homemade butter and jam. At 10am, Mary would appear in the kitchens to discuss events and menus. As soon as this finished, the kitchen maids were sent away to put on clean uniforms and prepare lunch. After that there would be tea, a popular, relatively new ritual at which ladies wore hats and gloves. The final task was dinner, which required a further change of uniform; a substantial meal which could go on for three hours.

Arthur's formal steps into society were marked by becoming Master of Foxhounds and Sheriff of Hull. He was not under any misapprehension as to why he had been asked to take on the Master of the Holderness Hunt. It was, effectively, bankrupt and no one else was prepared to do so. Arthur's own hunting had been fairly haphazard but he was a businessman and he was sure he could turn it round. He certainly kept it going, with a combination of badgering members for their subscriptions and occasional injections of his own money. There were, however, compensations. In January 1882, the Hunt met at Christopher Sykes's house, Brantingham Thorpe, where the Prince of Wales was staying.[120] The Master would most certainly have been presented to His Royal Highness. Hunt Balls were popular and extravagant affairs. When Prince Albert (Eddy), the Prince of Wales's eldest son, was stationed with the 10th Hussars in York in January 1888, he attended one at the Assembly Rooms in Beverley and stayed at Tranby Croft. He had become a firm friend of Jack Wilson.

Arthur was Sheriff of Hull from 1888 to 1889. It was a true recognition of his philanthropy and munificence. He was a generous benefactor to the City, and is especially remembered for the Victoria Children's Hospital, for which he served as Chairman.[121] His wife, Mary, plunged into all sorts of charitable functions and her very presence could guarantee success. There were more visits to Tranby Croft from Prince Eddy, cementing the Wilson's position in society. He also attended probably the most prestigious event in Arthur's year of office; the Sheriff's Ball. There were 700 guests, personally greeted by Arthur, wearing court dress and a sword. Mary wore a diamond necklace and tiara. The Prince led Mary out in the first dance to the enjoyment of the guests and her family. By now, the Wilsons had bought a larger house in London, 13, Grosvenor Crescent, Belgravia. There they entertained the Duke of Cambridge, Lord Randolph Churchill and Christopher Sykes, Arthur's neighbour in Yorkshire and a close friend of the Prince of Wales. In March 1889, Arthur was proposed for membership of the Marlborough Club, the Prince of Wales's elite private and highly personal Club.

The Wilsons had reached the zenith of their wealth and influence, and were fully accepted by Royalty and aristocracy. They were charming and benevolent. Their life could not be better but about to enter it was their nemesis, Lieutenant Colonel Sir William Gordon-Cumming Bt.

CHAPTER 8 - A Game of Baccarat

St Leger week at Doncaster Races in September was a firm fixture in the Prince of Wales's calendar. He thoroughly enjoyed his racing and the social arrangements surrounding the week. Often, he had one of his own horses running and that, coupled with lots to eat and drink, surrounded by friends and fragrant women, was something to which he much looked forward. He normally stayed with Christopher Sykes at Brantingham Thorpe but Sykes had virtually beggared himself in his lavish entertainment of the Prince and, nearing bankruptcy, could not afford to have him to stay again. He explained his dilemma to Lord Coventry, the head of the Prince's household, and Arthur Wilson's name was suggested. The Prince had met him before and Mrs Wilson had a name for being a first-rate hostess. The Wilsons, of course, were more than happy to have him and it would have given the family enormous pleasure and social prestige to have such a guest at Tranby Croft, their large country house. [122] The Prince might have stayed in more aristocratic surroundings, such as Welbeck with the Duke and Duchess of Portland, but it was to his credit that he felt it proper to recognise those who had contributed so much to the economy of the Nation. He would also have been aware that, given the vast wealth of the Wilsons, it was not going to be an uncomfortable week.

A good deal of care was taken, as always, with the names of those who were to be invited to the house party. They would have been discussed with the Prince and then, once agreed, passed to Mrs Wilson for invitations to be sent out. Heading the list were Lord and Lady Brooke. Careful planning of the bedroom layout at Tranby Croft might have provided an opportunity for the Prince to indulge in some amorous assignation. However, this was not to be. To Daisy's distress, and, no doubt, the Prince's, her step-father, Lord Rosslyn, had died in Scotland and she and her husband had to travel north for the funeral. However, there might be a chance to meet up later?

In attendance on the Prince were the Earl and Countess of Coventry and his equerry, the Hon Henry Tyrwhitt-Wilson. Other close friends were the Earl of Craven, Lady Brougham and Vaux, and Lieutenant General Owen Williams, formerly of the Royal Horse Guards (The Blues), who had been the Prince's equerry on the Indian tour. He was a particularly close friend and confidant. Lord Edward Somerset and his cousin, Captain the Hon Arthur Somerset and Berkeley Levett, a subaltern in the Scots Guards, were younger guests. Reuben Sassoon and Count Henry Lützow were examples of the wide circle of the Prince's friends who were not solely drawn from the ranks of the British aristocracy. Poor Christopher Sykes brought up the rear.

Arthur Stanley (Jack) Wilson, the Wilsons' son, joined his parents as hosts. Ethel, the Wilsons' daughter, with her husband, Edward Lycett Green, were included. Completing the guest list was a Miss Naylor.

Not originally asked, but included at the relatively last minute for reasons which are unclear, was Lieutenant Colonel Sir William Gordon-Cumming, Bt.[123] He had stayed at Tranby Croft for the Doncaster Races in 1885 and with the Lycett Greens at their house in York in 1888. He had also dined with the Wilsons in London, so he knew the family but not well.[124] The Wilsons would have known he was a close friend of the Prince's and, by any standards, cut a dash in Society. His presence would do nothing but enhance the house party.

The party was, therefore, an interesting mix. Had Agatha Christie been writing at the time, it would have featured as one of her classic whodunnits; all it needed were a couple of dead bodies and Hercule Poirot mincing in. There was, though, a slightly uneasy atmosphere. With no Daisy Brooke, the Prince of Wales lacked the stimulating female company that he so enjoyed. He had missed his tryst with her at Gordon-Cumming's London house and, understandably, would have been feeling frustrated. The other ladies were no compensation. He needed diversion. Did his fellow guests provide it?

Reuben Sassoon was a member of the famous Iraqi Jewish family, one of the richest in the world. Reuben, while not unamusing, was not going to be the life and soul of the party. It was unkindly said he only opened his mouth to put food in it.[125] Count Lützow was a Bohemian historian and critic. He had been a member of the Austrian Parliament and Chamberlain to the Emperor Franz Joseph. He was, though, a tireless advocate of Bohemian independence from the Austro-Hungarian Empire. In July 1888, he had narrowly avoided appearing as a witness in a criminal case, invoking Diplomatic Privilege as Charge d'Affaires at the Austrian Embassy.[126] Interesting to talk to, no doubt, but not known for a sense of humour.[127] Both these men would have been tolerated by the Prince but bored him pretty quickly. Young Berkeley Levett, although seeing himself as a somewhat dashing figure and a bit of a dandy, may have been out of his depth in the Prince's circle, particularly in the shadow of his decorated and experienced senior officer, Gordon-Cumming. Did he need to compensate for some lack of self-confidence? Later, he married a Bass brewery heiress and served as a Gentlemen Usher in the Royal Household. Edward Lycett Green was the son of Sir Edward Green, Bt, a self-made 'ironmaster' and Conservative politician. Green had married Mary Lycett and joined her name to the family surname. Edward, the son, described himself as a Master of Foxhounds.[128] Was the double barrelled surname an aspiration to gentry which was not quite there?

Was Gordon-Cumming, therefore, a late addition in order to provide amusement for the Prince, together with the court jester, Sykes?

The scene was set.

On Monday 8 September, the Prince of Wales travelled directly to Doncaster and inspected the course, from where he, and his party, went by special train to Hessle, the nearest station to Tranby Croft. The little station had been transformed; the waiting room had been luxuriously re-carpeted and furnished with oak tables and chairs in crimson velvet. Outside, every square foot was covered in green foliage and flowers. A triple arch had been built of yew and laurel, and bunting flew from post to post. A huge crowd had gathered and cheered as the Prince alighted, at about 5 o'clock, onto the red-carpeted platform to be met by his host, Arthur Wilson. Together they drove by coach to Tranby Croft where further welcoming arches, this time surmounted by white flowers in the shape of the Prince of Wales's feathers had been erected by the gardeners.[129] A Union Jack flew from the tower, together with the flag of the Wilson Line but not, surprisingly, the Prince's own royal standard. But no one appeared to notice in the euphoria of the welcome.

There was then time to settle in before the dressing gong went at 7 pm. Valets unpacked, clothes were pressed and shoes polished while guests met and mingled. Had Daisy been there, there might have been an opportunity for the Prince and her to snatch a moment of privacy; what the French call a *cinq à sept*.[130] One of the joys was that ladies dressed for tea without the constricting stays and corsets, so their clothing was looser and more comfortable for whatever might be in store. Dressing and undressing, or perhaps the other way round, was easily achieved in total privacy without the need for a lady's maid. Dinner was at 8.15. It was a magnificent feast, consisting of fourteen courses, with wines to match. There were round tables, each sitting eight people, so the Prince sat in the centre one, flanked by Mrs Wilson and Lady Brougham.

After dinner, the ladies withdrew, leaving the men to their port and cigars; ribald stories and, no doubt, teasing Christopher Sykes, invariably the butt of His Royal Highness's jokes. Joining the ladies later in the drawing room, the party was entertained by some singing by Ethel Lycett Green. She had an enviable local reputation as a musician and the Prince was never averse to listening to, and looking at, a pretty woman. In his early years, he might have even enjoyed a little dancing but now a portly 48, he looked for other divertissement, and suggested a game of Baccarat. The game was certainly played at Sandringham late into the night with 'a real table, and rakes, and everything like the rooms at Monte Carlo.'[131] This would not have pleased his host who had been infuriated the year before to catch his son and his cronies playing a drunken version for high stakes in the billiard room. He had confiscated the counters and forbade the game in his house. There was nothing, though, he could do about this now without giving enormous offence to his royal guest, so he allowed Jack to prepare the tables and, diplomatically, retired to bed leaving his wife in charge.

Given the host's views on Baccarat, there were no specific tables in the house, so Jack had to improvise with two card tables and an oblong one in the smoking room. The tables were different heights and the oblong one highly polished thus needing a cloth cover. Some curtain material was found which was not entirely satisfactory as the counters did not show up well, but it was all they had. On a proper Baccarat table, a white line is marked approximately six inches from the edge of the table and stakes are put out beyond this line.

Baccarat is not a game for skilled card players. In fact it is merely one of luck. Four packs of cards are shuffled together and the banker deals two cards face down, only to the people immediately on his right and left, and two to himself. One card, face up, is then dealt to each. All the other players sitting on the right and left of the banker form what is called a *tableau*. They put out their stakes but do not have cards. The banker then looks at his cards and offers one more card to the two people on his right and left. The aim is to reach a score of eight or nine. All cards are face value with aces worth one, and tens and Court cards nothing. The players declare and if the banker's are not as good, he loses to the whole of the *tableau* on that side.

That night, the Prince of Wales was the banker. Was anyone else going to volunteer? He enjoyed the power and relished being in control; something so absent from the rest of his life. He had his own, very elegant counters, made of leather and with a *fleur de lys* embossed in gold on the reverse. They were in various denominations and colours; not the possessions, one might think, of someone who disapproved of gambling. They had been given to him by an old friend, Sir Edward Hulse Bt. Reuben Sassoon, who was the croupier or 'accountant' for the evening, made a careful list of what each player won and lost. It was decided that the banker would be limited to £100, so stakes were prevented from being outlandish.

The Prince sat in the middle of the tables and, reading to his left, the *tableau* was Mary Wilson, Berkeley Levett, Jack Wilson, Sir William Gordon-Cumming, Lord Edward Somerset and General Owen Williams. Gordon-Cumming, an inveterate card player, although not a very good one according to his daughter, Elma,[132] had a piece of white paper in front of him, on which he kept a score of his wins and losses. He placed his stakes on the paper, which were seen more easily against the curtain material tablecloth. One method of play, used by Gordon-Cumming, was to double up his stake if it was a winner. So, if, say, a £1 stake won, a counter of £1 was paid out from the bank and left on top of the original stake, then a further £1 counter added from the player to make a £3 stake for the next round or *coup*. Inevitably, therefore, there was a certain amount of legitimate movement of stakes between *coups*.

As play continued into the evening, Jack Wilson convinced himself that Gordon-Cumming, sitting on his left, was cheating by surreptitiously increasing his stake when the cards were good for the player and withdrawing counters when losing. Horrified, he whispered his suspicions to Berkeley Levett, sitting on his other side. 'This is too hot. The man next to me is cheating.' Levett replied, 'Impossible.' 'Well, look for yourself.' Levett agreed, 'This is too hot.' Surprisingly, no one else appeared to have heard this conversation or, indeed, noticed anything curious about the play. In his turn, Levett had watched carefully and saw Gordon-Cumming increase his stake, when the cards were good, to be paid out by the banker on the larger stake. He was equally disturbed but nothing was said or done until the game ended and everyone went to bed.

Jack Wilson followed Levett to his room and asked him what they should do? 'My God! Think of it. Lieutenant Colonel Sir William Gordon-Cumming caught cheating at cards!' Levett wanted nothing to do with it. Gordon-Cumming was a highly respected senior officer in his Regiment and he wasn't going to become involved. He would rather do nothing and hope the problem would go away. Anyway, was what he thought he had seen, amount to cheating? Interestingly, though, he did not refute Jack's claim. Jack, realising he was going to get no support from Levett, then went and told his mother. She had seen no irregularity and was, of course, aghast; if this went further it was going to ruin her brilliant house party. She told him to say nothing but organise a proper table for the following evening. Desperate for help to lighten the load of this secret, Jack told his brother-in-law, Lycett Green, the following morning, and, he, not unnaturally, told his wife. Already, five people were in the know.[133]

A happy day was then spent at the races with lots of champagne, mingling with Society and everyone looking forward to a good dinner and evening at Tranby Croft. No one, particularly the Prince, Lord Coventry or General Williams had any idea of what was afoot.

Again the Baccarat table, this time a rather better one with a proper baize cover, was placed, now in the billiard room, and those who wanted to play assembled after dinner. That night a line was drawn in chalk, on the cover, six inches from the edge. The seating plan, with the Prince of Wales again holding the bank and General Williams being the croupier looked like this:

Reuben Sassoon

Mary Wilson	Arthur Somerset
The Prince of Wales	Lord Coventry
Lord Edward Somerset	General Williams
Berkeley Levett	Lady Coventry
Lady Brougham	Sir William Gordon-Cumming
Edward Lycett Green	Ethel Lycett Green

Jack Wilson[134]

It was not clear whether those who suspected the cheating had made an arrangement between themselves to watch Gordon-Cumming. If they hadn't, why was Berkeley Levett playing again? He had said, the night before, he had wanted nothing to do with it. The sensible option would be simply not to play but join the others in the drawing-room. Had he changed his mind? Perhaps he hoped that Gordon-Cumming would not be seen to cheat and then would he be in a good position to reject Jack's accusations? Lycett Green, who had only, of course, been told of the previous night's events, was in a good position, opposite Gordon-Cumming, to see what was going on. It wasn't long before he persuaded himself that the Colonel was, indeed, cheating. Did he want to catch out this eminent man? His reaction, though, was very odd. Instead of making a scene at the table or, rather better, taking the Colonel on one side at an opportune moment and having a quiet word with him, he left the table, went into the smoking room where he wrote a note to his mother-in-law, Mary Wilson, to outline what he had witnessed. He then gave it to a servant to give to her at the table. She failed to react, no doubt wishing the drama to evaporate but, in human nature, she could not avoid keeping an eye on Gordon-Cumming's play. Play continued but no one noticed any further cheating despite all those aware of the problem, presumably, keeping a very close eye on what Gordon-Cumming was doing. Gordon-Cumming was up £225 [£21,610] overall, which was about £100 [£9,603] more than anyone else, of course, all won from the banker, the Prince of Wales. The Prince, later, congratulated him on his good luck, which it was; unless he had manipulated that luck.

Further gloom added to Mrs Wilson's anxieties as, the following morning, Wednesday, news came that her brother, Henry, who lived not far away, had died. The family had to go into mourning but Mrs Wilson was determined this would not affect the race-goers and it was decided they would attend the races, but dressed in mourning. In the train, on the way to Doncaster, Lycett Green found himself in the same compartment as Lord Edward Somerset and could not resist telling him the story. Somerset promptly told his cousin, Arthur, who maintained that Lycett Green should inform Lord Coventry, the head of the Prince of Wales's household. He did so and Lord Coventry, who as a novice at Baccarat, probably didn't really understand the situation, told General Williams. Why Arthur Wilson, the host, was not told has never been explained. Perhaps it was thought that, with his well-known abhorrence of the game, it would only make matters worse.

That evening, when everyone was dressing for dinner, Gordon-Cumming was visited by Lord Coventry and General Williams but none of those who, allegedly, had actually seen the cheating. Solemnly, these two informed a shocked Gordon-Cumming that they had just come from a meeting in Coventry's room with Jack Wilson, Lycett Green and the two Somersets, and outlined the accusations. (Berkeley Levett had refused to join them.) They told Gordon-Cumming that the Prince would have to be informed. (Although he didn't admit it, Coventry had already done so.) Gordon-Cumming was livid and accused Coventry and Williams of believing statements from 'a parcel of inexperienced boys.'[135] Why these two worldly and senior pillars of society took such immediate action and completely failed to investigate the matter properly or seek an explanation from Gordon-Cumming in the first place, can only, it seems, be put down to their paranoia of involving the Prince in yet another scandal. Or was it something else? Gordon-Cumming demanded to see the Prince, hoping to put his case first, little realising that the Prince had already been told and had, effectively, made up his mind.

It is not difficult to imagine that that evening's dinner was a pretty sombre affair; a bereaved household and a potential scandal hanging over a number of heads. There was no Baccarat after dinner in view of the mourning, but Gordon-Cumming did get his way and have an interview with the Prince of Wales. Both Lord Coventry and General Williams, but none of the actual witnesses, were present. So no one knew exactly what had happened at first hand. Gordon-Cumming protested his innocence and explained how he had played the game (doubling up his stake) and maintained that others, who were pretty ignorant of the game, simply failed to understand the technique. He had his stakes on the white sheet of paper in front of him and, clearly, in his view, what Jack had seen was a perfectly legitimate way of playing the game. The Prince was unsympathetic, saying there were five accusers against him. He was merely relying on what he had been told by Coventry and Williams, who had not, themselves, seen anything. He completely failed to see any other side of the story. Maybe he didn't want to?

Gordon-Cumming was sent out of the room and the Prince of Wales then summoned Lycett Green, Jack Wilson, Berkeley Levett and the two Somersets. Lycett Green did all the talking and when the Prince turned to Levett to ask a question, the latter declined to answer on the basis that he was in Gordon-Cumming's Regiment. He would have been too well aware of the responsibility to report an officer to his Commanding Officer if he suspected him of conduct unbecoming.[136] To be fair to the Prince, not a professional soldier, this might well have escaped him but not General Williams who would have been even more aware of the regulation than the inexperienced Levett. Nevertheless, it was quite brave of Levett to stand up to the Prince.

Coventry and Williams then asked Gordon-Cumming to return and invited him to sign a hastily drafted statement which read as follows:

"In consideration of the promise, made by the gentlemen whose names are subscribed, to preserve silence with reference to an accusation which has been made in regard to my conduct at baccarat on the nights of Monday and Tuesday 8th and 9th September 1890, at Tranby Croft, I will on my part solemnly undertake never to play cards again as long as I live."[137]

The remainder of the paper was blank, so he would have no idea who the 'subscribers' were and who, and, more importantly, who had not, been sworn to secrecy. Additionally, on the face of it, it could be construed as an admission of guilt. It was unclear exactly when this document was drawn up, whether before Lycett Green's interview with the Prince or afterwards and, indeed, who suggested drafting it.[138] The most likely person was Owen Williams, the ringleader of the unfolding conspiracy.

Gordon-Cumming's initial reaction was to refuse to sign it and report himself to his Commanding Officer. With, he thought, five people against him, his chances of a fair hearing, though, would be negligible. He therefore sought the advice of his old friends, Coventry and Williams who, not unnaturally, urged him to sign. The alternative, Williams threatened, was that he would have to leave the house immediately and would be warned off every race-course in the land. Lycett Green had already said that if the document was not signed he would denounce Gordon-Cumming at the races in the morning. Quite how he was going to do that and the uproar that would have ensued seems to have escaped him. It was the last thing the courtiers would have wanted. Still protesting his innocence, the accused signed.

The Prince of Wales's attitude, at this juncture, was baffling. He totally accepted what he had been told by Coventry and Williams without question. For instance, there were not five witnesses to the cheating but three, Jack Wilson and Berkeley Levett on the first night and Lycett Green the second; the others had been told. It would have been quite simple and achieved the perceived aim of keeping the Prince out of trouble, merely for him to reject the accusation against his old friend and demand an apology from the various accusers for treating him thus. Silly boys, how could they possibly misinterpret the skilled playing of an experienced card player; an icon of respectability? With, perhaps a hint of a New Year honour for the host? End of story.

Without Gordon-Cumming seeing the document again, the following signed:

Albert Edward P
Coventry
Owen Williams
Arthur Wilson
A C E Somerset

Edward Somerset
E Lycett Green
A Stanley Wilson
Berkeley Levett
R D Sassoon

Where was Christopher Sykes's signature? Were he and the bold
Count, the Earl of Craven and Lady Brougham living in a land of their
own? What about Mrs Wilson and Mrs Lycett Green? They knew of the
accusation but had not been sworn to secrecy. Not much escapes those
'below stairs.' There must have been some sort of gossip in the servants'
hall. Why any of the signatories really thought it would remain a secret
for long, is highly questionable.

That evening Gordon-Cumming wrote a letter to Owen Williams on
Tranby Croft writing paper.[139]

Dear Owen,

I hope you will take an opportunity of telling the Prince of Wales how
entirely I was guided in my action yesterday by his advice & yours &
Coventry's. While utterly and entirely denying the truth of the
allegations brought against me, I thoroughly see how for my own sake,
as well that of others, it is essential to avoid an open row & the scandal
arising therefrom. It is difficult for anyone, however innocent he may
know himself to be, & however unstained his character may be, to come
well out of an accusation brought by numbers against me alone, & I
shrink therefore from doing as perhaps I ought, court a full and thorough
investigation.

[*illegible*] a cruel blow it is to me to know that any men, even if
strangers to me, should believe that I have deliberately cheated them at
cards, or to feel that men like His Royal Highness, Coventry and you,
against whom never a word has been said, should have been called on to
advise me on such a charge, & possibly believing yourselves that from
the fact of my signing that paper, I am in any way unfit to associate with
you & men like you.

Of course my word is suspect as regards credibility but it was quite
unnecessary. I should never under any circumstances have touched them
again.

As regards the money I won this week, I feel it impossible for me to take it. I believe it was mostly from the Prince. Sassoon need know nothing as to whether I [*illegible*] it or not, & as HRH will doubtless insist on paying, I should be [*illegible*] if in any way he may think fit, to a mission or other charity.

I intend to fulfil my engagements in Scotland and elsewhere as if this had not occurred, though with a heavy heart. This I owe to myself.

Again thanking you and Coventry,

I am

Yours ever,

W Gordon Cumming

Was this really the sort of letter a guilty man would write? He left Tranby Croft early the following morning. [The photograph of the house party is dated 11 September. This must be wrong as that was the day everyone left. It must have been taken the day before, the 10th, unless there was some ulterior motive for incorrectly dating it.] The Prince of Wales also left that day and stayed the night in York for the day's racing, then summoned Lord and Lady Brooke to have tea with him at York station, on their way north, on the evening of 12 September.[140] Did he want to unburden himself of this devastating secret or was it just that he missed Daisy so much?

Anyway, the case was closed.

Or was it?

CHAPTER 9 - The Gathering Storm

Everyone was safe; the secret remained tucked away in Tranby Croft. The Prince of Wales had secured the silence of the house guests and his mother was not going to find out. Those arch-courtiers, Williams and Coventry, had prevented a re-run of the Mordaunt scandal; the Wilsons and Lycett-Greens could look forward to further social successes and advancement and Gordon-Cumming, though privately bruised and tarnished, could still move freely in Society and his Regiment, albeit without playing cards.

The Prince of Wales had written to his son, George, from Tranby Croft on 9 September and from Abergeldie Castle on 16 September, mentioning 'Bill Cumming' but not alluding to any card playing and certainly no problem connected with it.[141] Nevertheless, Gordon-Cumming was worried. On 12 September, he wrote to the Prince. '...the secret is already in the minds of far too many, I fear, to remain one long, but the one thing that would serve to drive me to death or worse, would be the knowledge that your Royal Highness is now in any way altered your manner or tone to me when we meet, as meet we must, if I am to continue to live as I have hitherto lived in the world......But what I again wish to point out is, the only hope I have of remaining in the eyes of the rest of the world an untarnished English gentleman is that the said world should not be aware of any alteration in the courteous and friendly manner with which you have so long honoured me, and the forfeiture of your esteem is, Sir, believe me, the cruellest blow of all. I must apologise for even writing to your Royal Highness at all, and you must be well aware that I write in no way wishing to dictate to you, but I cannot help making this final appeal to show how utterly it remains in your power to utterly damn, morally and physically, one who has ever been a loyal and devoted subject to your Royal Highness.'[142]

The Prince did not reply but sent the letter to General Williams on 13 September:

'I received the enclosed from W.C. today. I should like to have your opinion and that of Coventry on the subject of its contents whether an answer is desirable, and if so what is it to be. The writer does not seem thoroughly to understand the gravity of his conduct, and when he alludes to "the forfeiture of my esteem", how could it be otherwise? He also still harps on the strings of being allowed to play whist with his brother officers. Naturally such a thing could not be allowed for a moment, nor does it coincide with his statement to us that he should anyhow have never touched a card again. It must always be very disagreeable for us who know what happened to meet him in future, & much will depend on his conduct and tact (if indeed he possesses the latter) what attitude we have to adopt towards him in society & in public. Kindly return me the letter after Coventry has seen it.'[143]

Needless to say, he did not reply having now got himself into a state where he regarded Gordon-Cumming as the arch-villain.

On 17 September, the Prince wrote again to General Williams. He now clearly regarded him as a man in whom he could totally put his trust and rely on him completely for advice.

'Many thanks for your letters of 13th & 15th with enclosures.[144] Our first letters crossed so I did not acknowledge your first one till I heard again from you. All you say in your letters is I think quite admirable & I agree with you that it is important to have a statement of what occurred, which explains why the "conditions" (which are in my possession) were drawn up. Will you kindly draw up a clear statement & then submit it to Coventry before sending it to me, so that you may both be agreed about it. I also agree that it would be better not to answer C's letter to me. What could I say? & I don't think he really expects an answer. As to the future all depends upon him & the tact he displays to those who know the awful secret. I feel so strongly on the subject, & have such horror of anything of that kind, that I don't consider any punishment too severe. Indeed we <u>have</u> dealt leniently with him solely to prevent a scandal, but I confess that I am horrified at the flippant way he treats the whole matter. I shall try before others not to be marked in my manner towards him, but the less he comes in my way the better. It is also impossible to be "hail fellow, well met" as formerly. I don't suppose also that Temple will be an "open house" to him as formerly. If he could only be induced to go away for a time, & avoid Country Houses this winter it would be the wisest course to adopt, but he has "brass" enough to "brazen out" anything! How can he ask you to give him "the benefit of the doubt", making out his accusers to be about the greatest scoundrels on record! It is altogether a most deplorable business, & is to me like a hideous nightmare! How an officer & a gentleman with everything to lose should behave in such a manner surpasses all human comprehension. With renewed admiration for the admirable & decided way in which you have carried out the terribly difficult task which has been thrown upon.'[145]

The Prince was now becoming very aware of the difficulties he and his courtiers had got themselves into and what a bad decision it had been to play it the way they did at Tranby Croft. The "conditions" were, of course, the infamous document which Gordon-Cumming and the guests had signed and the 'clear statement' was what came to be called the *précis*. It was, however, weighing badly on his mind and he wrote, yet again, to General Williams on 19 September:

'Many thanks for sending me C's letter & I am glad he has taken the hint, & his letter to you is a very proper one though short. I also hope with you that the scandal will never leak out, but we have as you say a perfectly good position, because the stipulation you insisted we should make if we maintained [ ], will effectively [ ] prevent a similar occurrence in the future & society in general will greatly profit by it! I have had some grouse drives & deer stalking this week, the former has been the most successful of the [ ]. Our weather is wonderfully mild for this time of the year. I heard from R. Sassoon that he had received no acknowledgement for the cheque that he sent from York last week!'[146]

Owen Williams then wrote the *précis* which he passed to Lord Coventry for comment. The latter accepted the 'description of what took place' but merely added that Miss Naylor had not been present as she had not joined the party until later. Williams then forwarded it on to the Prince who replied:

'I duly received the statement this evening which you drew up & which is signed by Coventry as well as yourself. Nothing could be better, & it states the facts perfectly clearly and concisely. It shall be locked up safely with the other papers. Let me also thank you for your letters of 20th & 24th. I think it right to mention for you information and that of Coventry that I had a letter from R. Sassoon a few days ago, who informed me that C. had cashed the cheque which the former sent him but never acknowledged its receipt even! After having told us that nothing would induce him to keep the money, this is a strange proceeding on his part. It only shows how little his statements are to be credited! He is I believe disporting himself in Scotland & I heard of him at the R. Sassoons!'[147]

Rumours were starting to filter into London Society that Gordon-Cumming had been banned from some of the casinos in Monte Carlo, but nothing substantial until he received an anonymous letter, in French, from 4 Rue de la Concorde,[148] Paris, dated 27 December. It read:

'They are beginning to talk much here of what passed at Newmarket this summer and of your sad adventure. If you come to Paris or Monte Carlo be very reserved and *do not touch a card*. They have talked too much in England.'[149]

Despite its inaccuracies, no one had any idea who had written it. Gordon-Cumming clearly thought Owen Williams was behind it and sent him a copy. The General denied all knowledge and refused to accept the obvious: the secret was out. Shortly, Gordon-Cumming wrote to him again, saying he had now heard from a lady, whose name he did not disclose, that the affair was being bandied about. He added that, as this was now common knowledge, his signing of the agreement at Tranby Croft was void as the promise of secrecy had been broken and, if the allegations were made public, he would 'fix on' anyone who repeated the slander.

How had the story got out? The story best loved by the newspapers and gossip-mongers, was that it emanated from Daisy Brooke. The Prince of Wales had met the Brookes at York Station after the Tranby Croft house party on 12 September and the implication was that he had told her then. Daisy, not known for her ability to keep a secret, and, therefore unkindly known as 'Babbling Brooke' was immediately suspected of being the source. It is possible but unlikely. The meeting between the Prince and the Brookes was relatively brief and, with her husband present, it is improbable that the Prince would talk even to Daisy about something which he had only recently agreed to keep secret himself.

Edward Legge, in his hagiography of Edward VII,[150] asserts, 'The American papers were quite wrong in attributing the "blabbing" to a well-known and popular English lady, for, as a matter of fact, she had nothing whatever to do with it. The tell-tale was quite another person, whose name was then only moderately known in English society. The statement of a London paper that it was one of the valets who "split" was just about as true as was the same journal's full-flavoured romance concerning the Prince's "debts".' [It was fairly common gossip that the Prince had run up enormous debts. This was true, to a certain extent, despite Legge's denial. The Prince's borrowings were seldom repaid]. Sadly, Legge does not come clean as to who this person was, even if he really knew.

The Prince was understandably worried. On 20 January he wrote from Sandringham to General Williams:

'I was not unprepared to receive your letter this morning, as both in London last week & here I have heard that Bill Cummings' name is in everybody's mouth, & I have also received a letter from Mrs Wilson on the subject. How the events which occurred at Tranby Croft have come out I know not, as I fell convinced that all those who knew of the horrible circumstances will have held their tongues. I have been questioned by several people & and it has been very difficult for me to evade telling the truth. I shall be in Town next Monday and should be very glad to see you and Coventry at 4 at Marlborough House to talk over the present position of affairs. F. Knollys had already written to you both to ask you to come & see me. I am glad that you are enjoying your visit to Lowther & I hope some day to see a place I have heard so much of.'[151]

The Hon Arthur Somerset, one of the guests at Tranby Croft, wrote an account, albeit not until April 1940,[152] but his guess is the most probable:

'How did it all come out? Nobody knows, but my own impression is as follows. It was, as I have said, a large party, so there were many in the house who whilst not in the secret could not fail to notice that something had happened, and they had signed no pledge not to speak of it. Also (although none of us knew of it) Sir W. had been detected at it before and there were several people aware of it. My idea is that one of these people, hearing from one of the party who were not in the know that something had happened at Tranby, followed by the disappearance of Cumming by a very early train the next morning, put two and two together and guessed what had occurred, met someone who was amongst the 10 who knew, cross examined him and as they seemed to know all about it he gave them the information, thinking they practically were already in possession of the broad facts.'

The leaking of the secret exposed a number of people to differing amounts of trouble. Obviously, Gordon-Cumming would be labelled a cheat and the enormous penalties that would bring. He would be finished socially and expelled from the Army. The Prince of Wales's part would confirm the population's view that he was an idle spendthrift, gambling away their money in a quasi-illegal game, in the company of a cheat. A summons, again, to appear in Court would infuriate the Queen and question the necessity for the Royal Family. The courtiers, Coventry and Owen Williams, with their botched cover-up plan, would have to live with the bad advice they had given the Prince and the consequent condemnation from the Private Secretaries to the Queen and the Prince. The Wilson family faced ostracism from Society for allowing the gambling to be held in their house and their subsequent inability to bury the problem. The younger players, Jack Wilson, Levett and Lycett Green faced ridicule and sniggering from their peers.

With the scandal now in the open, the scene dramatically changed. First of all, the position of the Prince of Wales was now exposed to risk. The whole conspiracy of Williams and Coventry to keep the secret, and the Prince, out of the public eye, lay in ruins. All the heat of the radical Press was soon to be stoked up against him; the puritanical prelates and non-conformists were to preach anti-gambling Sodom and Gomorrah from pulpits and, worst of all, his mother was going to be apoplectic with anger. His, and the Queen's, private secretaries, Knollys[153] and Ponsonby,[154] were desperate to keep the Prince out of the Courts and prevent any scandal touching the Monarchy. The Wilsons, Lycett Green and Levett were well out of their depth; they could only go with the flow and had no leader, apart from Williams and Coventry, to guide them. Williams and Coventry were hardly in a position to take that lead; they were beginning to realise what appalling advice they had given the Prince over the drawing up of the document and were way out of their league in now trying to influence the Prince in any way. Knollys and Ponsonby were in charge. As for Gordon-Cumming, his options narrowed to trying to clear his name in Court or ignoring the accusations of cheating, retire from Society, the Army and life as he knew it and never feature again; with the likelihood of, forevermore, being the butt of gossip, innuendo and the muck-raking journalists of his day. He had a number of friends in and out of the Regiment but also several enemies who would delight in his downfall.

There was still just time to avoid a court case and the accompanying bad publicity. It was, though, too late for the Prince of Wales to tell the Baccarat players they had made a mistake; he should have done that at the time and Williams and Coventry should have advised him to do so rather than drawing up the document. Gordon-Cumming did make one last effort to discuss it with the Prince.[155] The latter sent him a telegram refusing to do so and wrote to his old friend, Owen Williams on 25 January:

'I received a telegram yesterday & a letter today from Cumming begging me to see him tomorrow. I thought it better to decline & and sent a telegram to that effect yesterday. You had I think better write to him on the receipt of this that you wish to see him at Hill Street at 5 tomorrow & that he must not leave Town. After the interview which I shall have with you and Coventry tomorrow at Marlborough House at 4 o'clock we shall have to come to a determination as to what has to be done in this painful matter which is known not only in English Society but abroad you will then inform him of our decision as to his future course of action but he need not know beforehand of our interview.'[156]

Quite what the Prince thought he could do about it now is unclear. What 'future course of action' did he think he could order Gordon-Cumming to take? The players themselves could admit their error but they had no one to suggest it. With the arrogance of youth, it probably did not occur to Jack Wilson and Lycett Green. Berkeley Levett was the one person most open to some sort of get-out; he was, after all, a fellow officer in Gordon-Cumming's Regiment and it must have been very difficult for him going against a senior, and respected, Guardsman. He was too young and inexperienced, though, to take any kind of lead. Gordon-Cumming did try to persuade Levett and got him round to his house in Harriet Street. Levett though stuck to his guns but agreed to contact Mrs Wilson to see if anything (quite what?) could be done.

Next the Regiment and the Army were brought into it. Colonel Stracey, who was the officer commanding the Scots Guards – the two battalion commanders were lieutenant colonels – had not heard the story until Gordon-Cumming told him. He was appalled as well he might; he could see the disgrace besmirching the Regiment without even thinking about it. His immediate reaction was to tell Gordon-Cumming to leave the Regiment at once. The latter then told him he was taking proceedings against his accusers but would leave the matter of his Commission in his commanding officer's hands. In the meantime, Levett had returned to him to say that Mrs Wilson refused to go back on her word on the basis if she did so, all would be lost. She said, 'If any of you go back from your words, you are done for.'[157] She could clearly see her life as a society hostess crumbling before her eyes.

On 26 January, Gordon-Cumming saw Owen Williams and Coventry to ask their advice. As the matter was now public, they said there was no advice they could give. They must have now realised what bad advice they had given to the Prince; they had nowhere to turn. Clearly, nothing was forthcoming from their meeting with the Prince of Wales at Marlborough House an hour before. Owen Williams then produced the account, or *précis* as it was called, of the events as he saw them. Despite a number of errors, the account finished, 'The above is an accurate statement of all the facts of the case.' This had been 'cleared' earlier by both the Prince of Wales and Lord Coventry. It may have given the two courtiers some sense of righteousness and self-justification and a hope that they would not topple into the abyss they were now facing. The reality was that it may well have been the account they told the Prince, who then reached his opinion on that basis, but was it actually true? Gordon-Cumming's strongest objection was over the sentence that they had pointed out to him that signing the document was an admission of guilt, whereas it was *he* that had told *them* that by doing so, it was an admission of guilt. For the first time, Gordon-Cumming realised that his so-called friends, assuming his guilt, had gone behind his back to the Prince with the document before he'd even been told of the accusations. The 'advice' from these 'friends' was purely designed to have Gordon-Cumming sign the document with the least argument. It was nothing more than a conspiracy to shield the Prince and calm any hot-heads who threatened to expose the affair at the Races the following day.

The die was cast. Furious, Gordon-Cumming instructed his solicitors, Wontner's, on 27 January, to issue a demand for a retraction of their accusations, and an apology, from Mrs Arthur Wilson, Jack Wilson, Berkeley Levett and Mr and Mrs Lycett Green or proceedings would be taken against them for slander. In the meantime, Colonel Stracey had consulted other officers in the Scots Guards; some thought he should be thrown out, others that he should be given a chance to defend himself.

With that Stracey approached the Adjutant General, Sir Redvers Buller, with the advice that Gordon-Cumming should be allowed to retire on half-pay until the court case had concluded, and then his Commission reviewed. Buller agreed on fairly thin grounds that it was Gordon-Cumming who had reported the matter himself and the Prince of Wales appeared to accept him remaining in the Regiment. On 13 February,[158] Buller wrote to Ponsonby explaining what had happened and that it was important that no military enquiry should take place pending civil action. Stracey did not see the need to be so politically careful. He summoned Gordon-Cumming and told him, in no uncertain terms, that signing the document was an admission of guilt and that if he succeeded in Court, he would be allowed to retire. If he failed, he would be dismissed from the service.[159] Hardly a supportive statement from one's superior officer.

The Duke of Connaught,[160] the Prince of Wales's younger brother, and Colonel of the Scots Guards, to Knollys's infuriation, refused to become involved. Knollys wrote to Ponsonby on 15 February, 'The Duke of Connaught refuses to budge from Portsmouth even for a few hours to talk to the Prince about the Cumming affair, though he is Colonel in Chief (sic) of Cummings's Regt, while the Duke of Cambridge [the Commander-in-Chief] is playing the part of Antony, with Cleopatra up the Nile, in Egypt. The old idiot ought really to be ashamed of himself at his age making such a fool of himself and keeping away from his Post at home for nearly 3 months when Parliament is sitting for the greater part of that time.'[161] The fact is that the Duke of Connaught was being entirely sensible. If he had interfered on behalf of his brother, the world would have quickly concluded that Gordon-Cumming had been sacrificed to save the Prince of Wales.

The American newspapers were relishing the scandal:

For example The Daily Globe of St Paul, Minnesota, headlines of 7 February read:

Tummy is in Trouble

Prince of Wales Implicated in Malodorous Gambling Notoriety

An English Baronet Lets the Gay Feline Loose from the Bag

The Heir Apparent Played baccarat and now regrets it

The Whole Scandal to be thoroughly sifted in the Court of Law

*

Another way Knollys thought he could get at Gordon-Cumming was to have him blackballed from the Guards Club. Quite what that would have achieved is not clear. Knollys's obsession now was to prevent the Prince of Wales going into the witness box. He thought that if the Guards Club threw Gordon-Cumming out, then the Marlborough and Turf would follow. This, presumably, in his eyes, would so prejudice the case that it could not take place. The Guards Club Executive Committee was not that naïve. On 20 February, it convened a special general meeting of members with the motion that the Committee be empowered to conduct its own enquiry. The motion was defeated by 78 votes to 49. The Prince was furious, 'The decision of the Guards Club is a terrible blow to the Scots Guards; and I feel most deeply for the officers who have the honour of their Regiment so much at heart. Should Cumming, by any legal quibble, win his action, I think nearly every officer would leave the Regiment.'[162] It would not have occurred to him that some officers might well have considered Gordon-Cumming innocent and the whole affair a conspiracy to make him a scapegoat for something they might not wholly understand, but about which they would have been uneasy. Ponsonby also thought the result lucky for the Prince; had the Club expelled Gordon-Cumming it would have smacked of pressure from Marlborough House, the Prince of Wales's official residence,[163] which, of course, it was.

In March, it was inaccurately reported in some newspapers, that Gordon-Cumming had refused the offer of a retraction and that he wanted 'his day in court.' It was asserted that he required the jury to hear the case, his denial on oath and then merely specify the damages to which he felt entitled.[164]

With the instructing of solicitors and counsel for the Plaintiff and the Defendants, the case now developed into lawyers' preliminary skirmishes. The Instructions to Counsel for the Defendants, drafted by the wily George Lewis, lie in the Royal Archives.[165] In it, he outlines the case, and identifies its strengths and weaknesses while suggesting lines for Counsel to take.

First of all, they had to state that their accusation that the plaintiff cheated was true in substance and fact. This had to be substantiated with evidence. The difficulty here was that in the civil court, which this was, the burden of proof – *on the balance of probabilities* – was lower than the one in a criminal case – *beyond reasonable doubt*. However, the accusation that the defendants made against Gordon-Cumming was a criminal one; cheating.[166] The jury, therefore, were going to have to believe the defendants *beyond reasonable doubt*. This distinction would, of course, be beyond the understanding of the ordinary juryman, so it would depend on the explanation, and direction, of the judge.

Next, there were five defendants. For the defence this might have raised problems, to be exploited by the plaintiff's counsel, when their stories differed. Lewis thought it strange that Gordon-Cumming had taken action against the five when one (Jack Wilson) would have done. Was it to intimidate them, particularly, in the case of the two ladies, into a retraction? He was seeking £5000 [£480,100] damages from each defendant. Lewis drafted a similar statement for each defendant, in the most general terms; that they saw Gordon-Cumming cheating by placing a larger stake on the table after the cards had been declared. He hoped this would satisfy Wontner's, Gordon-Cumming's solicitors when they required answers as to exactly what their client was accused of. Lewis, who was, clearly, going to have to coach his clients, wanted to keep the detail to the absolute minimum and as vague as the law would allow to prevent forensic dissection of individual accounts in the trial.

There had been much coverage in the newspapers. The *World* and *Truth* very much supported Gordon-Cumming. Other supporters were *Star* and *Land and Water*. Did he leak material to them? Possibly, but there is no actual evidence that he did so. The editor of *Truth* had twice been convicted of libel, so was not a great stickler for truth. Lewis publicly claimed that Gordon-Cumming had tried to prejudice public opinion by issuing false and misleading statements to the Press. Counsel might consider cross-examining Gordon-Cumming on this, he suggested. *The Pall Mall Gazette*, on the other hand, appeared to display a more balanced picture. This was hypocritical of Lewis; he was the source.

There was no conspiracy, Lewis told *The Pall Mall Gazette*, of deliberately inviting Gordon-Cumming to Tranby Croft in order to do him mischief. Nor was there any hint that anyone was prepared to commit perjury against him: all were of impeccable stature and there was no indication that Gordon-Cumming had cheated before. In taking this line to Counsel, it must have been in Lewis's mind that this might have been a possibility. Was he writing it to alert Counsel to a possible attack in this area from the plaintiff's side? At the same time, Lewis drew Counsel's attention to the contents of a letter[167] Lady Middleton, Gordon-Cumming's sister, had written to Mrs Wilson on 7 February, in which she declared that her brother's court action was in no way a menace to the defendants whom he saw acting conscientiously, but were wrong. If, wrote Lewis, it *was* seen as a menace, was that actually what it was really intended to be; to bully the defendants into a retraction? Lewis, clearly, felt this was a strong card. He added that, while Williams and Coventry were not his clients, they had acted in their friend's best interests but had they made up their minds too quickly?[168] This was a small warning bell to Counsel. However, Gordon-Cumming could not say anything other than that Williams and Coventry were men of honour and integrity, which, indeed, they were. Additionally, while Gordon-Cumming was a friend of the Prince of Wales, his 'name should not be introduced unduly into the case.'[169] With the Prince of Wales being the key to the whole affair, quite what Lewis was getting at is unclear. Maybe it was to give himself a little overhead cover if things ultimately went wrong and he was blamed for inadequate Instructions by not persuading Counsel to keep the Prince's name out of it?

There were two real dangers to the defendants' case, Lewis believed. The first was Williams's so-called *précis*, which had been approved by Coventry and sent to the Prince of Wales via Knollys. It was sloppily written and contained a number of inaccuracies that Gordon-Cumming's Counsel would quickly identify. The second was even worse. This was the letter Williams had written to Gordon-Cumming on 28 January. In it he said, 'You are quite at liberty to tell Stracey [his commanding officer] that you signed the document under extreme pressure and the promise of secrecy, but you never acknowledged for a moment either to Coventry or myself the truth of the accusation against you. You signed by the strongest advice on the part of Coventry and myself who were deputed to present you with the ultimatum, and who were absolutely certain that unless you did so the accusations would be immediately made public & that therefore your signature was the only possible hope of the avoidance of a horrible scandal…you signed as the only way out of the impasse but in no way made any acknowledgement that you were guilty, but on the contrary strongly asseverated your innocence.'[170] This was a gift to Gordon-Cumming's Counsel; the defence of coercion. He had signed under such extreme pressure that no weight could be attached to the document. It also contradicted the theme of the *précis*. No wonder Lewis termed it 'indiscreet' and 'a letter to be regretted.'

However, the clever lawyer that he was, Lewis still sought an out of court settlement, although, of course, that was, primarily, to keep the Prince of Wales out of the witness box. His first tactic was to ask for a retraction by the defendants but this had already been tried and it was therefore unlikely to succeed now. The second was to persuade the military to change their minds and hold an enquiry prior to the court case. Apart from prejudicing the civil case, if the Army found Gordon-Cumming guilty of a breach of Queen's Regulations, or worse still, the Army Act, then the case would fall apart. Failing that, Lewis was not to be deflected. In his Instructions to Counsel, the fact that Gordon-Cumming had refused an enquiry [he hadn't, it was Buller's decision] before a tribunal composed of his fellow officers, who, in Lewis's mind, would have been on his side, showed that Gordon-Cumming had something to fear. Counsel was invited to use this in court.

On 13 February, General Buller reported to Ponsonby,[171] as a result of the Queen's close interest, that, 'Lord Coventry and General Owen Williams came to me and protested against his being allowed to retire upon half-pay...I absolutely declined to take action against him upon street rumours...until I had evidence to go on I would not interfere.' With that, Lewis drafted a response for Williams and Coventry to sign, formally acquainting the military authorities of the charges against Gordon-Cumming. That changed Buller's mind; Gordon-Cumming was suspended from duty as opposed to retiring on half-pay and a military enquiry was instigated. Wontner's, Gordon-Cumming's solicitors strongly objected and, after consulting the Lord Advocate-General, Buller rescinded his decision to hold an enquiry while civil proceedings were on-going. The Prince of Wales was furious and blamed Buller for not behaving decisively in the first place and ordering Stracey to act in order that any civil action would not have been contemplated.[172] Knollys echoed this in a note to Ponsonby of 15 February,[173] 'Buller, after calling up the witnesses decided to stifle all military enquiry, and leave the matter to be decided by civil law.... The civil action cannot come on before November at the earliest (so George Lewis tells me), and in the meanwhile this scandal is to be kept hanging over everyone's head and at the end of nine or ten months the whole affair is to be raked up again because Buller chooses to throw his mantle over Cumming, and refusing to have any sort of enquiry or a court martial, leaves the matter to be settled by a civil court. According to the line of conduct he has adopted, every officer, Non Commissioned Officer or private against whom a disgraceful charge is brought can evade it for months by merely getting hold of a solicitor and bringing a civil action against his accusers.'[174] This sort of attitude was not helping the Prince of Wales. He believed that his two friends, Williams and Coventry, had investigated the situation at Tranby Croft *before* persuading him of the course of action he took. Clearly, as he now realised, they had done nothing of the sort; they had merely believed, precipitately, what they had been told by others. The Queen wrote to her eldest daughter, Vicky, on 24 February,[175] 'I must at once correct an error which you seem to have made in thinking Bertie wishes to shield this horrid Mr Cumming. On the contrary he is most anxious he should be punished. The incredible and shameful thing is that others dragged him into it and urged him to sign this paper which of course he should never have done. He is in a dreadful state about it for he has been dreadfully attacked about it.' To give the Queen her due, throughout this terrible time for her son, she firmly supported him. When he refused to go to Windsor if she spoke of his gambling, uncharacteristically she capitulated and agreed not to mention it.

There was a last throw of the dice by the indefatigable Lewis. A short time before the start of the opening day of the trial, he came to Gordon-Cumming's Counsel, Sir Edward Clarke, with a message from Marlborough House. 'Sir Edward Hulse had given the Prince of Wales a box containing the cards and counters to be used in playing baccarat. The counters were large and of bright colours. On one side was the value - £10, £5, £1, or 10s. – on the other the feathers of the Prince of Wales. These were the cards and counters used on the evenings of the alleged cheating.'[176] It was suggested that the defendants should produce at the trial not these counters themselves, but others of the same size and colours, but without the gilt feathers. This was a ploy to make it look as though the Prince was as other men, and not carry with him personalised gaming chips which might portray an abnormal interest in gambling. Clarke refused to allow it.

There was now no turning back and the main players in this sensational court case were selected. Lord Coleridge, the Lord Chief Justice of England was to preside. Coleridge had been a successful barrister on the western circuit. 'He was tall and graceful, moving always with a certain slow dignity. His face was of classic outline, and the clear complexion and the soft blue eyes gave it something of feminine beauty. And indeed Coleridge was more subtle than any counsel at the Bar. His cross-examination was always painstaking and ingenious, and the more closely the witness was entangled in the net the more suave and gentle was the manner of the cross-examiner' Edward Fordham wrote in *Notable Cross-Examinations*.[177] In 1865 he had been elected Liberal MP for Exeter. When the Liberals came to power in 1868 under Gladstone, Coleridge, a good friend, was appointed Solicitor-General and, in 1871, he was promoted to Attorney-General. In 1880, as Baron Coleridge he was made Lord Chief Justice of England. He was involved in the celebrated Tichborne case and represented Constance Kent in the Road Hill murder.[178] His first wife died in February 1878 and he remarried 1885. He was now seventy and longed to retire to his lovely garden in Devon with his beautiful young wife. He had held high office for eleven years and had had enough.[179]

For Gordon-Cumming, Wontner's instructed Sir Edward Clarke QC. He was a steady, rather earnest man who, nevertheless, enjoyed the confidence of the public and Bar alike through his reputation for fairness and integrity. In 1886, he was appointed Solicitor-General but the rules, at the time, allowed him to accept briefs.[180] Barristers do not always have to believe their clients but must do the best by them; such is the power of the Law. In this case, however, there was no doubt that Clarke totally believed in Gordon-Cumming's innocence. His junior was C F Gill.

George Lewis secured Sir Charles Russell QC, an altogether more flamboyant member of the Bar than his opponent. His tastes - owning race horse and being fond of cards - were much more in line with the Prince of Wales's. Nevertheless, he was a shrewd and powerful cross-examiner and had the ability to express complicated points of law, simply, to juries. He had a touch of the Irish blarney and the self-confidence of the stage actor. He had, in the past, lost to Clarke, whom he called 'a clever little attorney,[181] which was probably not meant as a compliment. In his team was H H Asquith QC, destined to become Prime

Minister in 1908. Interestingly, Asquith's wife, the well-known beauty, Margot, carried on considerable correspondence with Gordon-Cumming in later years, as, of course, did Asquith himself, even when Prime Minister, with Venetia Stanley.

From a complacent and comfortable situation at the end of 1890, when the Tranby Croft card game problem had been safely swept under the carpet, the Baccarat players now faced a court case of sick-making stress, personal embarrassment and public ignominy. For all of them, life would never be the same again.

CHAPTER 10 - The Case for the Plaintiff

The trial[182] opened at 11 am on Monday 1 June 1891 in the Law Courts of the Queen's Bench Division, London, to extraordinary scenes. Edward Clarke wrote in his memoirs[183] that Lord Coleridge had appropriated half the public gallery and given tickets to his friends. He also had his pet ferret concealed under his voluminous robes.[184] The Prince of Wales occupied a chair in front of the Bench between the judge and the witness box. Lady Coleridge sat close to her husband's right hand to check that he had not gone to sleep; something which was becoming noticeable. *The Pall Mall Gazette* gleefully reported, 'Lady Coleridge, indeed, divided the honours of the Court with her husband. She looked as charming as ever, she nodded and smiled all round, the Court and galleries all sparkled with her friends, and as the case opened she borrowed the pencils and paper of the Lord Chief Justice at her elbow with delightful audacity.'[185] The rest of the Bench was occupied by fashionable ladies in front of whom, 'close to the footlights' sat one of the judge's daughters-in-law, Mrs Gilbert Coleridge, with a sketch book, busily drawing the actors in the drama.'

The draw was, of course, the Prince of Wales. The public had been well primed by the newspapers over the weeks before, with salacious tit-bits of murky goings-on in high places with thinly veiled suggestions of sex and skulduggery. 'Everybody is speculating as to how much of the rottenness of the English aristocracy will be exposed. It is believed that Sir Gordon-Cummings (sic) will expose a stream of corruption and deluge with infamy many of the best names in the English aristocratic circles.'[186] [Not prone to allowing truth to get in the way of good innuendo, the newspapers were light on the actual names of these English aristocrats]. To have a member of the royal family actually on view, in court, facing some possibly embarrassing questions, however, was just too good to miss. They were 'reliably informed' that apart from the brief appearance of the Prince in the Mordaunt case, no heir to the throne had faced court since Prince Hal before he became Henry V.[187] 'Sensational disclosures are confidently expected by society.'[188]

The jury, the *Pall Mall Gazette* reported, were, 'a sensible, commonplace, but not particularly bright-looking dozen good men and true, with unfair proportion, perhaps, of broken noses, but with untarnished reputation.'

The *Star's* reporter set the scene: 'It was ten minutes to eleven when Mrs Arthur Wilson, dressed in black with hat to match and wearing a blue fox boa, took her seat in front of Sir Charles Russell. By then the jury was sworn in and Lady Coleridge carrying her useful fan with which she, on the occasion of another big trial, tapped her slumbering husband while he drowsed through a weary address to the jury. Then, just when the public had finished admiring the peach-like complexion, the ivory teeth and the smart attire of the Chief's young wife, all lorgnettes and opera glasses were levelled dead on the chair on the left of the judge's seat, for the Prince of Wales wearing a black frock-coat and a big smile had located himself there with Sir Francis Knollys behind him.'[189]

Gordon-Cumming had entered court, with his solicitor, a little earlier, as *The Pall Mall Gazette* reported: 'his firm, set, handsome features steadily composed to the deadly issue… his complexion tanned by travel and adventure to a deep permanent red; the row of defendants, much more nervous and much less distinguished than the man they accuse, but with a certain clearness and decision of type not uninteresting in its way.'[190]

Lord Coleridge opened proceedings by asking Edward Clarke to indicate how long he would require His Royal Highness to remain? Clarke replied that he could not say whether the Prince would be needed as a witness for the plaintiff but he would address the matter in his opening statement. Coleridge reminded him that the Prince was not attending as a spectator but 'on the summons of the parties.' The Judge started as he meant to go on; putting pressure on Clarke. (The Prince actually attended the whole trial apart from the last day.)

Clarke opened his case by telling the jury that it was a simple question of whether or not Sir William Gordon-Cumming cheated at cards. He then outlined Gordon-Cumming's career and background, particularly stressing his personal friendship with the Prince of Wales for the last ten years, including staying at Sandringham three times. He spoke of Gordon-Cumming's relationship with the Wilsons and how he had stayed with them for the Doncaster Races in 1885 and dined with them in London. As far as the defendants were concerned, he did not know them apart from the Lycett Greens, slightly, as he had dined at their house in York. He stressed Gordon-Cumming's social background as landed gentry and his, not inconsiderable, military service, which included Levett as a junior officer in his Regiment. The game of Baccarat was explained, at length, to the jury. Edward Clarke then described the events leading up to the accusation of cheating and Gordon-Cumming's signing of the document swearing not to touch another card. He raised the matter of the *précis* written by Williams and Coventry. (This was one of the danger areas which Lewis had warned the defendants' Counsel about). Charles Russell pounced before the document was read, claiming that it was no part of the evidence against his clients, but he accepted it being read if General Williams and Lord Coventry were called as witnesses. Clarke replied that he would call only General Williams (it was, after all, he who drafted it.) He went on to read it.

At this point Clarke turned to two very significant points. The first was that the *précis* maintained that, 'It was agreed that they [the accusers] should all carefully watch the play the following night, when Sir William Gordon-Cumming was again observed most distinctly to repeat the same practices.' But, said Clarke, this was not the 'accurate statement of all the facts of the case,' sworn by Williams and Coventry because the defendants, in their preliminary statements denied agreeing to watch Gordon-Cumming's play on the second night. Secondly, it was inconceivable that, despite what had been written in the précis with regard to maintaining secrecy, that this matter could remain undisclosed. Was it really possible, he asked that two men of the knowledge and experience of General Owen Williams and Lord Coventry could have imagined that such a thing as this could be kept secret, when it was known to so many people? For example, there were ladies present, who knew about it, but had not signed the undertaking. The contents of the document, Clarke said, had even been published in the Press.

It was also important to realise that it had been said that Sir William Gordon-Cumming would not have signed the paper unless he knew that he was guilty. By now Clarke was reaching the nub of the case. He argued that precisely the opposite was true. The fact was that Gordon-Cumming never accepted any guilt; he was persuaded to sign the document, under the strong pressure of his old friends, Williams and Coventry, to avoid the 'horrible scandal connected with the playing of baccarat at Tranby Croft.' The reality was that playing card games of the baccarat type in private houses was hardly a scandal, even if it involved the Prince of Wales. Williams and Coventry had wildly exaggerated the threat. Clarke pointed out that if Gordon-Cumming was really guilty of cheating, he would have brazened it out and never signed such a document. There was simply no evidence that he admitted being guilty of cheating. Did, he asked, the Prince of Wales, General Owen Williams and Lord Coventry really believe Gordon-Cumming had cheated? Or did they think that, by getting him to sign such a document, a scandal would be avoided? If they really believed he had cheated then no document would have been signed and Gordon-Cumming would have been reported to his Commanding Officer in accordance with Queen's Regulations. The Prince and General Owen Williams, as Army officers, knew that perfectly well, although the Prince, as a 'titular' officer could have been forgiven for not actually remembering it. Lord Coventry, not a soldier, but a man of integrity, bound by rules of honour, could not have allowed Gordon-Cumming to remain a member of the various Clubs to which they all belonged if he really believed he was a cheat. Forcing Gordon-Cumming to sign the document was tantamount to accepting that he was not guilty of cheating but only attempting to avoid scandal.

The courtiers, Clarke maintained, did not believe it but the defendants did. Gordon-Cumming briefed Clarke that he did not think they made the accusations through any malice or unfairness but they believed they had seen him do what they alleged. In the *précis*, it was asserted that Gordon-Cumming had been seen to add to his stake when the cards were in his favour and withdraw counters when they were against him. However, in their preliminary statements, the defendants now stated that they never saw him withdraw part of the stake when the cards were unfavourable. So Williams and Coventry were inventing an accusation which was never actually made.

Clarke then explained how Gordon-Cumming was playing, by what would nowadays be called 'doubling up'; adding to an original stake when one has won, in addition to the payout from the croupier. So, if the original stake was, say, £1, the player would be paid a winning of £1. He would leave that on the table and add another £1 stake for the next round, making a total of £3 in front of him.

Edward Clarke ended his opening statement with a resounding and emotional defence of his client, clearly explaining the penalties if the jury found against him. He finished, 'I do trust that Sir William Gordon-Cumming may go away from this Court, when your verdict is given, back to the life of honour and repute that he has led hitherto among his fellows, that he may still wear in your service, and in his country's service, a sword that has never been stained but with the blood of his country's foes, and that he, as he has risked his life for you and yours in times gone by, may, in his hour of peril here, find protection in your instincts of justice.' At the close of Clarke's opening speech the crowded court room cheered and the judge angrily exclaimed, 'Silence, this is not a theatre,' which Clarke found, 'in the circumstances, rather amusing.'

Gordon-Cumming now went into the witness-box. The *St Paul Daily Globe* of Minnesota reported, 'While giving his testimony today, Sir William Gordon-Cumming was the typical aristocrat. He leaned easily on the edge of the witness-box, coolly surveying the court and the evidence, seemingly confident of himself and his case.'[191] Although Clarke had covered the relevant parts of his life in his opening statement, it was important for the jury to hear the detail from the plaintiff. Clarke took him through his background, Clubs and military service. He checked that he had stayed at Sandringham in 1881 and twice since, and that he had previously stayed at Tranby Croft for four days in 1885 during Doncaster Races. Gordon-Cumming replied that Ethel Lycett Green was at Tranby Croft in 1885 when she was unmarried but that he had seen the married Lycett Greens in York in 1888 or 1889.

Clarke then took him through the events of Monday evening. He confirmed that the Prince of Wales held the bank, General Owen Williams was the croupier and Reuben Sassoon was in charge of the counters. Gordon-Cumming explained how he had kept the 'score' on a sheet of paper, with two columns of B [bank] and P [players] and dotted under each when they won. The tables were different heights, so that losing stakes had to be handed up to the banker from the lower table; Gordon-Cumming sometimes did so on his piece of paper. He went on to run through his 'system'. 'When I stake a £5 counter and win, that will represent £10, and I should then add a third counter in front of me, which will represent a second coup of £15.' He was sitting between Lord

Edward Somerset and Jack Wilson opposite Owen Williams. No one had made any comment about the play.

The following day, everyone had gone to the Races and that evening again played cards but this time in the billiard room with a different table. The bank was held, as before, by the Prince of Wales and Owen Williams the croupier. Gordon-Cumming said he remembered sitting with Lady Coventry between him and Owen Williams. He helped her with her counters as she was inexperienced in the game. Ethel Lycett Green sat on his left and Mrs Wilson on her left. He particularly noticed that Jack Wilson had a run of 'novice's' luck, winning five 'coups' in a row. No one said anything about the play but the Prince, at the end of the evening, commented on his good fortune, at which Gordon-Cumming showed him the scores on his sheet of paper, saying, 'How could I help winning with such a tableau as this?' He had won £225 over the two nights.

On Wednesday morning came the news of the death of Mrs Wilson's brother. Gordon-Cumming suggested to her that they should all leave but she replied that she hoped they wouldn't. They therefore went to the Races as planned. At about 8 pm that evening, Owen Williams and Lord Coventry came to his room. Lord Coventry said that, 'Some of the people staying here object to your manner in playing Baccarat' and that he and Owen Williams had gone to the Prince of Wales. Gordon-Cumming asked them what he had done? They replied that they didn't know precisely what but they distinctly asserted he had been guilty of foul play. Gordon-Cumming totally rejected the charge but, as they were old friends, he was happy to put the matter entirely in their hands and would do whatever they thought best. He said that he wished, though, to have an interview with the Prince of Wales.

Later that night, the Prince of Wales saw him in the company of the two courtiers. He said to Gordon-Cumming, 'What can you do? There are five accusers against you'. Gordon-Cumming left the room while the Prince conferred with Owen Williams and Lord Coventry. At about 11.30 pm, he was summoned back into the room but the Prince of Wales was not there. He was given a document which he was asked to sign and told this was the only way to avoid a horrible scandal. He said, 'This would be tantamount to an admission of guilt'. If he didn't sign, he was told, people who brought the accusation would tell the whole story at the racecourse the following day. On the recommendation of his two friends, he then signed the document, but, being a well-known card player, he warned them of the comment and curiosity which would arise when he refused to play cards. He was told the spokesman for the party was Lycett Green. Clarke finished by asking him, 'Did you cheat at baccarat that night?' 'I did not.'

After lunch, Russell began his cross-examination, interrupted by a number of ladies sweeping in late, to his obvious annoyance. Russell followed his brief by asking Gordon-Cumming to confirm that those he knew or had met even briefly before the house party, were people of honour and integrity and bore him no ill will. Gordon-Cumming agreed that he had written to his sister, [Lady Middleton], 'they are acting perfectly conscientiously in the matter and they believe they did see me resort to foul play.' Did Gordon-Cumming agree that there was nothing scandalous in playing a quiet game of Baccarat for relatively low stakes in a country house? He did. [It was an important point for Russell to make as it discredited any suggestion, in Gordon-Cumming's view, that it was a scandal for the Prince of Wales to play Baccarat; therefore why later sign a document to cover it up?[192]] Russell then went through the rules of the game, possibly to ensure the Lord Chief Justice, who described it as resembling *vingt-et-un*, and the jury understood. He went on to suggest ways in which cheating might occur by increasing the stake after the banker had declared his hand. Under questioning, Gordon-Cumming explained how he held his hands on the table in front of him, with a pencil and paper, taking the scores, and that sometimes he put his stake on the paper but not the rest of his counters. Russell now started to put pressure on him by suggesting he had increased his stake by adding counters when the cards were favourable. This was resolutely denied. There was considerable detail of what amount had been placed when and who sat where, to which Gordon-Cumming responded that he could not remember. Neither could he recall Lycett Green leaving the table and a note then being brought in to Mrs Wilson.

When Owen Williams and Lord Coventry had approached him, late on the second night, with the accusation of cheating, had he asked what the detail of the accusation was? They couldn't answer, except that he had been seen cheating. He was told five people had made the accusation. Did he ask who they were? No, not until after the interview with the

Prince of Wales. Why did he not confront them? It was not suggested that he should. 'Sir William Gordon-Cumming, as a Lieutenant-Colonel and a man of the world, in a matter of this kind did you need any suggestion of what you ought to do?' said Russell, sensing a gap in the armour. 'I had lost my head, Sir Charles, on that occasion. If I had not lost my head I would not have signed that document.' Was he told that Lycett Green refused to sign the paper but wanted to confront him and have it out? No, he had no recollection of that. [This was a spurious point. This happened later when Lycett Green was signing the paper. Russel knew, perfectly well, that Owen Williams and Coventry, having got this far, would not let Lycett Green undo the good work by having a public row]. But he had not lost his head so much that he did not seek an interview with the Prince of Wales? No, it was his first thought. When he was told who his accusers were, did he say they were but a parcel of boys? He couldn't recall saying so. Did he remember saying anything about referring the matter to the Duke of Cambridge, and General Owen Williams saying he would not be as lenient as them? No, nothing of the kind. Russell had scored some easy but important points by making suggestions, which were legitimately refuted by Gordon-Cumming through lack of memory, but would have registered in the minds of the jury. A clever barrister's ploy.

Russell then addressed the signing of the paper. Did Gordon-Cumming think that in signing the paper he was doing a dishonouring act? A foolish one and since giving it thought, yes. It seemed to be an admission of guilt. Why sign it then? It was put to him by old and trusted friends that, with five accusers, he had no chance of clearing himself and that a horrible scandal would follow in which his name, his Regiment and everything would suffer unless he signed the paper. A scandal to which the name of the Prince of Wales would be attached. How? It would not be desirable that the name of the Prince of Wales should be associated with a game of Baccarat with an officer who had been accused of cheating by his hosts or by the people of the house in which the Prince of Wales was staying. But it was an innocent game? It was a scandal for a man in his position.

Finally, Russell turned to a letter of 11 September which Gordon-Cumming had received from General Owen Williams in response to his of the 10th. Before doing so, however, he asked Gordon-Cumming whether he thought his friends were advising him, in his best interests, as a guilty man? No, he did not believe they thought so at the time. But he changed his mind twenty-four hours later after signing the document. Was it on their advice alone? Yes. Why then in his letter to Owen Williams did he write, 'I hope you will take an opportunity of telling the Prince of Wales how entirely I was guided in my action yesterday by his advice and yours and Coventry's.' He did so, he said, because he thought the paper had been submitted to the Prince before he saw it. The letter was left for Owen Williams at Tranby Croft after Gordon-Cumming had gone. Owen Williams's response was brief; he had shown the letter to the Prince of Wales and Lord Coventry. However, a memo, signed by the three of them was attached. In it, they declared that they had dealt with Gordon-Cumming as leniently as they could under the overwhelming evidence against him. As far as they were concerned, if he complied with his undertaking then silence on their part would be strictly maintained. He added that the money he had won would be forwarded to him by Mr Sassoon.

The second day of the trial saw Russell resuming his attack on Gordon-Cumming by producing a further letter written by him to Owen Williams from his London house. Gordon-Cumming had 'stepped back into the witness-box, fresh and collected,' according to *The Pall Mall Gazette*. 'Nothing but the tint of his gloves was changed from yesterday.'[193] But the letter betrayed a sense of gloom, 'I have little before me to make life worth living.' Russell was relentless; did Gordon-Cumming, after receiving Owen Williams's letter have any doubt that they believed he was guilty or that they were acting, as far as they could, to shield him? No. And the Prince? And the Prince. What, asked Russell, had changed between 13 September and now? Russell, in asking this, employed the advocate's trick of disguising the question a number of times so that the witness was uncertain as to its point, thus sounding difficult and uncooperative. 'I am asking the question which I have put to you. I will repeat it now for the third or fourth time, and I hope you will kindly attend.' The answer, of course, was that Gordon-Cumming lived in the hope that the events would remain secret and he could live his life as before. However, when the matter became public property, he realised it would be taken up by his Clubs, his Regiment and his friends.

Russell then brought up the anonymous letter of 27 December from Paris, revealing the secret, which Gordon-Cumming sent to Owen Williams. [There were a number of letters exchanged between Owen Williams and Gordon-Cumming; on the whole copies were not kept and many destroyed – Gordon-Cumming admitted he was not in the habit of keeping letters – but the defendants' solicitors had refused to show any kept by Owen Williams to Clarke. This gave ample opportunity for Russell to confuse the jury with who wrote to whom, when.] However, Owen Williams's letter of 29 January to Gordon-Cumming was important because it referred to Gordon-Cumming's reason for signing the document. 'You are quite at liberty to tell Stracey [the Regimental commander] that you signed the document under extreme pressure and the promise of secrecy, but that you never acknowledged for one moment either to Coventry or myself the truth of the accusation against you.... Therefore your signature was the only possible hope of the avoidance of a horrible scandal.... You signed as the only way out of an impasse but in no way made any acknowledgement that you were guilty.' This is exactly what Russell's instructing solicitors had warned him of because it gave Gordon-Cumming the defence of coercion; he had been forced into signing the document under pressure without admitting guilt. Russell sensibly glossed over it and asked about Gordon-Cumming's contact with the military authorities. Gordon-Cumming explained the procedure of informing his commanding officer of the allegation and the steps available to the Army. He said he had offered to retire on half-pay. Russell then switched to establishing at what stage Gordon-Cumming had decided to bring proceedings against his accusers. Gordon-Cumming was vague on the date but Russell, clearly, was trying to insinuate that, while still in communication with Owen Williams and Lord Coventry, he had actually, secretly, instructed solicitors in the case. Russell turned to Gordon-Cumming's attempt to persuade Berkeley Levett to drop his allegation. Why did Gordon-Cumming see him? To find out specifically what Levett and the others had seen him do and explain to him what a mess he was now in. Levett said he saw something. But what? He shuffled, he didn't quite know. Gordon-Cumming then asked him to go to Mrs Wilson to see if a formal retraction of the accusation might be made. Later Gordon-Cumming received a letter from Levett saying nothing could be done. At that point, Gordon-Cumming maintained, he instructed solicitors. After some legal wrangling over the submission of a letter marked 'Private' from Gordon-Cumming to Lord Coventry, which was not allowed, Russell ended his cross-examination. It had been a powerful performance, leaving Gordon-Cumming bruised but by no means defeated. Clarke, in re-examination, stressed a few points. He underlined the inaccuracies in the précis which Gordon-Cumming had not seen until the end of January. He confirmed that the letters from Owen Williams were addressed to him as 'Dear Bill' or 'My dear Bill' and that when his solicitors applied for copies of the letters he had written to Owen Williams and Lord Coventry, his request was refused.

Then, what the Country had been waiting for; the Prince of Wales in the witness-box. Clearly nervous, he, nevertheless, answered firmly and confidently. Clarke ran through his relationship with Gordon-Cumming and then the events of the two night's card playing. Was there anything to give him the smallest suspicion as to Gordon-Cumming's play? Nothing whatever. There was no indication of any bad play until the evening of the 10th? No. Who then told him? Lord Coventry. He said the statement came from five individuals. The Prince did not see any of them until after his interview with Gordon-Cumming and then only the three men, not the two ladies. Did the Prince agree with the contents of the précis? Yes. What happened to it and the document signed by Gordon-Cumming? They were sealed in an envelope and Sir Francis Knollys put them in a safe place until the trial. Russell cross-examined. How long after the event did he see the précis? About a week. Russell ran through the people the Prince had seen. '(Mrs Wilson) said very little,' the Prince replied shortly. Did he suggest drawing up the document to be signed by Gordon-Cumming and the others? No, it was Lord Coventry and General Owen Williams. Did he want to act as leniently as he could with Gordon-Cumming? Most certainly.

Clarke reached the nub of his case. The Prince quite clearly had taken Coventry's and Owen Williams's accusations at face value, without questioning any of the people who had, ostensibly, witnessed the cheating. Additionally, he fully accepted the précis, despite its inaccuracies. The *Los Angeles Herald* of California reported, 'Though it lasted only twenty minutes, the examination of the Prince evidently wearied him exceedingly, and made him extremely nervous. He kept changing his position, and did not seem able to keep his hands still.

When a question more pressing, more to the point than usual, was put to him, the Prince's face was observed to flush considerably, and then pale again, showing the state of nervousness in which he found himself.'[194]

At that point, an extraordinary thing happened. A small juryman, sitting at the back of the jury box, jumped to his feet as the Prince of Wales was leaving the witness-box, and said, in a Cockney accent,[195] 'I should like to ask one question. Are this jury to understand that you as banker on these two occasions saw nothing of the alleged malpractices of the plaintiff?' The Prince answered courteously, 'No; it is not usual for a banker to see anything in dealing cards,[196] especially when you are playing among friends in their house. You do not suspect anything of the sort.' 'What was your Royal Highness's opinion at the time as to the charges made against Sir William Gordon-Cumming?' 'The charges appeared so unanimous that it was the proper course – no other course was open to me – than to believe them.' It was utterly wrong that the Judge allowed the juryman to ask a question in the first place and then to seek, secondly, an opinion from the witness rather than to seek pure evidence. Clarke, feeling that there should be no doubt as to the Prince's failure to notice anything untoward, remarked to the Prince's retreating back, 'I take it that the answer to the first question is "No."' It was probably the question he should have explored in more depth himself.

The final witness for the plaintiff was General Owen Williams. Clarke summarised his close friendship with Gordon-Cumming and the Prince of Wales, then confirmed that he had been an ordinary player on the first night at Tranby Croft, then croupier for the second, which meant he shared the profit or loss with the bank. The first evening, the Prince had been banker and croupier, so would have dealt cards and handled the counters. When did he hear of the allegations against Gordon-Cumming? When Lord Coventry summoned him to his room on the 10th. In the room were Lycett Green, Jack Wilson, Berkeley Levett[197] and the two Somersets. Lycett Green gave the account of the events. Prior to dinner on the 10th, had he heard any statement as to the alleged facts by anyone other than Lycett Green? No. When did he draft the statement summarising the facts? Sometime later, as accurately as possible. The statement (the *précis*) of what Lycett Green had told him was produced in court.

He believed it was necessary to make the Prince of Wales aware of the allegations. Did he, asked Clarke, agree to make a suggestion of how to handle this before meeting the Prince? Yes, in consultation with Lord Coventry. Had he seen Gordon-Cumming at the time he made the suggestion? No. Or any statement from anyone apart from Lycett Green? No. So he and the others agreed that the matter should be hushed up before Gordon-Cumming had been seen at all? Yes.

'At that time you were under the impression that there were five witnesses against him?' queried Clarke. 'We were.' 'The document was signed by a number of persons who did not profess to have seen foul play?' 'Undoubtedly it was.' 'Then the expression "Signed also by the gentlemen cognisant of the facts of the case" means "gentlemen who had been informed of the matter".' 'Yes.'

The court listened intently as Clarke made the important point that Owen Williams and Coventry relied solely on Lycett Green's account on which they briefed the Prince of Wales. They, and others who signed the undertaking document did so without having witnessed any cheating. (Of the defendants, the only people who thought they saw Gordon-Cumming cheating were Jack Wilson, Lycett Green and Berkeley Levett, after he had been told by Jack. Mrs Wilson had been told by Jack, Lycett Green by Jack and Ethel Lycett Green by her husband.)

On being cross-examined, Owen Williams maintained it was his 'impression' that he was told (by Lycett Green) that, in addition to increasing his stake, Gordon-Cumming had withdrawn counters when the play was against him. It was also his 'impression' that Lycett Green and Jack Wilson agreed to watch Gordon-Cumming the second night.

Owen Williams accepted that he when he explained the purpose of signing the document to the others, Lycett Green demurred. He said that the matter should be settled immediately; the idea being that it should be made public and that he should confront Gordon-Cumming now. Owen Williams persuaded Lycett Green that, by signing the document, Gordon-Cumming was effectively admitting his guilt. Lycett Green then agreed to maintain silence.

On confronting Gordon-Cumming with the document, Owen Williams and Coventry told him, '… that unless he signed it he would be requested to leave the house on the following morning, and proclaimed over every racecourse as a cheat.'

On being asked about his letter of 28 January to Gordon-Cumming, Owen Williams said it was in response to an emotional one from his old friend, he replied, '… that he had not in any way acknowledged his guilt, and that he had signed the document under extreme pressure.'

Clarke wound up the examination. Owen Williams accepted that, at the time, he had nothing but the statement of Lycett Green and Jack Wilson and the tacit acquiescence of Berkeley Levett. The statement of Lycett Green was the sole material on which the accusation was put to Gordon-Cumming? Yes. Did he recall, on or before he wrote the précis, being told that Berkeley Levett had not seen Gordon-Cumming cheating on the second night? No, Berkeley Levett told him he had seen him cheat.

'That, my lord, is the plaintiff's case.'

How did it go for the plaintiff? Both Clarke and Russell were at the top of their form; very little escaped them and they glossed over the danger areas. Gordon-Cumming himself was, as one might expect, cool under fire and revealed little of the tension and anxiety he must have felt. The Prince of Wales acquitted himself well, even when questioned by the courageous juryman. Owen Williams? Torn between being a genuine old friend of Gordon-Cumming's and the duty he felt to his future king, he managed well enough over some shaky parts of his testimony, but, in the end, he had failed his mission, which was to prevent the Prince from appearing as he did now. Nevertheless, the Prince clearly thought Williams had done well. He wrote to him, on the same day, from the Marlborough Club:

'I feel I must write two lines to congratulate you on the admirable manner in which you gave your evidence. Nothing could have been better or more calm & collected. I feel convinced it will carry great weight even with the intelligent (?) jury! Tomorrow will be an interesting day.'[198]

All still to play for.

CHAPTER 11 - The Defence

On Wednesday 3 June 'the scene in front of the huge iron gates [of the Law Courts] resembled for all the world that which may be observed at the entrance of the pit of a leading theatre on the first night of a long-expected play. For fully half an hour before the time they would open, the carriages, now well known, had been depositing ladies and gentlemen, who pressed forward so as to be in a favourable position for getting as soon as possible into the room, and when the bolts were drawn there was a rush that would have done credit to a regular first night gathering or football team,' the *Pittsburg Dispatch* reported and continued. 'Perhaps the best dressed woman in the crowd of fashionables who have come to regard Lord Coleridge's court as their happy hunting ground, was Lady Coleridge, who wore a black empire costume with a white and rose-pink spotted vest and creamy silver gauntlets. She is a beautiful woman, and her very becoming costume made her one of the centres of attraction. She undoubtedly formed a charming adjunct to the administration of justice, and the pleasant way in which she looks around the court for her friends and nods at them, smiling as she does so, seems to convey the idea that she has a delightful sense of the property in the whole proceedings by virtue of her relation to the presiding judge. Her smiles and the pretty dimples she shows when she smiles have been freely commented on as proving the infinite amusement she derives from her attendance, and above all the pretty little "cheeky" absence of awe for the majesty of the law, which is proved by her behaviour under the very eyes of the great Lord Chief Justice himself, have done much to make the court very pleasant.'[199]

The equally elegant Sir Charles Russell opened the case for the defendants. He was slightly late, arriving after the Prince of Wales and Lord Coleridge. Was it to make an impression as he swept in, bowing and profusely apologising? It certainly did not dent his self-confidence.

'Sir William Gordon-Cumming, dignified and apparently confident in spite of the general belief the "celebrated case" was going against him, [had earlier] entered the court with his head erect and his grey eyes flashing scorn in the direction of his enemies and took up his accustomed place near his counsel. The plaintiff is a much better looking man than his portraits now in the show windows make him out to be. His tanned, soldierly features are clear and firm and he has a mouth and chin which denote determination. The anxiety and worry which the baronet has suffered are beginning to leave their traces on his face and are shown in his weary look and dark circles which can be plainly noticed around his eyes.'[200]

There were five defendants in the case; Mrs Wilson, wife of the owner of Tranby Croft, their son, Arthur Stanley Wilson, known as 'Jack', their daughter, Ethel, Mrs Lycett Green, and her husband, Mr Edward Lycett Green and lastly, Lieutenant Berkeley Levett of the Scots Guards. In his Instructions to Counsel,[201] their solicitor, George Lewis, was puzzled that there were five when one, Jack Wilson, would have been enough for Gordon-Cumming to make his case against. Was it to intimidate the witnesses, particularly the women, he wondered? Was it an attempt to drive a wedge between them by attacking their differing versions of events? He thought that Gordon-Cumming had been badly advised although he noted that he sought £5,000 damages against each one.

Russell pointed out that there were actually nine people in the case. Apart from the plaintiff and the five defendants, were the Prince of Wales, General Owen Williams and Lord Coventry, all with vital roles in the 'melancholy story.' Russell began by demolishing Gordon-Cumming's view that the defendants were mistaken, despite conscientiously believing what they saw. Given that they made their statements on different days, in good faith and 'honesty of intention', this was impossible. The defendants were not involved in any of the interviews between Gordon-Cumming and the Prince of Wales, General Owen Williams or Lord Coventry, nor were party to any advice, right or wrong, given to him. Indeed, Lycett Green wanted to have it out, on the spot, as he feared that if this was not done then Gordon-Cumming might, in time, turn on them and charge them of falsely accusing him. He was only persuaded not to do so by the signing of the document, promising that Gordon-Cumming would never play cards again; in what Russell called 'humiliating and degrading terms.' Russell warmed to his theme that Gordon-Cumming was a dishonourable man, taking no steps to rebut the foul slander until he found it impossible to slip out of the army, so then, and only then, turning upon the defendants. He had been accused of cheating and had – to use his own expression – virtually admitted his guilt. It was inconceivable that had he been innocent he would not have taken immediate steps to vindicate himself. He said he had lost his head but he is a man of the world, wrote careful and considered letters to Owen Williams and is cool in the witness box. Although dishonoured in front of his friends, he was content to continue to maintain his place in society until the matter became public property. Despite his suggestions to modify or withdraw the charges, the defendants, with regret, refused and were determined to tell their story. Russell then took the jury through the précis, underlining the dates, inferring that Gordon-Cumming took no action until the matter was being openly discussed at the end of January and then tried to cajole Berkeley Levett, as a loyal officer in his Regiment, to drop the case. (Russell, patronisingly, called him 'young Mr Levett'). Meanwhile, Russell alleged, Gordon-Cumming tried to leave the army on half-pay. However, when he found out that the army would conduct its own inquiry but postpone it if there were a civil case, he only then took proceedings against the defendants.

Russell then ran through the events at Tranby Croft. The problem he had to overcome, was whether there had been any conspiracy amongst the defendants to watch Gordon-Cumming on the second night, the 9[th.] The defendants denied that there had been any collusion between them to watch Gordon-Cumming specifically but a table would be arranged to make cheating difficult. But watch they did. Levett deliberately did not do so but Jack Wilson, who had witnessed it the night before, and Lycett Green, who had been told about it, certainly did. It was suggested, in the précis, that Gordon-Cumming withdrew part of his stake when the cards were unfavourable, but the defendants never alleged that.

Lycett Green's slightly odd behaviour – leaving the table when he had seen the cheating, writing a note to Mrs Wilson, which was then sent into her by hand of a servant – was not satisfactorily explained, but Russell then asserted that Mrs Wilson and Mrs Lycett Green saw the cheating. The account of the various interviews and consultations was then run through. While carefully avoiding making any judgment on the wisdom of the advice to the Prince of Wales or course that was taken, Russell emphasised that Gordon-Cumming's actions were not those of an innocent man. He explained that the speed at which Owen Williams and

Coventry reached their conclusion that Gordon-Cumming had cheated was due to the independent evidence of the five accusers. In the face of this, Gordon-Cumming had failed to ask exactly what he had been accused of, who his accusers were, when they said it had happened, and to confront them right away. He was content, Russell maintained, to say he was innocent and that no one should believe a 'parcel of boys.'

Russell wound up his opening remarks by telling the jury that the scandal was not that the Prince of Wales was playing baccarat but that he was involved in a game in which one of the players cheated. The signing of the document was not, therefore, to protect the Prince but to guard the secret of the fact that Sir William Gordon-Cumming was dishonest. If he had not signed the document, he would have been publicly denounced as a cheat. Gordon-Cumming signed to protect himself, not the Prince. He was not a man who had lost his head; it was a carefully thought out performance to protect his own honour. These proceedings were only taking place because Gordon-Cumming had failed to leave the army on half-pay without an inquiry.

Russell handed over to his Junior, H H Asquith, to handle the first defendant, Arthur Stanley Wilson, known as Jack to differentiate him from his father of the same name. Sallow and looking younger than his age of twenty-two, he was the vital witness as the first person who had seen Gordon-Cumming cheating. He had met him before, he said, when staying at Tranby Croft. Asquith went through the seating plan on the first night and then the rules of the game. Jack had played the game many times and knew the rules well. It was important to ensure that the jury knew exactly where people were sitting in relation to Gordon-Cumming. On the Prince's left was Mrs Wilson, then an empty chair or an unidentified person, then Levett, next to him was Jack, then Gordon-Cumming and, on his left, Lord Edward Somerset – the left tableau as it was called.

Yes, he most certainly observed where the plaintiff placed his stake. He placed it on the top of a sheet of white notepaper which he had in front of him. Once or invariably when Jack saw him? Invariably, he thought, but he may have done it once or twice in another way. His usual practice? Certainly. And there was no line on the table at that time? No.

The middle table was higher than the side ones. Where did Jack and Lieutenant Levett place their stakes? Both placed them on the higher table. They stretched across and put them on the higher table. Before the Prince dealt the cards did Jack look round the table? Yes, to see how the people were playing - whether they were playing high or not. Did he notice what stake the plaintiff had put in front of him? Yes, one £5 counter. This was before the deal. On what was it placed? On the sheet of notepaper. What was the colour of the counter? Red. He looked round to see what other stakes were being played.

The cards were then dealt. Which side won? His. Did he notice what sum was paid to the plaintiff? £15: three red counters. There were three red counters on the sheet of paper? Yes.

When the dealer came to pay Sir William Gordon-Cumming at the end of the round how many counters had he in front of him? Three. On the top of the sheet of notepaper. Did he then notice anything with reference to the plaintiff's stake? When Lord Edward Somerset was taking up the cards. A member of his tableau, he was seated immediately on the left of the plaintiff. As he looked across at Lord Edward Somerset about to take up the cards he noticed Sir William sitting with his hands in front of him and there was one £5 counter on the top of the sheet of the notepaper. He was sitting with his hand over the £5 counter, leaning forward. Lord Edward Somerset picked up the cards, and Gordon-Cumming leaned over to see what cards he had got. At the same time Jack saw something red in the palms of his hands, and immediately knew it could be nothing less than one of the £5 counters. Lord Edward had a natural - a nine and a court card. Immediately he saw this Gordon-Cumming opened his hands and let drop three more £5 counters. He was paid £20 on the coup.

What was the next thing he noticed about Gordon-Cumming's play? He was sitting with his hands in much the same position. Jack could not say for certain who was then taking up the cards. Whoever it was drew a very bad card, which made them baccarat - that is nothing. Immediately Gordon-Cumming saw this he drew back his hands to his own pile, which was in front of him, to the bottom of the sheet of notepaper, and let fall counters – an unknown quantity - into his own pile.

Jack was sitting next to Mr. Berkeley Levett, and whom he knew to be a brother officer of the plaintiff.

Directly he saw this he turned round to him and whispered, "My God, Berkeley, this is too hot!" "What on earth do you mean?" "This man next to me is cheating." "My dear chap, you must be mistaken; you must have made some mistake. It is absolutely impossible."

"Well, just look for yourself." He looked; and a few coups afterwards he turned and said, "It is too hot."

Before Levett made that remark, he had seen the plaintiff's hand in a suspicious place, but he did not like to look too closely.

Was Levett looking? He thought so. After what he had told him it would have been a natural thing for him to do. After Levett had said this did he notice anything in the plaintiff's play? He saw him win one distinct coup again. He did not know who was taking the card; at any rate the card was favourable. This time the plaintiff did not have his hands in the same position as he had the first time. He had them back over his own counters. He had £5 down at the edge of the table. The only thing Jack could see close to the paper was a £2 counter, and this, with the pencil the plaintiff had in his hand, just pushed over the edge of the paper and half-way up. He was paid £7.

Still during the first evening, did he notice anything else in Gordon-Cumming's play? Nothing that he could specify. If he had been asked the next afternoon, he could have specified half a dozen more cases.

How long did he play that evening? About one hour and a half hours. After the game was over did he go to Mr. Levett's room? Yes. What did Levett do in his room? He threw himself down across the bed.

What was it he said? He said, "My God! To think of it - Lieutenant-Colonel Sir William Gordon-Cumming, Bart., caught cheating at cards!" That was the first thing he said. Jack asked, "What on earth are we to do?" Levett said, "For goodness' sake don't ask me. He is in my regiment and was my own captain for a year and a half. What can I do?" Jack then said to him, "I know what I shall do. I shall have a talk with my brother-in-law in the morning." He then left the room and went straight to his mother's room. He told her that he had seen Sir William Gordon-Cumming cheating at cards. She was surprised and distressed at what he told her. She said, "For goodness' sake, don't let us have a scandal here."

Jack then explained how he had organised the butler to arrange a new table, covered in baize, with a chalk line drawn round it. He told his mother that would stop him cheating.

On the morning of Tuesday, 9th September, as he walked with his brother-in-law, Lycett Green, he told him what he had seen the night before. He mentioned that Levett had also seen something. At first, Lycett Green was very indignant, but Jack told him that he would never think of saying such a thing unless he was absolutely confident of it. Did Jack say anything to him about the change of the table? Yes; he told him he had done his best to stop any recurrence of it. Jack said, "He will not be able to do it tonight at any rate, as we have so arranged the table that I don't think it is possible."

Is it true that at this time, or at any other time, he and Lycett Green agreed to watch the play? No, absolutely untrue. Did he agree with anyone to watch the play? No, with nobody at all.

Jack then went on to explain the table arrangements for the following night's play. It was a three foot wide table, capable of sitting twenty or so people. A chalk line had been drawn round it, six inches from the edge. The Prince of Wales sat in the centre, with his back to the fire, with General Owen Williams opposite, acting as croupier. Gordon-Cumming sat between Lady Coventry and Mrs Lycett Green. Jack sat next to her with Lycett Green on his left. He was not sure where Levett was, but somewhere on the opposite side of the table.

The first time he noticed anything odd was when Gordon-Cumming was helping Lady Coventry with her cards, having staked £5 himself. The Prince lost that coup, so had to pay out. As he heard that, Gordon-Cumming nudged a £10 counter just over the line, four inches away from the original £5 stake. The Prince paid out on the £5 stake, failing to notice the £10 counter. Gordon-Cumming said, 'I beg your pardon, sir, but there is another 'tenner' here that you have forgotten,' and the Prince of Wales said, 'I wish you would put your stake in a more conspicuous place,' and paid him. On a further occasion, when he knew the cards were favourable, he flicked another £5 counter over the line, with his pencil. Jack maintained Gordon-Cumming cheated again but he could not provide details.

The following day he went to the races and shared a compartment in the train with Lycett Green and the two Somersets. They agreed that the matter should be put in the hands of Lord Coventry. Jack had earlier spoken to his mother and Mrs Lycett Green who told him what they had seen. On return Berkeley Levett joined the four of them in the compartment and when told what they intended, asked to be left out of it on account of his embarrassment being a fellow officer of Gordon-Cumming's.

He then covered the detail of the interviews they had with General Owen Williams and, later, the Prince of Wales.

'The Court adjourned for luncheon in the midst of this testimony, and the Prince of Wales again honoured Lord Chief Justice, Lady Coleridge and her party with his presence at luncheon, while such celebrities as Lords Coventry and Somerset and General Owen Williams, who had failed to bring luncheon which their better ballasted friends had provided themselves with, had to fight for refreshments for themselves and the ladies of their parties around the public house bars of the neighbourhood, which were packed to suffocation by the common herd.'[202]

After lunch Sir Edward Clarke began his cross-examination. He established that Jack was twenty-two on 30th July last year, had no occupation and didn't do very much. He had left Cambridge, he thought, about two years ago. He had not completed a full course and was only at Magdalene College for a year. He explained he did not do much work there, and thought it rather a waste of time. This raised, unsurprisingly, much laughter in the court. His father thought it a waste of time as well and it would be better for him to leave. In order that he might waste more time? No. He went into his father's business for a month. To waste more time there? No. He worked very hard for a month but has not returned to business since then.

Like all good barristers, Clarke knew perfectly well what the answers were going to be before he asked the questions and it did not take him long to reduce Jack to the picture of an idle waster with too much money. He went on further to probe Jack's gambling habits. Yes, he had played Baccarat a number of times at Cambridge and in places he couldn't remember with people whose names he wasn't prepared to divulge. He had played the game with Lycett Green and at Tranby Croft until his father forbade it. While his memory was seemingly vague, he did, he said, recall the events at Tranby Croft in detail. He agreed that when Lycett Green told the story to Lord Coventry on the night of the 10th, it was largely what Jack had told him. He accepted that Lycett Green had seen no cheating on the 8th but was merely relating Jack's account.

Clarke then turned to the précis written by General Owen Williams, signed by Lord Coventry and agreed by the Prince of Wales. Due to the inaccuracies it contained, it was quickly becoming an embarrassment to the defence. Was the statement made by Lycett Green in Jack's presence accurate? More or less, though not quite. Did he use the word 'systematically' in relation to Gordon-Cumming's cheating? He thought so but could not swear that he did. Did Lycett Green say that he had had told him that Gordon-Cumming withdrew stakes when the cards were unfavourable? No, he did not say that. Did Lycett Green tell the three gentlemen (Williams, Coventry and the Prince) that Mrs Wilson had noticed the cheating on the 8th? No. And that she had told her husband? No, certainly not. 'This conduct had also been noticed by Mrs Arthur Wilson, who informed her husband of what she had seen. So, Mr and Mrs Lycett Green and Mr Levett having been also made acquainted with the facts, it was agreed that they should all carefully watch the play on the following night. Is that statement correct? No, it is entirely wrong.

Jack's memory, under Clarke's relentless questioning was starting to fail him. Vague phrases like: That I cannot be quite certain about. I think he did. My idea is that he did. In fact, I am nearly certain of it, although I could not swear. And, I do not remember the exact words. And, No; I cannot say what he said. So, there was no such statement made as to an agreement to watch on any day? No, absolutely nothing. To make it absolutely clear to the jury, do you think there is anything that might have slipped your mind? Certainly. After nine months one is quite liable to forget a few of the facts or forget the details. Forget the details? Yes. Clarke had him on the ropes.

He continued the pressure by pursuing relatively small details of the tables, tablecloth colour and so on, but, each one further demonstrating Jack's faulty memory. He took him through the colour and value of the counters. Did he play Baccarat on any system? No, just as fancy struck him. Did he know the system of *coups des trois* – in other words, if you win £5 you add that £5 and another £5. If you won then you would get £15, making £30? Yes, of course, there are various ways of playing. The questioning continued over the number of times an individual handled the cards and the number of coups that happened during the evening. Jack's replies were increasingly elusive and evasive. Clarke then turned to the piece of paper in front of Gordon-Cumming on which he was noting the gains and losses. Jack accepted that the paper was in full view of all those round the tables.

The Lord Chief Justice sought clarification, as well he might. Mr Wilson, you maintain your answer is substantially the same – that he [Gordon-Cumming] had seen the card? Yes. And having seen it, he put on more counters? That is exactly what I mean.

With much relief, particularly for Jack, the court adjourned for the day.

The alliterative headline writers in the United States, ushered in the fourth day of the trial:-

Racy, Rich and Rare[203]

Bummy "Baccaraw" Business Brought Close to a British Baronet

Wilson Wondered at William's Winning Way and Watched

Cumming Clearly Caught Converting Cold Counters Into Coin

Lords and Ladies Linger and Listen to Leading Lawyers

Others were more sombre: 'It is safe to say, however, that both the plaintiff in this libel suit, Sir William Gordon-Cumming and the defendants, to say nothing of the Prince of Wales, have not shown up in very bright colors. Even the Prince of Wales's best friends are said to admit unwillingly that the testimony he gave was far from being a nature to reflect credit upon the future King of England and Emperor of India. At this stage of the proceedings it is safe to say that Cumming will lose the case.'[204]

Jack Wilson was still in the witness box. The strain on the 22 year old was starting to show. An unkind journalist suggested yesterday had probably been the hardest day's work he had ever done in his life.[205] Sir Edward Clarke continued to challenge Jack's memory in a clear attempt to persuade the jury that his evidence was shaky and unreliable. Jack accepted that George Lewis [the defendants' solicitor] had taken down his sworn statement.[206] Yes, they had played the game with the Prince of Wales's counters which he had never seen before or since. No, he had not told his father; he thought telling his mother and brother-in-law (Lycett Green) was enough. He thought the chalk line on the table the following evening would prevent cheating. No one had said anything to Sir William or his two friends and the five people in the know sat down to play cards again the following evening? Yes, Jack didn't think his word alone against Gordon-Cumming would be believed. He was doubtful of Levett's support.

Clarke could see that members of the jury were starting to question the evidence of this young man. He twisted the knife further. Was it usual to play Baccarat with a chalked line, across which the stakes were placed? Yes. Did Sir William again keep his score on a piece of paper? I think so. And put his counters on the paper? No, they were over the chalked line. How far was the chalk line from the edge of the table? About six or seven inches. As the table was very narrow, and the chalk line being drawn six inches from the edge, it would leave only a small space in front. The line could easily be seen. Correct? Yes.

Jack thought he could remember Sir William keeping the score on the piece of paper in front of him. He did not know whether anyone else was doing so. He sometimes did himself but could not recall whether he had done so that night. It was too long ago. However, he did remember winning £30 the first night and £25 or £30 the second, playing for low stakes both nights. On the second night, after about twenty minutes, he thought he noticed something wrong. He was not sure whether he was the only person to do so. He thought Sir William's hands moved in a suspicious manner but he could not be certain.

Clarke asked him why he hadn't said anything when he saw Gordon-Cumming cheating? There were ladies present. But both ladies knew of the misbehaviour, why should that therefore inhibit him? It would not be a gentlemanly thing to do when ladies were present. Coupled with that, his brother-in-law was hot tempered and he did not want a scene over the card table. So he played on for an hour, staking his own money on the success of the cards which Gordon-Cumming was backing? Taking winnings which were obtained by the cheating he alleged on the part of Gordon-Cumming? No.

Jack left the witness box. Despite being portrayed as an idle playboy, he had, with some memory lapses, stuck to his story under rigorous interrogation by Sir Edward Clarke. Although flustered and nervous, his clear description of what Gordon-Cumming was alleged to have done was not unconvincing.

It was now Berkeley Levett's turn. For him, this was a worse ordeal than for Jack Wilson; he was torn between loyalty to the Prince of Wales, loyalty to an respected senior officer in his Regiment and his disciplined inclination to do the right and honourable thing.

Charles Mathews, one of Russell's Junior Counsel conducted the examination. He took him through the events of the first evening which were now becoming very well known to the court. It was, though, only after Jack had drawn his attention to it that he thought he saw Gordon-Cumming cheating. Later, in Jack's bedroom, when they were discussing it, he implored Jack not to do anything for the sake of the man and the Regiment. But he said he would consult his brother-in-law. Levett really wanted to keep out of it and the following evening deliberately did not watch Gordon-Cumming playing. When returning from the races on the second day, he shared a compartment with Lycett Green, Jack Wilson and the two Somersets. They discussed the matter and decided to approach Lord Coventry; Levett begged to be left out of it owing to his awkward position. However, later that night, he accompanied all the others to the Prince of Wales's room.

The Prince of Wales asked him if he had seen what went on. Courageously, he said as a member of the same Regiment he wished to be left out of the matter. Notwithstanding that, later he signed the document.

On 25 January, Gordon-Cumming asked him to go round to his house in London. On arrival, it was clear what Gordon-Cumming wanted to talk about. He was not asked to withdraw but to say he was mistaken. He replied that for Gordon-Cumming's sake and for the sake of the Regiment he could, but he knew there was one man who would not; Lycett Green. He had to say he had seen Gordon-Cumming adding to the counters. However, he would contact Mrs Wilson to see what could be done.

He explained that nothing could be done from Mrs Wilson's point of view and that, when on Guard the following day, he had seen Jack Wilson, also without any further result. He met Gordon-Cumming by chance in Piccadilly soon afterwards, having received a letter from Gordon-Cumming's solicitors, which he forwarded on to Lord Coventry. Subsequently, he received a letter from Gordon-Cumming, the gist of which was there was nothing further that could be done and it would have to be seen through to the bitter end. Gordon-Cumming said he was sorry that Levett had had anything to do with it.

Sir Edward Clarke cross-examined. He suggested to Levett that, having been told by Jack Wilson he had seen Gordon-Cumming cheating, he then expected to see him doing so rather than by some accident or mistake? No. He definitely saw him adding to the stake. On the following night, he was sitting opposite Gordon-Cumming but deliberately did not watch his play.

He did hear Lycett Green's statement to the Prince but could not remember the detail or verify the accuracy, therefore, of the précis. How did he know that, while he was prepared to say he was mistaken, Lycett Green was not? Because he knew what sort of man he was.

Lycett Green, probably the key man in the whole saga, was now called as a witness. 31 years old, tall, fair-haired, he wore a monocle. Son of a wealthy iron-master, he was, like Jack Wilson, a man of 'independent means.' What effect was his evidence going to have on the jury?

At this stage had Clarke missed a vital point? General Owen Williams had never been asked outright, 'Whose was the ultimatum you spoke of in your letter to Gordon-Cumming?' and 'Who was going to denounce Gordon-Cumming next morning on Doncaster Racecourse?' The only people who would do so were the Wilsons or their spokesman, Lycett Green, which meant their role was perilously close to blackmail. The ultimatum, of course, was directed also against the Prince, Lord Coventry and General Williams, all of whom had an interest in preserving the secrecy of the scandal. Gordon-Cumming was going to keep them all out of trouble by signing the document. It is understandable, therefore, why they exerted such 'extreme pressure.'[207]

Herbert Asquith took up his brief. Lycett Green confirmed he was the son of Sir Edward Green, MP for Wakefield, and that he had married Ethel, daughter of Mr and Mrs Arthur Wilson about six years ago. He lived in York and was a Master of Foxhounds. He had been present on the first night (8th) at Tranby Croft but had not played baccarat as he went to bed early. The following morning Jack told him that he had seen Gordon-Cumming cheating and so had Berkeley Levett. He told his wife and that evening they played cards. They had not reached an agreement to watch Gordon-Cumming's play. He had no doubt that he had seen Gordon-Cumming push a counter over the chalk line when his cards were favourable. His first instinct was to jump up and expose him however, with ladies and His Royal Highness present, he did not want to make a scene. So he left the room and wrote a note to his mother-in-law which the butler took into her. He returned to the room and continued to play. The next day he went to the races.

(After the lunch adjournment, the jury foreman handed the judge a vulgar and abusive letter which he had received. Lycett Green had also received one which he gave to the judge. Coleridge assured them that the appropriate steps would be taken. Sadly, there is no account of either what the letters contained or what His Lordship's steps were.)

After the discussion in the train returning from the races, Lycett Green went to Lord Coventry. In General Owen Williams's presence, he told them what they had seen and said he was willing to confront Gordon-Cumming. He said his wife had also seen the cheating, confirmed by her mother. After dinner, he was summoned to the Prince of Wales's room with the two courtiers, both Somersets, Jack Wilson and Berkeley Levett. He could not remember exactly what he had said. Yes, he remembered the Prince asking Levett something, but Levett had excused himself from answering as he was in Gordon-Cumming's Regiment. The Lord Chief Justice asked him what Levett said. He told him he had seen cheating.

During the meeting, he said that if there was any doubt, he wanted to be confronted with Gordon-Cumming. Somerset's account is more florid, 'HRH said, "I must tell you Gentlemen, that Sir William most strongly denies it." Whereupon Lycett-Green, a fearless and obstinate Yorkshireman, said, "Does he Sir? Then have him here and I will tell him to his face that he is a cheat and a liar." But he was pacified by it being pointed out to him that by signing the paper Sir W practically admitted his guilt.'[208]

Charles Gill, Clarke's Junior counsel, began his attack. (Gill was well known to the public as a rising star of the legal world).[209] Lycett Green made no note or memoranda of the events? No. So what he was saying is entirely from memory? Yes. His recollection was proving as vague as Jack's even to the extent of not remembering whether he had made a formal statement to the Prince. Gill managed a cheap laugh by asking him his occupation – Master of Foxhounds. [The occupants of the court were left to their own imagination, possibly putting him the same idle camp as Jack Wilson, which, of course, was exactly what Gill wanted.] He knew nothing of any record that had been kept [the précis]? No. But he was chosen or constituted himself as spokesman? He didn't know; he was older than his brother-in-law. He had heard the précis read out and

General Owen Williams being asked as to its accuracy, particularly the passage where he claimed that Gordon-Cumming had 'systematically' placed a larger stake on the table when the cards were in his favour? He could not remember the exact words; he would not absolutely swear. He had not stated that he saw Gordon-Cumming withdrawing stakes when the cards were against him nor had he said that anyone had agreed to watch him the second night. How did General Owen Williams then come to write that in the précis? The Judge disallowed the question on the ground that counsel could not ask the witness how General Williams came to do anything. [Nevertheless, clever Mr Gill had planted a question into the jury's minds – why was the General making this up or was he?]

Gill took Lycett Green through the game of Baccarat, exposing him as someone who had a fairly peripheral knowledge of the game. He answered the questions with a string of, 'I do not know', I cannot do so', I cannot say..', I cannot remember..', I do not understand the question.' Gill then turned to the first day at the races. Upon this particular day he had been at the races all day entertaining a party there? Yes, with the house party. He was he assisting, as host, to entertain. Gill claimed not to know what people in society did at races, but other people lunch on these occasions? Yes, Lycett Green admitted they lunched. The lunch went on all afternoon, Gill supposed? No, and if he insinuated Lycett Green was drunk, he was not. Gill warmed to his theme, 'We have heard of the profuse hospitality of the Wilsons, and I presume they were entertaining everybody at the races?' 'Oh, not anybody.' The judge pretended not to understand the question. Gill, darkly, 'But the jury will. I am in hopes that the jury will understand many things that are not on the surface.'[210]

The cross-examination continued in much the same vein with Lycett Green either deliberately being vague in his answers or because he genuinely could not remember. He came over as evasive and insouciant, even short tempered; the events must have been much clearer in his mind than he pretended. He would have discussed them with the family and certainly with his wife, let alone the smooth solicitor, George Lewis. He was not pressed on what would have happened had Gordon-Cumming not signed the document. Was he really going to carry out his threat of public disclosure at the races? How? He did not say what would have happened had he confronted Gordon-Cumming that night. Duel at dawn?

Hardly. Gordon-Cumming was far too much a man of the world and experienced soldier to feel threatened by one such as Lycett Green. The jury would not have warmed to him and Gill ensured they didn't.

Ethel Lycett Green, his wife, who came next, was very different. She was small, elegant and neatly dressed. She gave her evidence in a calm, confident way. Sir Charles Russell was determined to make up for the set-back of her husband's performance. She had been married to Lycett Green for six years and had three children. She had played Baccarat a number of times before and had been taught how to by Gordon-Cumming in 1888 when he dined with them. She had met him before she was married when he had stayed at Tranby Croft. She was a great friend of a 'near relation' of his who lived in Yorkshire [his sister, Lady Middleton. It was curious she did not name her.] She noticed nothing strange on the first night except that Gordon-Cumming seemed to be very lucky, winning handsomely. She recalled the Prince of Wales asking Gordon-Cumming to place his counters where they could be seen and Gordon-Cumming replying that they were on the sheet of paper in front of him.

The following morning her husband told her that her brother had seen Gordon-Cumming cheating. She was profoundly shocked and it must have registered deeply in her mind. That night Baccarat was again played but on the new table with the line drawn in chalk. Was she, subconsciously, fearful that the cheating would re-occur? She was sitting on Gordon-Cumming's left with Lady Coventry on his right. She explained that she had seen him increasing his stake when the cards were good. She demonstrated to the court how he held his hands and used a piece of paper and a pencil. It was very clear and particularly dramatic coming from a person with the closest view possible of what happened. Apart from the Prince's remark about seeing the counters, it was curious that neither he nor Lady Coventry nor General Owen Williams, the croupier and therefore not actually playing, could have failed to see what Ethel had. Nevertheless, her evidence was transparently sound and believable. She was not in the least upset by Clarke's attempts to break her recollection. He even produced the name of someone called Bowles, who had seen her play, badly, before. She denied ever having met him. It was not a good point for Clarke to have made, merely confusing the jury and making Ethel look even more composed and confident in her denial.

The following day, Friday 5 June, Mrs Wilson followed her daughter into the witness box. For the aristocrats in the courtroom, was there a whiff of *bourgeoisie* about her? Was she really a hostess up to handling a visit from Royalty and then the shock of potential scandal? Interest was palpable. Russell took her through the events which were now becoming well known to the jury to the point of tedium but there were aspects of Mrs Wilson's evidence which were going to be very interesting. During the first night, she detected her son catching her eye, but did not understand why until he came to her room later and told her that he had seen Gordon-Cumming cheating. Asking what he should do, she said, 'I cannot let you speak about it. Oh, you must not speak. We cannot have a scandal in our house.' Jack Wilson told her he would have another table produced for the following night at which it would be impossible to cheat. She did not want to trouble her husband, who came to bed late, with the problem.

The following night she sat on the Prince of Wales's left and the matter had completely passed out of her mind until she had the note from Lycett Green. When he returned to the room, she shook her head at him, but certainly watched what Gordon-Cumming was doing. She saw him push another £10 counter to join his original stake of £5, and was paid £15. He did this on two occasions. On the morning of the 11th, she took leave of the Prince of Wales, on account of her brother's death. She did say to him that she had seen Gordon-Cumming cheating because she feared it would damage her son in some way. The Prince said, 'Oh no; nothing of the kind.' Sir William also left early that morning without saying goodbye but leaving a note expressing his condolences and explaining his sudden recall to London.

In cross-examination, Clarke asked her whether she had mentioned the matter to anyone? Not at all, it was in her interests not to do so. While she had not signed the document, she had promised the Prince not to say anything. She said nothing to her husband about it as she hoped the cheating would not re-occur. He did not like the game and, 'He did not think it wise for young, hot-headed boys to play high.' It had been played before at Tranby Croft with the bank holding some £300 to £400. Why, if she had been told someone had been cheating, did she allow the game to be played again the second night? She did not want to have to give a reason for doing so and cast 'an imputation on the character of the whole of [her] guests.' She had told the Prince of Wales that her husband didn't like the game but that they were such a 'staid and non-gambling party' that she didn't think any harm would come of it. Mr Wilson was conspicuously absent from the rooms where the game was being played, on both nights. Curiously, she said her husband played on the first night. This simply was not true; no one else mentioned it in their statements and it was nowhere in either Counsel's Instructions. However, Clarke was, seemingly, concentrating on her agreement to play happening on the second night and failed to fasten onto this blatant lie.

She thought the new table arrangement the following night would prevent any cheating. How could it have gone out of her mind when Jack had reminded her just before she went into the billiard room? She had lots of other things to think about. Why did she not break up the party after receiving Lycett Green's note? She did, as soon as she could. Three-quarters of an hour to an hour later? It could not have been done at once. Half an hour after midnight? Yes. Clarke continued to question her on the exact ways in which she had seen Gordon-Cumming cheating. She was clearly embarrassed in having to explain her reaction and particularly why General Owen Williams, the croupier whose duty it was to assess stakes, recovering from those who lost and paying out those who won, hadn't seen anything odd about Gordon-Cumming's play. 'I felt very uncomfortable and very unhappy.' As well she might.

The benign 53 year-old George William Coventry, the 9th Earl; courtier and Conservative politician was next. As a former Captain of the Gentlemen-at-Arms, as well as Master of the Horse, he was as close to the Prince of Wales as anyone. While General Owen Williams was the prime mover in the cover-up operation, Coventry, because of his relationship with the Prince, was an important player. It was he who maintained that because Gordon-Cumming was such a friend of His Royal Highness, they had to tell the Prince what had happened. Coventry ran through his recollection of the various meetings and interviews. 'General Williams and myself had expressed the desire that this matter – this accusation – should be kept as secret as possible, by binding all those who had seen the transaction over to secrecy.' Was there any suggestion that Sir William had lost his head? No. Coventry advised him to sign the document, commenting that the Commander-in-Chief or his Commanding Officer would not be so lenient. To the court's delight,

Coventry's private diary was produced and the entry for 10 October read aloud. It covered the drafting of the précis and the undertaking signed by all the participants. 'We believe we have done our duty to society', he wrote. There were inaccuracies in it, and the précis which Coventry had signed, and he blamed this on his deafness and therefore not hearing precisely what some people had said. Nevertheless, the précis had mentioned that the accusers had agreed to watch Sir William on the second night when quite clearly, they hadn't, and that the undertaking was to avoid a scandal and keep the Prince's name out of it. This was utterly contrary to Sir Charles Russell's suggestion that the document was signed in order to preserve Gordon-Cumming's integrity.

But he and Williams decided that if they subsequently met Gordon-Cumming they would treat him as if nothing had happened. So, he agreed, Sir William would retain his rank in the Army and membership of his Clubs.

Incredulous, Clarke asked how could he and General Williams, very old friends of Gordon-Cumming, concoct a document to be signed by him which would be an admission of guilt before they even saw him? They thought it the only way out of the difficulty. But he had no idea of Gordon-Cumming's reaction to the accusation? No. Coventry's performance was not as good as it should have been; despite his twinkling eye, patrician demeanour and voice, he was as evasive and shifty as some of the others, and it was not all to do with being deaf.

The case now closed in preparation for the final speeches. While there had been some devastating evidence against Gordon-Cumming, witnesses had been muddled and less than candid. Statements conflicted with others and there were substantial inaccuracies in the précis and Lord Coventry's recollections in his diary. The jury was now in the hands of the eloquent barristers and the experienced judge.

CHAPTER 12 - Closing Stages

It was now the turn of learned counsel for the defendants and the plaintiff to persuade the jury to accept their clients' story. Having heard the evidence, hammered by examination, cross-examination and re-examination, the jury would have been swayed this way and that. They could be forgiven for being occasionally muddled. The barristers now sought to embed, in simple terms, the critical facts of their case in the jury's minds. The judge would then sum up even-handedly, with points of law and, if necessary, direct the jury.

The suave Sir Charles Russell, for the defendants, began. His task, he said, was a comparatively simple one. It was a question of whether the evidence was satisfactory that, on the nights of 8 and 9 September last year, Sir William Gordon-Cumming cheated at cards. Gordon-Cumming had admitted that the defendants conscientiously believed that they saw him commit the acts of cheating. They were given the chance to withdraw their accusations but it was impossible for them, in all honesty, to say they were mistaken. The damning things they had to say about Sir William were 'rather in sorrow than in anger.' Mrs Wilson had been cross-examined on her conduct on the two evenings in question. Her reactions and what she did was not the issue, but whether she was telling the truth of what she saw. Allowing the game to be played at all, contrary to her husband's earlier objections; then not telling him of the allegations; continuing with the game the second night and not stopping it after Lycett Green's note, was reasonable under the circumstances. To do anything else would have raised scandal then and there.

Both Lord Coventry and General Owen Williams had been attacked for their advice, since they could not have believed Gordon-Cumming guilty of cheating, because they allowed him to continue his career in the army, and they reached a premature conclusion as to his guilt based on barely considered evidence. However, they advised him to sign the document, which no man who was really innocent would have done. They relied on the independent evidence of no fewer than five witnesses. Sir William failed to confront his accusers, which was not the reaction of an innocent man. His cheating could not possibly be mistaken for the system he said he was employing. The leniency with which he was dealt with by his old friends and the signing of the document was to preserve the secrecy of Gordon-Cumming's conduct.

It had been suggested, continued Russell, that the evidence came from 'a parcel of boys' and two ladies inexperienced in playing Baccarat. This was not true; they had played before. In any case, it was hardly a difficult game. It needed no experience to see that if a player increased his stake after the cards are declared, that was cheating. The fact that others had failed to see the cheating was understandable. The Prince was busy dealing the cards and others, playing a friendly game in a country house, would not have been over vigilant. Just because five saw the offence and seven did not, that was no cause to disbelieve the five. The inconsistencies and inaccuracies in the précis and Lord Coventry's diary were irrelevant since the contents had not been seen, or agreed, by any of the defendants.

The real question was one of the evidence. Did the witnesses appear credible and truthful? Did they have an ill motive? How well did they stand up to cross-examination? Lycett Green's lack of memory, for which he was severely attacked, was merely to take great care that he did not commit himself to words which he may or may not have heard during the events. The suggestion that he had over-indulged at lunch at the races and at dinner that evening was without foundation. It was not mentioned by anyone else and therefore had no vestige of truth. There was no evidence that there had been any plan concocted to watch Sir William play the second night.

The court then adjourned for the weekend. Queen Victoria was intensely worried about the situation and wrote, a little later, to her daughter Vicky (Princess Royal, Dowager Empress of Germany). 'This Trial is indeed dreadful. I hope & think there is no doubt that the verdict will be given agst. Sir Wm G Cumming as the evidence is perfectly clear - but even if it is not - he will be turned out of the Army & society.......The whole thing must do Bertie harm I only pray it may be a warning.'[211] Then again, 'He must give up gambling & high play or the result may be most dangerous. I have written vy. kindly but vy. earnestly to him - and you shld. say a few words too, for the Monarchy almost is in danger if he is lowered & despised.'[212]

On Monday 8 June, Sir Charles Russell opened with the honeyed words of the Victorian barrister, 'Gentlemen[213] of the jury, I have a grateful recollection of the attention you were good enough to pay to the observations I addressed to you upon Friday, and I do not intend to repeat anything I then said; indeed, I hope that it will not be necessary for me to make a very lengthy demand upon your attention, although I feel that you will not grudge the necessary time for the elucidation of this matter.'

He went straight to the evidence against Gordon-Cumming, urging the jury to concentrate on that rather than any other suggestion his opponent might make. The defendants honestly believed they saw what they said they saw. Therefore the only course open to the plaintiff's counsel was to say the whole thing was an invention. There were eleven undoubted acts of cheating, possibly thirteen. The chain of evidence was as follows; Jack Wilson saw acts of cheating, Levett's attention was drawn to it, he rejected it with indignation then saw it. Lycett Green saw it, walked out of the room, informed Mrs Wilson, then she saw it. Mrs Lycett Green also saw it.

There had been attacks on Lord Coventry and General Williams from the plaintiff's side but it was clear that, although possibly precipitately, the conclusion they reached was a judgement based on the evidence. The subsequent actions by Gordon-Cumming confirmed their decision. He did not boldly meet the accusation but did something that, in secrecy, would give him a chance of preserving his good name. Parts of Sir William's evidence were unreliable; he denied he was told that Lycett Green wanted to confront him, but three witnesses said he was. He said he was advised not to confront his accusers but would an innocent man not ignore that advice? He denied he made any reference to the Duke of Cambridge or his Commanding Officer but the Prince of Wales, Lord Coventry and General Williams all said he did. It was clear that Lord Coventry and General Williams, in their wish to shield Mrs Wilson's feelings to avoid a scandal, dealt with him more leniently than they otherwise might.

When Gordon-Cumming signed the document, he rightly construed it as an admission of guilt and was told just that by Coventry and Williams. Nevertheless he signed it, explaining that he did so because he lost his head. There were five people who saw him cheat and another three who reached the same conclusion based on the evidence. If he thought he had done an unwise thing, why did he not say so? In an immediate exchange of letters with General Owen Williams, Gordon-Cumming made no protest of innocence and took no further steps to refute the accusations. It was not until January he met and corresponded with Coventry, Williams and Levett. Then he saw Colonel Stracey in an attempt to retire on half-pay. This was not allowed and he then sought Levett's help to persuade the accusers that they were mistaken. Levett would have done so but Lycett Green, he knew, would have none of it.

In summary, Gordon-Cumming was content to be regarded as a cheat in the eyes of his close friends as long as it remained a secret. When he tried to leave the army and was refused, his only option was to take proceedings against his accusers for vilifying him. He quoted Owen Williams's acceptance that he signed the document under pressure but the pressure was that if he didn't sign, he would be exposed as a cheat on Doncaster Racecourse. The difficulty was not getting *him* to sign but Lycett Green to do so, failing which Gordon-Cumming would have been denounced.

On the one hand, there were, he said, five unimpeachable witnesses and on the other, the denial of a man who's own conduct gave little weight to that denial. Sir William Gordon-Cumming was tied hand and foot by a chain of evidence, of which not one link had been broken.

Russell finished, 'You must now do your duty. So far as I am concerned I leave the case in your hands, with the fullest confidence that the truth will prevail, and that justice will be done.'

In Sir Edward Clarke's opening statement for the plaintiff, he had adopted a soft and conciliatory approach in order to give the defendants, even at that late stage, the opportunity to admit they could have been mistaken and withdraw their accusations. That failed, so he now had to go on to a full-blooded attack. No one was to be spared, including the Prince of Wales. '...here, in the Royal Courts, where justice is administered by the judges of the Queen, I shall speak freely even of the most illustrious of my fellow subjects,' he said. There could be no misunderstanding of what he was about to do. He had done well to demolish much of the witness's evidence by highlighting their vague recollections and imperfect memory, and identified the inconsistencies in the précis and Lord Coventry's diary but there remained the difficulty of the signing of the document and Gordon-Cumming's subsequent behaviour. Additionally, though, an important factor was that he genuinely believed Gordon-Cumming to be innocent.

Clarke started by saying that Sir William could have called twenty-three witnesses (the jury must have blinked) for the twenty-three years he had held Her Majesty's commission, associating with the most illustrious and honourable men in the land and 'never doing an act which diminished in the slightest degree the regard and esteem they felt for him.' There had been the hope, therefore, that the defendants and his friends would have recognised that and accepted his denial. It was disappointing that they had not taken that chance. Not only had they instructed their counsel to maintain the charges in the face of his denial on oath but also to make insinuations that he had tried to slip out of the army on half-pay to avoid an inquiry, for which there was not one shred of evidence.

The Wilsons could have been put in the witness box first so that everyone could find out exactly what Gordon-Cumming was accused of doing. [In fact, before the trial, Wontner's, Gordon-Cumming's solicitors, had tried to find out the particulars of the charges but their application was, for some reason, denied.] However, Clarke considered a better course was to put his client into the witness box to defend his honour from the start. He would have assessed Gordon-Cumming as a robust defendant under hostile cross-examination, and he was right. There were two threads to the case against him. The first was that the evidence, in the word of the defendants, was 'damning' and the other was that his three friends, the Prince of Wales, Lord Coventry and General Owen Williams believed him to be guilty. The reality was that Lord Coventry and General Owen Williams cannot have believed him guilty and allowed him to continue in the service of the Crown and be a member of the clubs to which they all belonged and enjoyed the social life. It would have been too embarrassing to bump into him if they genuinely believed he was a cheat. They desired only to avoid a scandal and gave advice to the Prince of Wales as to how this should be done, which he unwisely accepted. It was suggested that, even if Gordon-Cumming won his case, his signing of the document would be an offence against military discipline, necessitating his removal from the army. If that was so, it would be impossible, Clarke suggested, for Gordon-

Cumming's name to be removed from the Army List and the Prince of Wales's and General Owen Williams's to remain. The court was stunned at this. The implication was clear – if Gordon-Cumming was to be dismissed from the army, then not only would a senior general, but the Queen's son and heir would have to stand down as well.

The *Los Angeles Herald*, 'This bold statement seemed to completely take away the breath of the audience, and caused by far the greatest sensation of the entire trial. A hushed murmur of astonishment, not unmixed with dismay and some irritation, swept over the court room. One must thoroughly understand the almost religious worship of royalty which prevails throughout Great Britain to clearly understand the full meaning of the crushing significance of the solicitor-general's words, aimed directly at the heir apparent.'[214]

Russell had, unsurprisingly, tried to brush the précis aside as irrelevant in considering whether its contents were accurate or not. His problem, maintained Clarke, was that the defendants had made statements showing the précis to be inaccurate. Was it not curious that, given the account had been written soon after the event, later seen by the defendants but, in court, they produced different versions? Russell had also suggested that if Sir William won his case, then the Wilson family must have committed perjury. That was not so; Gordon-Cumming had never said they were lying but were merely mistaken in what they thought they had seen. The hospitality at Tranby Croft was 'large and generous.' Without suggesting that anyone was actually drunk, the conviviality was substantial – on the first race day the Prince's horse had won, then the next, the excitement of the St Leger; very good food, lots of wine and brandy, and smoking at the card table both evenings. Clearly people were hardly in the atmosphere of cold judgement as they were in court today. Who, he asked, would you prefer to believe, the Prince of Wales, Lord Coventry and General Owen Williams or Lycett Green? Owen Williams had drafted the account soon after the event but Lycett Green and his younger friends had made statements which, on no less than six occasions, disagreed with those facts. The important point was that the hostile opinion that the Prince of Wales, Lord Coventry and General Owen Williams had formed against Gordon-Cumming was based on statements made to them by Lycett Green. Did the defendants agree to watch Gordon-Cumming the following night? Had he withdrawn stakes when the cards were against him? This was borne out by the précis, General Williams's oral evidence, Lord Coventry's diary and evidence that Lycett Green was 'determined to watch the person the following night.' Yet Lycett Green says it was not what he said on that evening; he said nothing about withdrawing the stakes and he said nothing about agreeing to watch. Clarke put it to the jury that surely a near contemporaneous account was infinitely more reliable than the recollections of the witnesses today? He wound up this vital part of his statement, 'And so, in closing my dealing with this record written in the following week, I point out that it is the best evidence which you have, because it is the evidence which those three gentlemen gave within a few days of the occurrences. I point out to you that, being the best evidence you have or can ask for, it is in direct contradiction to the evidence of the five persons upon whose testimony you are asked to destroy Sir William Gordon-Cumming, and I point out to you that it represents, and must represent, the story which has been told to, and accepted by, His Royal Highness and Lord Coventry and General Owen Williams at the time when they told Sir William Gordon-Cumming that the evidence was overwhelming against him. You will find, accepting the statement of the defendants' witnesses for the moment that it is incorrect. You then come to see the fact that His Royal Highness and General Owen Williams and Lord Coventry accepted the accusation of guilt, accepted against their friend and companion and comrade of years this statement which was put before them that night, and they accepted a statement against him which his accusers now say they never made at all.'

Clarke reminded the jury that when an allegation was made against someone, he was entitled to know of what, exactly, he was accused. In this case all the plaintiff knew was the general point that he had been seen to cheat by placing a larger stake on the table after the cards had been declared in his favour. This was Lycett Green's statement which was echoed word for word by the other defendants, drafted by the same solicitor. Without more detailed information on the charges, it seemed to Clarke that it was important, therefore, to cover, in his opening, the various ways in which a system of playing Baccarat could be played to show that it was possible for an inexperienced and careless or prejudiced observer to construe as cheating. Clarke used the example of the conjuror who brings people into a state of mind in which they expect to see a thing, and then they see it. Nobody except Stanley Wilson [Jack] saw any foul play except a person who was expected to see it and who had been told beforehand that he was going to see Gordon-Cumming cheat. 'The eye sees what the eye brings the power of seeing.' How could Sir William possibly have intended to cheat by using the most conspicuous and easily identifiable counter, the red £5, if he thought he would have any chance of success? His stakes were even on a white sheet of paper. On top of that, both the banker and the croupier have a vested interest in making sure the stakes are properly put down and do not exceed the amount in the bank. At no point did either the Prince of Wales, when banker, or General Owen Williams, when croupier, see anything untoward. Nor did either of the two Somersets or Tyrwhitt Wilson [the Prince's equerry], who were playing, see anything. It is true that it is not an absolute defence to bring six men to say they saw nothing against three who did. However, this was something occurring over a small table with a number of people in close proximity; the only people who saw it were those who thought they were going to see it. Clarke reminded the jury that he had asked Berkeley Levett in cross examination whether, 'At the time you saw what you have described, do you suggest that you made up your mind that it was done dishonestly?' What was the reply? 'I had been told he had been cheating.'

By now Clarke was in full swing, and the court hung on his every word.

However, what happened the next day? Instead of going, quite properly to his father, a man of honour and reputation, and indeed the host and owner of the house, Jack Wilson went to 'an experienced counsellor, a man of the ripe age, I think, thirty-one, or something of that kind – Mr Lycett Green – whose capacity is that of a Master of Hounds who hunts four days a week [one can almost see the sardonic curl of Clarke's lip], and Mr Lycett Green promptly takes it up; he feels that the whole reputation of the family has been committed to him; and instead of going to Mr Wilson, who was entitled to know, he goes and tells *his* father, who is not entitled to know at all, a member of Parliament it is true, but there are members of Parliament whose advice one would not desire to ask in matters of this kind – he goes and tells his father, takes his father's advice, and then for the most foolish of all reasons he tells his wife. Why should he tell Mrs Lycett Green? He says proudly in the witness box that he has no secrets from his wife; and he went and told his wife, Mrs Lycett Green, the daughter of the house, that Sir William Gordon-Cumming was accused of cheating at cards. He had no right to tell her the story on this occasion. But they had the most charming family party that was ever known. The Wilsons are told, Mr Berkeley Levett is told, Jack Wilson tells Lycett Green and Mrs Wilson, his mother, Mr Lycett Green tells Mrs Lycett Green, and there are five of them all agog to know whether Sir William Gordon-Cumming will or will not cheat the following night. They have a Baccarat table prepared; there is not the slightest doubt that that they thought it was prepared for the purpose of preventing Sir Gordon Gordon-Cumming from cheating, and having this table prepared arrange themselves to sit down to play baccarat with the cheat who in their belief had been discovered.'

'Furthermore,' Clarke went on, 'what about the extraordinary behaviour of Mrs Wilson? When they sat down at the specially prepared table, she had completely forgotten, she said in evidence, that Sir William had been caught cheating the night before. Not only that but that her son told her, just before they went into the room that all would be well as the chalk line on the table would prevent any cheating. So there she is, sitting down with the brother of a dear friend of hers, who has, it is suspected, been cheating. How ridiculous to expect any jury to accept such a story.'

It appeared that, on the second night, all the people who knew Sir William had been accused of cheating were sitting very close to him. Was this accidental? 'Sitting immediately opposite to them is Mr Berkeley Levett - within three feet. When I heard that dimension mentioned I thought it must be a mistake, that you could not have got a table so narrow as three feet to play at, but it is so - the table has been measured, and therefore within a distance as near as *that* [he demonstrated with his arms]you have Mr. Berkeley Levett sitting opposite to Sir William Gordon-Cumming during an hour and a half of Baccarat play, and he saw nothing wrong whatever in his play and says: "I looked away and did not observe." Curious behaviour for an officer of the Scots Guards to sit down immediately opposite a lieutenant-colonel of that Regiment, knowing that that lieutenant-colonel was alleged to have been cheating. He knows that there were at least four people to whom the secret had been confided sitting there, and that at any moment one of them might put his hand down on the table and say, "That was not the stake you had there when the cards were dealt." I do not envy Mr Berkeley Levett's feelings during that hour and a half. It is a pity he had not the felicity of Mrs Arthur Wilson, who succeeded in forgetting it altogether.'

Clarke paused to let this sink in. He was reaching the nub of his case. 'But what happens next? The esteemed Master of the Hounds comes on the scene. Mr Lycett Green had said he was going to watch the play to detect any cheating. There is no doubt about this at all. It is in Lord Coventry's diary, written the next day - not even twenty-four hours' later - that Mr. Lycett Green said he was going to watch, and that if they found him cheating they would denounce him. Quite right. That was the proper attitude. It is at the card-table, and nowhere else, that the cheating at cards should be denounced and pointed out. To save up an accusation like that, to be friends with a man you are going to accuse, and then to bring the accusation against him in circumstances which would make it impossible for him to say anything but "In the name of God, I am not guilty" - that is not the conduct of an honourable man, and it never has been; but Mr. Lycett Green is a Master of Hounds, and hunts four days a week. That is his job, and being the ripe old age of thirty, is the man chosen to represent these young men, and he has the fullest intention, that if he sees Sir William Gordon-Cumming cheating, will denounce him. What happened? He says that he saw Sir William Gordon-Cumming push a blue counter over the line, and that it aroused his suspicions; but nobody else of the five suggests that ever they saw a blue counter pushed over the line. That rests on Mr Lycett Green's evidence alone, but, clearly, he did not think detected cheating then, because he had made up his mind to act promptly and vigorously whenever the act of cheating was detected. However, the next thing that happens is the incident which undoubtedly did occur, the asking for the £10 more.'

By now it was apparent that Clarke had the attention of the whole court. The Judge listened intently as he explained that it is the only incident to which there is more than one witness, and there are three. What was the incident? 'Sir William Gordon-Cumming had a £5 counter staked, Mr Arthur Stanley Wilson has said. We do not know whether it was on the scoring paper. The £5 counter was on the table four inches beyond the line; then the £10 counter, the brown counter, was pushed, he says, just over the line; whereas Mr. Lycett Green, speaking of the same incident, says just on the line, but well away from the £5 counter. Then the banker loses and has to pay, and Sir William Gordon-Cumming says to the banker, the Prince of Wales, "There is another £10, sir, to come here." The Prince then says, "Give him another tenner, Owen" (speaking to General Owen Williams, the croupier), and "I wish you would put your counters so that they can be seen better," or something of that kind. The moment Mr Lycett Green heard that said by His Royal Highness, his loyal heart was quite satisfied that there was something wrong. He jumped up from the table. He felt that he had seen an act of cheating, so what was he going to do? This Master of Hounds knew what ought to be done. He knew that if you think a man is going to cheat, and you find him out doing so, that then and there, on the spot, at any cost, you should make the accusation, or ever thereafter hold your peace about it. You will recall he had told Lord Coventry that if they found him out they would denounce him. He jumped up, full of valiant resolution, and then changed his mind. He went away, and - wrote to his mother-in-law!'

There was considerable laughter in the Court. Clarke was on the crest of a wave.

'It is not my fault,' he said, 'if when putting these things, it appears to be a laughing matter. It is no laughing matter to the man I am defending here in this Court. However, it is ridiculous to talk of evidence of people like this as evidence upon which a life is to be ruined and a reputation wrecked. Lycett Green gets up and goes into another room, writes the note, and sends it to Mrs Wilson.'

He reminded the jury of the odd little incident that occurred when Sir Charles Russell was describing Mr Lycett Green's conscientious and high-minded conduct. Clarke's lip curled as he described the magnificent tones of elevated morality of his learned friend, "Mr Green saw this. He got up from the table; he would not play again. He did not sit down to play." At which his colleagues behind him began tugging at his gown, and told him he was making a mistake, and he said, "Well, he did sit down, and played for the rest of the evening." Mr Lycett Green came back to that room again, sat down at that table with the man he called a scoundrel in the letter he wrote to his mother-in-law, and went on peacefully playing during the rest of the evening - this Master of Hounds - and bottled up the accusation until the night after the Leger, when probably he felt a little more valiant, and he thought he might make it stick. But not so brave that he didn't ask to be covered if Sir William takes proceedings against him.

At this point, Clarke turned to the most important point; Gordon-Cumming's behaviour when all this was going on. Look at what was happening, he urged the jury. For instance, "Owen, give him £10 more," surely this sort of thing would have checked any inclination to cheat, supposing there had been any such inclination, and would have exposed the sleight of hand? Had Sir William Gordon-Cumming been cheating, and deliberately cheating, these whisperings of Mr Stanley Wilson and Mr Berkeley Levett on the first night, the getting up from the table of one of the players, and the sending the note in by the butler to the hostess, could not have escaped his attention, and must have stopped it. Nor was it conceivable that if he had been cheating he would have called upon His Royal Highness to pay an extra £10, knowing that he dishonestly pushed that £10 counter forward and only put it at a place where its position would attract attention and comment. But, what then? Lycett Green's note was handed to Mrs Wilson. Up to that moment, on neither night, had Mrs. Wilson seen any cheating at all, but when Mr. Lycett Green wrote that Sir William Gordon-Cumming was a scoundrel and was cheating, she said she saw it at once. But the evidence she gave to the court is ridiculous. Mrs Wilson was further away from Sir William Gordon-Cumming than the Prince of Wales, General Owen Williams, Lord Edward Somerset, Captain Somerset, Mr Berkeley Levett, and Lady Coventry. Yet she said that she saw a £10 counter on one occasion dropped, and a £10 counter on another occasion pushed so openly over the line that she wondered the others did not see it. She might well wonder the others did not see it. There were three of them looking for it, Mr Lycett Green, Mrs Lycett Green, and Mr Stanley Wilson, and none of them saw it.

The jury is asked to believe, said Clarke, on the witness's evidence that with all the resources and cleverness of a conjuror, that Sir William Gordon-Cumming was manipulating the counters, and flicking them, or pushing them, or dropping them, or withdrawing them, and that he was doing all this with such remarkable and discriminating skill that he could be seen by everybody who expected to see him, and by nobody else. The only possible way of testing and gauging the evidence of people who make charges like this is by asking them to say what else was happening. They were asked, "What did he stake the next time?" and they could never say. "What did he stake the time before?" They could not recall on any occasion, and though, if these people were right, their attention must have been riveted to the table and they would have watched, one would think, what happened immediately afterwards. Not one of them can say what he staked before or what he staked afterwards, though the answer to that would demonstrate at once that he was playing the system which has been described by Stanley Wilson, and, before anyone knew how important it was, by Sir William Gordon-Cumming himself.

At this stage, Clarke was reducing the evidence of the witnesses to shreds; the very danger that Lewis, the solicitor, had warned Russell about, when having statements from five different people, despite his expert coaching.

Clarke, sardonically, had the Master of Hounds in his sights again. When Lycett Green was cross-examined as to the state of things on that evening, he could not say whether Sir William Gordon-Cumming had a piece of paper before him. Or whether he was using a pencil. Smoking? Don't know. Or did he have a tumbler in front of him? Cannot remember. Clarke maintained that the moment one deviated from the matter of cheating, memories appeared to lapse. He knew very well they had been coached in their stories but when away from the script, they floundered.

Clarke told the jury he was not seeking a verdict for his client on merely sympathetic grounds or one of pity, but on one based on the argument and analysis that there was no evidence upon which they could convict a gentleman of such an offence. He reminded them that there were others outside the Court who were interested in the case who were looking with the keenest eyes on what has been said from beginning to end. He was clearly referring to the Royal Family without saying as much. But it would have been very clear to the jury what he meant.

Having dealt with the factual evidence, Clarke then turned to the insinuations. 'He must be guilty because his friends, the Prince, General Owen Williams, and Lord Coventry, thought that the evidence was overwhelming.' Lord Coventry and General Owen Williams have distinctly said that they believed in the accusation that was made against him. With regard to His Royal Highness, remember the careful terms in which His Royal Highness answered the juryman's questions. Two questions were asked; and the second question was an important one, as to whether His Royal Highness believed in this accusation. It was noticeable that His Royal Highness, with an expressive movement of the shoulders, said, 'They seemed so strongly supported - unanimously so - by those who brought them forward, that I felt that no other course was open to me but to believe what I was told.' Those were the exact words of the answer, and there was no doubt that His Royal Highness was clear, when he dealt with this accusation, that he was in possession of the evidence of five witnesses. But he had nothing of the kind. The unanimous story of the witnesses was nothing but the statement of Mr Lycett Green, supported by answers to questions of His Royal Highness to Mr Stanley Wilson, and by one particular answer from Mr Berkeley Levett. Mr Berkeley Levett said that His Royal Highness had listened to the statement of Mr Lycett Green - he had asked questions of Mr Stanley Wilson as to the details of that statement, and then he turned to him and said, 'I believe you saw it too?' Upon which Mr Berkeley Levett said, 'Well, it is a painful thing for me (or some words of that sort), because he is an officer of my regiment, but I did.' That was all Mr Berkeley Levett said to anybody, and the details of the accusation were not mentioned. The circumstances under which Mr Berkeley Levett had seen it were not mentioned, and it is impossible to say whether the question was asked, the vital question, 'Had your mind been put on the idea of cheating before you saw it?'

All the so-called overwhelming evidence was solely what Mr Lycett Green said, supported by the answers of Mr Stanley Wilson, and by the only statement, as far as the Prince was concerned, from Mr Berkeley Levett. Then General Owen Williams and Lord Coventry, before they approached Sir William Gordon-Cumming, had made up their minds what would be the best thing to do. They probably had not finally decided on the course that they should adopt, but before they saw Sir William Gordon-Cumming had suggested one to the other, 'Let us have a promise from him not to play cards again, and a promise of secrecy, and then it will be all at an end.' How Lord Coventry and General Owen Williams ever persuaded themselves that they could honourably adopt that course is incomprehensible. This man had been their friend for years, he had been the comrade of General Owen Williams for thirty years; they had been together as soldiers; they would have shared each other's dangers; they would willingly have laid down their lives for each other had they been together, they very likely have done so travelling through the world. However, the moment this accusation is made against him, made by people like this, meeting in this way, evidenced by this fragmentary statement, supported only by the confirmation of otherwise almost silent witnesses who agreed with what was being said at that moment, before they ask him whether there was any foundation for it or not, they suggest to each other, 'Suppose he signs a paper that he will not play cards again, and then we get a promise from these people that they will not take any further notice.'

To Edward Clarke, this was totally incomprehensible. He genuinely believed in the innocence of his client and he could not see how anyone could convict on such contradictory evidence and then be so let down by his friends. How he must have despised Owen and Coventry and, to a lesser extent, even the Prince himself. Clarke was now in full flow and later maintained his closing speech was one of his best. He even had it privately published but on sale, in 1891, for one shilling.[215]

Had not Sir Charles Russell made such a strong point of it, Clarke asserted he would have gladly refrained from commenting. However, Russell had said, indignantly, 'Is it possible that a man of honour should sign that which he is told, and which he knows, will be read and accepted as an acknowledgment of his guilt, when he himself knows that he is innocent?' Clarke retorted, 'Is it possible that men of honour, after twenty or thirty years of friendship, applied to by their comrade to advise him in the circumstances of the time, could advise him to sign a document which would condemn him, as they believe, if ever the scandal comes to be discussed. [This is] a document which they have already told his accuser, Mr Lycett Green, will be a safeguard and protection to him in case Sir William Gordon-Cumming ever brings an action against him for the slander?' He could not understand it, and could not imagine the thoughts that must have been in the minds of General Owen Williams and Lord Coventry. Though, there is one explanation he had hinted at in his opening speech. The reason was to save the Prince of Wales. He had suggested in his opening speech that it was the idea of scandal attaching to the Prince of Wales that had induced the signing of this document. Clarke had put it as mildly as he possibly could, but Russell would not have it, and proceeded to cross-examine Sir William Gordon-Cumming, 'Sir William, Baccarat is an innocent game? Certainly. You do not see any scandal about playing Baccarat? None.' Of course not; he was playing Baccarat himself. Sir William thought, as a great many people thought, that there was no harm whatever in playing Baccarat, and in Clarke's opening speech he put it very mildly that he did not see anything very seriously wrong with those who, having ample means and leisure, choose to enjoy themselves by games of this kind. But Russell disagreed. He insisted that there was no scandal affecting His Royal Highness - that the only possible reason for the courtiers suggesting this to Sir William Gordon-Cumming was that they felt that he was finished, that the evidence against him was so conclusive and overwhelming that he never again under any circumstances could hold up his head, and that it was in mercy to him that they suggested this writing and this settlement. Russell would not admit that it had anything to do with the Prince of Wales.

Clarke then had this to say. 'Sir William Gordon-Cumming and those who share the society which he then enjoyed were entitled to choose their amusements, and they may not think that there is any scandal about playing a game like this. Nevertheless, there are a great number of people whose knowledge of gaming principally is that a club is raided and the people prosecuted for playing Baccarat there, or an innkeeper loses his licence because betting on horses is allowed on his premises. There is a large part of the community who have a keen and abiding feeling that this unhappy incident ought never to have been allowed to occur, because the circumstances were those which are at variance with the feelings and the consciences of the people. What did Lord Coventry and General Owen Williams, when they were considering this matter, think would be said if the scandal was all over Doncaster racecourse the next day? They knew it would be said that at a country house at Yorkshire, the master of which disapproved of the playing of Baccarat within its walls, that a game had been played. They thought that they would be rendering a good service to His Royal Highness, if they took a course which would allow the whole matter to pass into oblivion.' Clarke went on to stress that while it was impossible to understand the feelings which the courtiers had at the time, there was a strong and subtle influence of royalty, which had coloured past history with 'unknightly and dishonouring' deeds done by men of character because they gave their honour as freely as they would have given their lives, to save the interests of a dynasty or to conceal the foibles of a prince.

This was dynamite. Clarke was asserting, in the full light of the court, and public, that Owen and Coventry had deliberately set up the document to save the Prince from embarrassment. Not to save their friend.

The Sun, New York, wrote, 'A slight ripple of applause, which was promptly suppressed, broke out in the court as the eloquent jurist uttered the last words in a most touching and impressive manner.'[216]

'There was no doubt,' he said, 'what was in the minds of Lord Coventry and General Owen Williams. It was perhaps a generous and a loyal feeling, but, the irony is this. It is known what they felt. There is no argument about it. It does not depend upon the speculation of a lawyer, or the inference from the ambiguous answer to a question. It is in Lord Coventry's diary, written the next day, contradicting every syllable of the speech which, in ignorance of that diary, Sir Charles made when he was opening his case. This is what was written, "We were induced to recommend this course because we desired, if possible, to avoid the scandal which would naturally attach to the publication of the circumstances, and to keep the name of the Prince of Wales out of it; and also out of consideration for our hosts, Mr and Mrs Arthur Wilson, who are at this time in domestic affliction."

There is absolutely no argument about it; this was the reason for keeping it secret. If there are any mitigating circumstances in relation to the conduct of General Owen Williams and Lord Coventry in allowing their old friend to take this course, for which he is now denounced, there must be something to be said for the loyalty on the part of Sir William Gordon-Cumming. He knew as well as Lord Coventry that the scandal would be an unpleasant one. He knew it would cause pain to the Prince whose friendship he had enjoyed for so many years. Sir William was intensely loyal to the Prince who had been kind to him. He owed much to the Prince of Wales and if Lord Coventry and General Owen Williams were to be approved of for advising their old comrade to sign the paper, which they knew doomed him to a life of suspicion, misery and ultimate dishonour, then Sir William Gordon-Cumming should, at least, have credit too. He, protesting he was not guilty, asking to be sent to his colonel, or the commander-in-chief, for investigation, when the paper at last is brought to him. He is told that unless he signs it he will the next day be denounced as a cheat. He refuses to sign it, but eventually turns to his friends and says, "Coventry, you are an old friend of mine. Owen Williams, we have been comrades for years. Advise me what to do." They advise him to sign it. This was the loyalty of the man, who sacrificed himself, as his old friends were willing to sacrifice him, in order to save the reputation of the Prince of Wales whose kindness during many years, whatever may happen in this trial, will always be a recollection he is entitled to remember with pride. It has been said that his conduct in signing this must condemn him. The book is closed, the account made up, the evidence concluded, and that the signing of that document condemns him for all time. What was in the minds of the people who suggested his signing that document? Amazingly, my learned friend asked if there was a suggestion that, in the light of the generous hospitality of Tranby Croft, Sir William Gordon-Cumming was drunk on that night of the 10th. The brief insanity of drink might, perhaps, be an easy explanation but there was no such proposition. The Prince of Wales, General Owen Williams, and Lord Coventry were all parties to him to signing that document, and the terms which were embodied in it. What did they think? Did they think that this was going to be kept a secret? They say they did. If they are to be believed, their reliability must be accepted at the expense of their good sense. Who could have imagined it would be kept secret? The next day, on Doncaster racecourse, the party from Tranby Croft appeared, and Sir William Gordon-Cumming was not with them. The question is asked at once, 'Where is Sir William Gordon-Cumming?' 'Oh, he went to town this morning', to people whom he probably had made arrangements to meet. Again, he is not to go to Mar. He has been a friend of the Duke of Fife, and has arranged a visit there, and he has to send an excuse not to come. What questions would be asked then? Or, what happens the next time he goes to the Officers' Mess; an honourable man, with the consent and the concurrence of the Prince of Wales, General Owen Williams, and Lord Coventry? The officers arrange a game of whist. Instead of sitting down as usual, he says he is not going to play, and he must make some excuse. Lord Coventry, of all men in English society, perhaps, to whom one might fairly have thought one could appeal as a man of sense, as well as a man of honour in difficulties of this kind, said, "I never thought it would come out, and as to what was to happen if it were talked about, I never thought about it at all.'"

Clarke then went on to explain the slightly complicated factors surrounding Gordon-Cumming's military commission. When Gordon-Cumming realised the matter had become known, he went to Colonel Stracey, his commanding officer, and put it before him. If, soon after the matter had taken place, say, in September, October, November, or December, he had sent in his papers and asked to retire on half-pay and said no more, he probably could have done so and secured his honourable retirement. However, when he had told Colonel Stracey what had taken place, it was impossible for him to retire upon half-pay without a mandatory investigation. This was the first time Colonel Stracey had heard of it but could not allow an officer to retire upon half-pay without informing the military authorities that there had been a serious accusation against that officer. So he was, effectively, in limbo, both militarily and socially. Yet, when he eventually read the précis, again he asked for advice. His so-called friends had no advice to give him. Their views had been bound and closed up by the idea of this never coming out at all. They had treated him as a friend afterwards. They had shaken hands with him after he had signed what they called a dishonouring document. They had met him at the clubs; General Owen Williams had written to him, 'My dear Bill.' Lord Coventry had written to him, 'Dear Sir William,' and 'Yours truly, Coventry.' His so-called friends were now faced with what they should have foreseen all along. They were finished. They had no advice to give him at all.

He had to make his own decision. Right or wrong, he determined upon a public examination of the facts. He applied for a copy of the record. Until he got a copy of the record he could not tell who had actually made the statement against him. On 5 February he received a copy, and on the 6th a writ was issued against every person mentioned in it as having made a statement to his discredit. The trial has been speeded up, in order that Gordon-Cumming should be able to come into Court to vindicate himself. He was first into the witness-box, to face a cross-examination which has terrors for men who have shameful secrets to conceal, or a disgraceful past to reveal to the world, but has no terrors for a man who could come into any Court, and face any cross-examination which envy or malice could suggest, knowing that 'whatever record leapt to light, he never should be shamed.'

Sir Edward finished with a powerful exhortation to the jury; 'I ask you, in his name, to clear him of the charge. It is too late to undo much of the mischief which, however this case was treated, could not but arise from this discussion. It may be too late to save the reputation of some of those who have been mentioned in the case; it is not too late for you to prevent the completion of the sacrifice of a gallant officer to the desire to keep a painful secret quiet. The motto of his race is "Without fear." He came without fear into the witness-box, for he had nothing to conceal. He sits without fear at this moment, for he believes, as I believe, that honesty is safe in the hands of a British jury, and that he has good reason to hope that the result will happen, which I believe will not be unwelcome to some of those upon whom I have been obliged to make sharp comments - that result which will assure the Prince, General Owen Williams, and Lord Coventry, that they made an honest but a sad mistake - that the man they had known and honoured was worthy of their friendship and their esteem - a result which will wipe a stain from a noble service and a gallant regiment, and will send Sir William Gordon-Cumming back, with that title-deed in his hand, to public service and private friendship, which will be written in the verdict given by you that clears him of this foul charge.'

The *Pittsburg Daily Dispatch*, Pennsylvania reported, 'Sir Edward Clarke's plain language throughout when he referred to the Prince of Wales, and when he made the assertion that the précis was prepared by Lord Coventry and signed by Sir William Gordon-Cumming solely in order to shield the Prince of Wales from scandal, caused one of the greatest sensations of this sensational trial, and those who heard the remarks made in court were so impressed with them that they were generally discussed afterwards and were commented upon and other circles far into the night and early morning.'[217]

San Francisco's *The Morning Call* wrote, 'Sir Edward Clarke's speech was regarded as a most eloquent and telling effort, and as he closed his remarks there was a burst of spontaneous applause, cheering and hand-clapping throughout the court, which caused the Lord Chief Justice to shout, "Silence! This is not a theatre." The Lord Chief Justice's call had the desired effect and the applause stopped, but as Sir William Gordon-

Cumming rose from his seat a minute later, and while the Prince of Wales and Lord Coleridge were still on the bench, there was a renewal of the cheers and hand-clapping, of which the plaintiff appeared to take no notice. The jury, it was plainly evident, appeared greatly impressed with the speech of the Solicitor-General and as he ended it the remark was heard throughout the court: "Cumming will get a verdict, or at least the jury will disagree."'[218]

Sir Edward Clarke, in his memoirs, maintained it was one of the best speeches he had made in his life.

The Court adjourned to await the Lord Chief Justice's summing up the following day.

CHAPTER 13 - Charge to the Jury

The seventh and final day of the trial, 9 June, was the one everyone had been waiting for; the Lord Chief Justice would sum up and despatch the jury to their deliberations. The Prince of Wales, who had attended every day so far, was disappointingly absent. He had decided to go to Ascot; no doubt rather more congenial but was it that he really want to avoid facing the final judgement? It was by no means clear who was going to win the case. A great deal depended on the judge's summing up.

As Coleridge settled himself in, a curious thing happened. A flustered and excitable General Owen Williams rose to his feet and addressed the judge. 'My lord' he said, 'as a witness in this case I have to ask your lordship's protection. Yesterday the Solicitor-General, in the course of his speech, thought proper to accuse Lord Coventry and myself…..'

Clarke quickly interrupted, 'My lord, I ask your Lordship that no statement of this kind should be allowed to be made in Court. General Owen Williams has no privilege here.' Indeed, Clarke was correct. Williams had no business to address the judge.

Coleridge should have stopped him there and then but, ignoring Clarke, he said, 'What do you want protection from?'

'We were accused of crime, my lord - of an abominable crime.'

'I do not now recall the expression; but I am afraid the law is inflexible.'

'We were accused of sacrificing an innocent man.'

The judge, 'In the discharge of his duty there is no control over the proceedings of counsel.'

To which Williams replied, 'I was going to ask to be put into the witness-box in order to refute the statement which counsel made without any evidence or justification. I ask it, my lord, with great respect.'

'Counsel must always speak under the sanction and the control of their professional duty, and I am afraid that if you consult authorities you will find that there is absolutely no restraint on the language of counsel when it is relevant; and, indeed, it is very doubtful whether there is restraint when the language is not relevant.'

'I only thought it due to myself, my lord, to apply to be put into the witness-box and refute that statement.'

'I am afraid I cannot allow you to do that.'

While Coleridge properly prevented Williams going any further, he should have immediately stopped him saying anything. Williams had, without knowing it, planted a small seed of uncertainty in the minds of the jury. Had he also betrayed his real feelings? Perhaps justifying, to himself, the abandonment of his former friend?

The judge began by explaining the law of slander to the jury in that Gordon-Cumming had complained that the defendants had defamed him. He also said that anyone who cheated at cards should be guilty of a misdemeanour, and punishable accordingly.

'Therefore the charge in this case is a charge against Sir William Gordon-Cumming, on which, if he had been indicted in a Court of criminal justice, he might have been found guilty, and, if found guilty, he might have been punished.'

Critically, he did not explain the difference in the burden of proof between a criminal charge and a civil action. A criminal charge, to which he had just referred, requires a higher standard of proof, that of 'beyond reasonable doubt' to the lower one in the civil court of 'on the balance of probabilities.' Was the jury therefore to adopt the higher level on the basis that what Gordon-Cumming was accused of was a criminal act or the lower which was slander? The judge failed to direct them.

He went on to explain the difference between libel and slander, and the distinction between defaming someone in writing or by word of mouth. But if a man is charged with a criminal offence, although that was only by word of mouth, a legal action is possible. In this case, therefore, Sir William Gordon-Cumming having been accused of an indictable offence, has the option of bringing a case against his accusers if he wants.

To a certain extent this was irrelevant; no one was accused of writing anything that became public. Gordon-Cumming was bringing a case for slander, not because he was accused of a criminal offence i.e. cheating.

In this case, it was merely a matter of what was true, the judge went on. The only question was whether the words the defendants spoke in relation to the plaintiff were the truth. It was as simple as that. If they did speak the truth, and the jury found that the defendants spoke the truth, then the verdict ought to be for the defendants. If what they have said is not true, that Sir William Gordon-Cumming did not in any common and ordinary sense cheat at cards, then the verdict ought to be for him. If the verdict was for him, then there was the question of damages.

The judge explained that Gordon-Cumming was not seeking damages or 'to make a fortune out of the pockets of rich defendants,' but to clear his character.

If there was any reason to suppose that there was any spiteful intention to oppress, to crush, to annoy, or to destroy the defendants - that ought to be considered. If, on the other hand, Sir William Gordon-Cumming, although a gallant soldier, failed to do anything to reduce or have the charge withdrawn, then there would be no grounds for increasing the damages beyond what was proper in relation to the verdict, said the judge.

However, what clearly worried the judge was a completely separate point from that of damages. Earlier in the trial, Gordon-Cumming's counsel had hinted at matters hidden below the surface. 'We have come here to try an important, but a simple issue,' Coleridge said, 'and not what there is beside that issue in the public mind, in the public press, or in our own minds. Presumption must not stand in the way of evidence, and belief must not stand in the way of truth. In a case of this kind, exciting great public interest, as the state of the Court for a week has shown, and as the placards in the streets also show, it is most essential that things should not enter into your mind to affect the case which has not been proved before you. Before the facts are subjected to the sifting of a Court, before they are proved upon oath, and before that oath has been tested by the proper and reasonable process of cross-examination, it is certain that things will be stated, and that colour will be given to transactions which, upon fuller and fairer investigation, will be found to be absolutely untrue and unreliable.'

Nowadays judges are more in the habit of warning jurors *before* a trial to avoid television and newspapers. Was there something more to this though? Were there shades of a cover-up? Was there rather more to the story than they had been told? Why did the judge take such trouble – and at length – to warn the jury of this in his summing up and not before? Any damage done by exposure to the Press would have already been done. Was Coleridge worried about innuendo affecting the jury? There had certainly been hints of 'other matters' not before the court. Even the doziest juryman would have wondered what they were. There was clearly a whiff of something they had not been told.

The judge then exhorted them to put aside their personal views of the ethics of playing baccarat. He quoted a late archbishop who said that 'gambling is an excessive, extravagant, and injurious habit, and holds it to be wrong and sinful because it stimulates, and often cruelly and fatally stimulates, the vice of covetousness and the desire of getting money out of other people's pockets without paying.' But Coleridge stressed that they were not his words and his Bench was no pulpit. 'The actors in this case, on both sides, have a perfect right as long as they keep within the law - and from prince to peasant there is but one law, and I hope and trust that in this Court it has often been shown to be so - prince and peasant alike have a right if they think to spend their time in pursuits which do not suit you and me perhaps - in which you and I very likely should not like to spend our lives. This is a free country. We do as we like, and others do as they like.'

This was a defence against the anti-gambling brigade who had been vociferous in condemning what the Prince and his cronies had got up to. Playing baccarat in public, say in a pub, was most certainly illegal. But that wasn't what was being tried in this court, the judge was saying.

'The question is a simple one - not an easy one, but a simple one. The question actually before you is: did Sir William Gordon-Cumming cheat? There is one other matter before I come to the actual question of the cause referred to in the Solicitor-General's (Clarke's) very able speech. He said yesterday, in substance and in much better language than mine, that the eye of man sees what it expects to see, and that you were to disregard a good deal of the evidence in this ease, or, at all events, to subject it to a very severe discount, because the people who came to speak of the particular acts of cheating went into the room where they saw them with - I will not say a pre-determination, but with an expectation to see them, and that therefore what would not have been proved to another person was proved to them. That is an old saying, but a perfectly true one, and it was very well put to you yesterday.'

Did the witnesses expect to see cheating, was what he was saying. His inference was, yes, look at it like that but treat it with caution. Clearly this was guidance to dismiss Clarke's clever "see what you expect to see" theory.

The judge reminded the jury of the charge. It was that on two nights - 8th and 9th September last - the plaintiff, at Tranby Croft, the house of Mr Arthur Wilson, cheated at cards. The question is, did he in truth add to his stakes several times on the 8th and several times on the 9th. He proposed to recall, first of all, the evidence of the defendants, and for this reason: 'in this case the ordinary relations of parties are reversed, and it is the defendants upon whom is thrown, by the action of Sir William Gordon-Cumming, the proof of the affirmative.' What he is saying here is that the onus lies on the defendants to prove the case, not on Gordon-Cumming to defend himself. But, in a sense, the whole trial was actually based on Gordon-Cumming defending himself against a charge of cheating.

The Lord Chief Justice then ran through the evidence of Jack Wilson, until he reached a point where he talked of a 'coup d'état, 'but it was some French term used to describe a certain way of playing,' he said.

This was too much for Clarke. 'Coup de trois, my lord. It consists of playing three coups in succession, according to a certain rule.'

Whether, despite endless coverage of the system in court, the judge really did not understand or forgot how it worked can only be guessed. Alternatively, he was deliberately fogging the minds of the jury or demonstrating that it was unimportant. The truth is that he probably didn't really understand the system and if he didn't, what hope had the jury?

He defended Berkeley Levett's unenviable position as a fellow officer in Gordon-Cumming's Regiment and then turned to Lycett Green's performance as the person upon whom the storm had fallen.

He said he had been made great fun of by the Solicitor-General (Clarke) and he probably made Mr Lycett Green - if he was in Court - very uncomfortable. However, it was for the jury to say whether Mr Lycett Green was not a witness to the truth. The defendants all seemed to have received with utter incredulity the allegation that the plaintiff had cheated at cards. The Solicitor-General, he suggested, had forgotten that the position was not an easy one. There were many ladies there. It was not only that Mrs Arthur Wilson, Mrs Lycett Green, and Lady Coventry - whose names have been heard - were there, but there were also Lady Brougham, Mrs Owen Williams, and Mrs and Miss Naylor; and therefore, with these six ladies present in that room, can the young man be very much to blame for not having a row before these ladies?

There was no Mrs Naylor. The judge was wrong. He was also clearly supporting Lycett Green's weak excuse for not challenging Gordon-Cumming there and then for fear of offending the ladies.

It was now becoming very clear, perhaps not to the members of the jury, but certainly to the lawyers in court, that the judge was firmly going against Clarke and Gordon-Cumming. He appeared to be supportive of Lycett Green's actions and the dilemma he faced with powerful men like the Prince of Wales in the house and having to accuse a senior Guards officer like Gordon-Cumming of disgraceful conduct. He rather put down Clarke's sneers about Lycett Green being a Master of Hounds, 'We have had our laugh and enjoyed it. Now we must ask ourselves gravely whether there was anything unreasonable in what Mr Lycett Green did.'

Coleridge then went on to give a splendid dissection of social attitudes in Victorian England, and a patronising defence of the middle classes. 'Before we go further into a far more serious part of the case - the conduct of the parties afterwards - let us consider the positions they themselves occupy. On the one side you have Sir William Gordon-Cumming - a person of rank, gallantry, character, and position, intimate with some of the most distinguished people in the country, and visiting great houses - going with the Prince of Wales to this place, invited to the Duke of Fife's, and moving in this high society - a baronet, soldier, and distinguished servant, a man who was received at Tranby Croft with the Prince of Wales as an honoured - and, I should not wonder, as rather a prized guest - a gentleman the Wilsons were rather glad to have there.

On the other side, you have Mr and Mrs Wilson. Mr Wilson is, I understand, a man of mature age, of large wealth, made in the honourable pursuit of merchandise and shipbuilding - Wilson of Hull, certainly known to most people who have nothing to do with Hull - a man of whom it is no disgrace to say that his great position, his wealth, his power of entertaining these great people, have been the result of hard work. Mrs Arthur Wilson, no doubt, has risen with her husband. No doubt it was to her an agreeable thing to have these great people in her house. I say ninety-nine people out of a hundred, whatever they may say out of Court or in the newspapers, would be very glad to have the Prince of Wales, Lord Coventry, and Lord This and Lady That, in their houses -

and I daresay Mrs. Arthur Wilson found a pleasure in having these people there. Mr Arthur Stanley Wilson [Jack] has been a great deal laughed at. He went to Magdalene College, which, I fancy, enjoys the reputation of not being the slowest college at Cambridge. After spending a little time there, his father thought he was not doing much good, and took him away, and he lives at home where, as a young man, no doubt, he was exceedingly glad to live. But why should he be attacked for that? He was very glad to know Mr Berkeley Levett and these people; it is very natural he should. Mr Lycett Green has been flown at. He is a Master of Hounds. Well, Masters of Hounds are rather proud of writing M.F.H. after their names. It is not as great as K.G., of course, but it is something. Certainly, in the box, he gave his evidence like a man, but it pleased the learned counsel to fly at him because his father was an engineer. As a sensible man he would not wish to help that, and, of course, he could not; but I cannot see why a man's father should be thrown in his face because he is an engineer, sits for a great place in Parliament, and has had rank given to him by Queen. I cannot understand....'

Clarke, 'I did not say so, my Lord.'

'If you did not, Mr Gill did.'

'I don't think so, my Lord.'

The judge warmed to his theme, ignoring Clarke. 'I do not see why he should have been laughed at because his father was an engineer. He is married to Mrs Lycett Green, and is son-in-law to Mrs Wilson. I daresay he would have had a sense of pleasure in meeting the Prince of Wales and General Owen Williams. Is there any harm in that? I cannot see that there is, and what is more to the point, would it make them at all likely to be prejudiced against Sir William Gordon-Cumming? I should think not.'

An unnecessarily spirited defence of the idle youth, one might think.

The judge now tackled the essential points of the cover-up. 'Lord Coventry and General Owen Williams must have said to themselves, "Now this is an awful thing about the Prince of Wales; this is a most serious business for the Prince to be mixed up with; it will be a bad thing for him; it will be a bad thing" - I won't say for the monarchy, but for the *entourage* of the Prince of Wales.' He went on to make some platitudinous remarks about how lucky we were to live under such a

Queen and our sacred institutions but what he was effectively doing was justifying the conspirators' actions in shielding the Prince.

Coleridge reminded the jury of the sequence of the accusation and Gordon-Cumming's reaction. 'When accused, what does the plaintiff (Gordon-Cumming) say? He says, "I am not guilty." Did he say, "Confront me with my adversaries and let me have this out?" No. Did he say even, "Give me names in detail of the persons who accused me? No. When he said, "I should like to go to the commander-in-chief," they said, "Go, let him go." Did he go? No. He goes to the Prince of Wales, and before the Prince of Wales he denies in the strongest way that he has been guilty of these acts. The Prince of Wales talks to him and says, "You know you have got all these people against you," and he says, "I should like to have the commander-in-chief made acquainted with it." "Very well," says not the Prince of Wales, but either General Owen Williams or Lord Coventry, "by all means; only I don't think you will find that the Duke of Cambridge will be so lenient to you as we should have been."

After some consideration they draw up the paper - that is Lord Coventry and General Williams - they undoubtedly had determined upon drawing up something like it before, and in that view I agree with the Solicitor-General,' the judge admitted.

Grudgingly, the judge has to accept that there was a form of pre-meditated action by the courtiers, even if it didn't reach the conspiracy threshold at that point. He is also craftily criticising Gordon-Cumming's immediate reaction.

So, 'They took a paper to him and asked him to sign it. I am far from saying that from his point of view there is nothing in the matter, but it is not a very serious point; however, their account is that, "We pointed out to him it would be an admission of guilt," and he says that it was he and not they who in the first instance said as much.'

The judge belittles what actually *was* a serious point. Did Gordon-Cumming say it was an admission of guilt if he signed the paper or did the courtiers say so first? Obviously it was discussed and if Gordon-Cumming said so immediately then, quite clearly, he was very aware of the danger he was to face before the courtiers muddled their way through.

The document undertaking never to play cards again was signed by Sir Gordon-Cumming. Having signed it, he said, "Well, but this is very serious; do you mean to say that this would prevent me from playing my playing sixpenny points, at regimental whist?" General Williams said, "Certainly, you cannot."

The understanding was that he was to leave the next morning. The whole thing was conceived with the idea of keeping the matter quiet. But, having signed the paper, how he could dream of going to the races the next day, where he knew ten or twelve people were in possession of the secret, passes his comprehension, the judge exclaimed. That evening Gordon-Cumming acted with what carelessness he could command, he added.

The judge was determined to show that Gordon-Cumming's defence that he had signed the document when he lost his head was implausible. 'What the plaintiff signed was well known. That he knew it would be used as conclusive against him he did not deny. He knew it was a confession of guilt. Men act very differently about these things. Sir William Gordon-Cumming has had it said in his favour, and with perfect truth, that he was a gallant officer, who had stood up under fire, who had served his country bravely, who had been of great use to the Queen and the people of England; a man of forty-two years of age, who had lived all his life amongst gentlemen of the highest society, and he says that he was so taken aback, so overcome by circumstances, that he signed the document when, to use his own strong and graphic expression, he had "lost his head." General Owen Williams and Lord Coventry both said he had not; and both said he showed no outward signs of it. He discussed the matter carefully, took time to consider, he argued with them, and eventually signed. After he had signed he made a not unnatural attempt to get a sort of qualification introduced about the regimental mess, but that was refused. The question is, could a man of age, position, ability - could he have acknowledged the charge made against him? He had time to consider the matter well before he signed. It was not as if they came, so to speak, with a pistol to his head. He had an adequate and reasonable time to consider the matter. I should have thought that a man of honour, if he were innocent - apart from the consideration to which I would draw your attention presently - would have said, "What, I, Sir William Gordon-Cumming, sign a document which is to write me down a card-sharper. If there are twenty persons who have said that I have done it, I, in my own mind, am perfectly certain that I did nothing of the kind." It is said that before that he had shown by his conduct that he was maintaining his innocence.'

What, of course, the judge did not say was that a real guilty cheat would have refused to sign the paper and bluffed his way out of it. A genuine card-sharp could not possibly have admitted to such a deed. This was a very clear direction to the jury to ignore the 'lost his head' defence of his actions. The judge completely failed to balance this with the possibility that a man, despite his personal courage and cool headedness, could behave very differently under alien circumstances.

The judge continued, 'I think there was evidence that he was told that Mr Lycett Green was only too anxious to be confronted with him.'

Lycett Green knew perfectly well that was a hollow threat. Under no circumstances were the courtiers going to allow him to disclose the saga the following day. The judge must have realised this.

The Lord Chief Justice pressed on. It had been suggested that Lord Coventry and General Owen Williams treated the plaintiff harshly. But it is not whether they had or not, the question is what the plaintiff did under that pressure. Rightly or wrongly, these two gentlemen came to the conclusion that the evidence of these witnesses must be conclusive, and, rightly or wrongly, they came to the conclusion that the conduct of Sir William Gordon-Cumming confirmed that. They were sensible men, and they saw that neither in his desire to be confronted with his accusers, nor in his desire to go to the Commander-in-Chief, did he really persevere, and the conclusion they came to was one undoubtedly hostile to the plaintiff. It must be said also that the Prince of Wales, who came as a witness, and who swore to speak the truth, he also, it is clear, was of the same opinion, though he did not say so.

The point here is that the judge is, effectively, endorsing the courtiers' and the Prince's decision based on evidence of others. They exerted such pressure on Gordon-Cumming that he, virtually, had no option but to sign to avoid a scandal. That aspect is simply not put before the jury.

The judge glossed over the military authorities' part in the case and whether the Prince and General Owen Williams should remain on the Army List. 'It is enough for me to be an unhappy lawyer; I do not want

172

to be an Imperial soldier.' He probably did not really understand the position; Williams had retired, so was not on the active List anyway.

He then referred to the précis, denigrating it as not being evidence in the case at all. This is nonsense. Quite clearly there was a statement recorded in the précis - "He systematically placed a larger stake on the table than he had originally laid down, and when the cards were against him he frequently withdrew a portion of his stakes, and by this means defrauded the bank." But, in court, the witnesses said, "We don't think he withdrew his stakes. We do charge that he cheated by adding; but we do not charge that he cheated by subtracting."

These are two quite conflicting statements. The judge says, 'It seems to me, however, to be profoundly indifferent - only a very small matter.' Hardly; it was a direct contradiction between what was written immediately after the event and the witnesses' present evidence in court.

He continued. It is clear that, as Lord Coventry said in his evidence, they wanted to stop a scandal, to be lenient to an old friend, and to prevent the name of the Prince of Wales being brought in connection with it; but they also wanted to disarm Sir William Gordon-Cumming, and would only agree to the condition of secrecy if he signed the promise not to play cards. And so they said: "We served society very well, because we stopped cheating on the part of Sir William Gordon-Cumming and also stopped a scandal." As to the affair being wholly maintained a secret with so many people acquainted with it, two of the twelve being ladies, how they could think secrecy would be preserved? Yes, indeed.

The real point, which the judge brushed aside, was that the 'conspirators' had decided on Gordon-Cumming's guilt based purely on statements of others, who had now withdrawn some of their accusations. To diminish the discrepancies in the précis, as he did, was disingenuous. He then covered Gordon-Cumming's exchange of letters with General Owen Williams suggesting that they were hardly those of a man tricked into signing a document against his will. 'On 11th September,' said the judge, 'he has £228 as his winnings, in a draft drawn to his order by Mr. Sassoon. He endorses it, pays it into his bank, and there the matter has rested from 11th or 12th September to the present time. We are now in 9th June. Gentlemen, would you, if you were accused of cheating, and if you had signed a paper saying that on consideration of silence being

173

maintained you would never touch a card again, and if you had written to your friend thanking him for his very great kindness, would you touch that money? Would you have paid that £228 into the bank? I pass no opinion, I merely ask you the question.'

As well he might; it was hardly hypothetical. His opinion was all too clear for the jury to see.

He was clearly driving the stake into Gordon-Cumming. He told the jury not to read too much into the fact that General Owen Williams wrote, 'Dear Bill.' This was purely out of kindness, he said, it did not suggest any presumption of innocence on Gordon-Cumming's part.

In Clarke's speech, the judge said, he maintained 'the true solution of this, or nine-tenths of it, was to save the Prince of Wales.' However, the judge, after somewhat sycophantically commiserating with the Prince having to carry out so many boring public duties, declared that introducing Baccarat, and playing it for a couple of nights, in someone's house would hardly have done much harm to the Monarchy or the Prince of Wales. Nobody would think the worse of a hard-working man spending the evening in this way among his friends, the judge suggested.

The judge was making it quite clear that he thought there was no harm in the Prince playing Baccarat and it was hardly the stuff of scandal. Why then should he be so protected from even a whiff of disgrace?

A man might accept death, but he would not accept dishonour, the judge said. Is it believable that an innocent man – a perfectly innocent man – would write his name on a dishonouring document, on a document which, in fact, stated that he had cheated and taken money out of the pocket of the Prince of Wales by craft and sharping, simply that it might not be made known that the Prince of Wales had played Baccarat for very moderate stakes? Are not the consequences far too great for the cause? Is it not putting an incredible weight upon it to suppose that any gentleman in the circumstances would allow himself not to die but to be called a card-sharper and a cheat for the rest of his life, for fear it should be known that the Prince of Wales had done something of which many people would disapprove?

This could hardly be classed as unbiased direction to the jury. It was a defence of the Prince's lifestyle and a clear disbelief that anyone would sacrifice their honour over an innocuous game of cards. The judge had deliberately glossed over discrepancies in the witnesses' evidence. He had failed to guide the jury on the balance of probabilities. He allowed a juryman to ask a question of the Prince of Wales. He had dismissed Gordon-Cumming's defence of the extreme pressure put upon him. He blatantly expressed the view that no innocent man would have signed the document, completely failing to balance this with the opposite that neither would a guilty man. On any interpretation of the judge's actions, there is only one conclusion; that they were totally biased against Gordon-Cumming.

'And now I send you to your duty. You have a very grave and a very important duty. You have sworn to perform it, as God shall help you, according to the truth. You must not, and you will not, I am sure, perform it in any other sense than the single, simple, unalloyed desire that truth and justice should prevail. You must remember that the consequences are not yours, but the duty is, and I send you to do your duty in the noble words of a great man many years gone - I divert them from his purpose to adapt them to this case - when you pass your judgment upon Sir William Gordon-Cumming I pray you recollect your own.'

The judge must have been congratulating himself on a job well done. A Knighthood of the Garter in the offing?

The jury retired at twenty-five minutes past three.

The Nation held its breath.

CHAPTER 14 – Verdict

The jury was out for thirteen minutes.

'Gentlemen, are you agreed upon your verdict?'

'We are.'

'Do you find for the plaintiff or the defendants?'

'The defendants.' With those two words Gordon-Cumming's reputation disintegrated. His world crashed around him.

An eyewitness recalls what happened.[219]

'When the clerk of the court suddenly announced the jury was ready to return there was a movement of surprise throughout the audience, the short absence of the jury being regarded as decidedly unfavourable to the plaintiff. Everybody may be said to have been in a breathless state when the jury entered their box, looking rather frightened and very nervous. The announcement of a verdict for the defendants was received with a slight hissing from the galleries where the ladies were congregated and upon the part of some of those in the body of the court who were in sympathy with Sir William Gordon-Cumming. The court officers had some difficulty for some time in suppressing these marks of, principally feminine, disapprobation of the verdict. They were, however, eventually suppressed and the court adjourned.

When the verdict was announced Sir William Gordon-Cumming, to all appearances, was the most unmoved man in court. He folded his arms and looked straight at the jury, but otherwise did not move a muscle, his face not showing the slightest trace of emotion. Lord Middleton, his blood relative, however, flushed scarlet and then turned very pale. Mrs Arthur Wilson and Mrs Lycett Green were evidently badly frightened when they heard the hisses that greeted the verdict. The two ladies stood for several minutes whispering earnestly with their counsel, and then accompanied by their respective husbands, passed slowly out of court with bowed heads, nobody speaking to them, and to all appearances the objects of much dislike. 'The Wilsons win,' as if by magic spread from the court room to the crowds outside, and from there all over London, and it was again made evident as the defendants drove away, by the chilling manner in which they were regarded, that popular sympathy was with the plaintiff.

In the meantime how different was the greeting extended to the defeated litigant, to the unsuccessful plaintiff, Sir William Gordon-Cumming. While the defendants were with sinking hearts leaving the courtroom, he remained calmly seated in his usual place. When the Wilsons had disappeared the baronet stood up and gratefully, smilingly shook hands with Sir Edward Clarke and others who pressed around him, with many cheering words of sympathy for the man whose career was thus blighted beyond all hope. Then, accompanied by Lord Middleton, he walked out of court by a private exit, followed by the pitying glances of the ladies, who still remained in the galleries, anxious to have a last glimpse of the victim of the Tranby Croft baccarat playing. As the proud-looking baronet and Lord Middleton left the court there was another instance of the different manner in which the general public looked upon the victorious defendants and the defeated plaintiff. Sir William and Lord Middleton were no sooner recognised as they entered the latter's carriage than they were loudly, repeatedly and enthusiastically cheered by the dense excited crowds.'

It was now the moment for Gordon-Cumming's friends and enemies to reveal themselves. The latter were only too glad to see the potential fall of someone they feared and disliked; others, despite his arrogance and womanising, were steadfast friends and would remain true to him, particularly his old Regimental colleagues.

One person, though, stood out from all the others: his fiancée, Miss Florence Garner. Florence's cousin, Frances Lawrence, had married Lord Vernon of Sudbury Hall. Through the Vernons she had met William Gordon-Cumming. She found his dashing good looks, charm and sophistication irresistible. In his turn, he was bewitched by her beauty and mischievous sense of humour. Although some twenty years separated their ages, his title and her fortune sealed the affair. They had become engaged well before the trial. Despite his urging her to break off the engagement due to the court case, she resolutely refused.

However, apart from the catastrophe of the baccarat scandal, Florence had her own heartbreak: she was the orphaned daughter of an American industrialist and his wife.

Florence's father, William Thorn Garner, was a genial 34 year-old New York millionaire and philanthropist, who had made a vast fortune from the cotton mills in New York state and considerable property interests.[220] He was reputed have an income of about $2 million [$44,800,000] a year and be worth between $19 and 20 million [$426 – 448 million]. Alternating between a large summer house on Staten Island[221] set in twenty-five acres with magnificent views over New York harbour, Brooklyn and Jersey City, and their residence at No.8 East 33rd Street, close to where the Empire State Building now stands, his family of wife, Marcellite and daughters Marcellite ('Lita') eight, Florence ('Flip') seven and Edith two, led a blissful and carefree life. Unsurprisingly, living where he did, Garner had taken up sailing and five years previously had been made a member of the prestigious New York Yacht Club. With no shortage of money, his schooner *Magic* had beaten the America's Cup winner *Comet* in what the Press called the most exciting race of 1874. There was a rumour that he had wagered a considerable amount of money on the race, and funded largely by his winnings, he had built the *Mohawk*. At 330 tons, she was the largest sailing yacht in the world and fitted out with the utmost luxury. The yacht was not merely an object of great beauty but competed well in competitions and was capable of standing up to bad weather. Additionally, she was a marvellous place in which to entertain the *glitterati* of New York. Garner was a popular Vice Commodore of the Club, particularly after building an outstanding galleried clubhouse in nearby Stapleton and earning public gratitude by arranging for the North Shore Ferry Company to provide a cheap ferry service by beating off the overcharging Vanderbilts' Staten Island Railroad Company.

At the clubhouse pier on Thursday 20 July 1876, the Garners' guests assembled for a gentle sailing trip to be followed by a good dinner on board. Guests included Marcellite's brother from Chicago, Louis Montant and Gardiner Howland of Howland & Aspinwall, textile merchants, Colonel John Schuyler Crosby, a Civil War hero, and two young ladies, Adele Hunter and Edith May, daughters of prominent local families. The Garner girls were considered too young for the party.

Although the sea was grey and choppy and the sky overcast, a large number of boats were afloat that afternoon. The *Mohawk's* crew prepared to cast off. The crew was a large one, headed by the 'sailing master', Captain Oliver B. Rowland, and included a mate, a boatswain, two quartermasters, a sailor and a fifteen-year-old cabin boy. But it was not a happy crew. Rowland was a strange, eccentric character. Harsh and dictatorial, he had run away to sea at the age of ten. He had commanded mostly trading coasters before joining the *Mohawk* the previous November. Uneasy to work for, he inspired animosity and distrust. Nevertheless, he appeared to have a good relationship with his employer.

By the time the guests were ready, storm clouds had gathered in the west. Was it safe to sail, Rowland was asked? 'I think there'll be a nice breeze when the tide has turned, Sir,' was the reply.

At high tide Garner gave the order to get under way. It began to rain quite heavily, and the Garners hurried their guests down into the comfortable saloon. Other yachtsmen, realising a storm was brewing, were rapidly taking in sail, and onlookers were concerned to see the *Mohawk* had not done the same. Captain Johnson, a local boat owner, was watching from the beach, 'There'll be an accident very soon, if they don't look out,' he remarked. At that, the wind caught the *Mohawk*, which heeled over onto her side in the water.

There was panic on board as her crew battled to get her upright and under way again. Attempts to reduce sail were hampered by the sloping deck. Down in the saloon a sudden lurch was felt. Nervous glances were exchanged before Garner dashed up the companion-way, followed by most of the other men. One of them stayed below with the ladies.

Small boats were launched from the shore and made towards the stricken vessel. On land, experienced sailors looked on helplessly, unable to understand why the crew of the *Mohawk* appeared to be acting so slowly. The yacht had righted herself after the first squall, but as far as they could tell, no efforts were being made to slacken the mainsheet or get her head round. At that moment the next gust arrived, and they saw her go over broadside again.

This time the crew were unable to lift the *Mohawk* out of the water, which was running over her rails and beginning to fill the boat. Rowland battling to keep control of the helm, saw Garner in the gangway and shouted across at him, 'For God's sake come out, Sir, and get your friends. We've lost steerage way. The ship's going to sink!' He refused to believe him at first, 'Oh no, Captain, I don't think there is any danger.'

But at last he was persuaded he was serious, and hurried back inside. Rowland was never to see him again.

The women screamed as the whole of the saloon tipped sideways. One clung to the mantelpiece to avoid being thrown across the room. Another two were not so lucky, and found sofas and chairs sliding towards them. They heard the cry, 'For God's sake bring up the women!' Marcellite's brother must have become trapped behind the door of the state room cabin and was never seen again.

Colonel Crosby fought his way across the debris to Edith, and managed to guide her across the cabin and push her up the companionway, where Montant and Howland were waiting to help her up on deck. Montant reached down to grasp her, but found himself being hit by something which caused him to lose his hold. Crosby was able to catch her and shoved her to the top of the steps, where she stood dazed and breathless.

By this time the water was pouring in. Peter, the young cabin boy, standing between the stairway and the saloon door, was overwhelmed. Inside, Garner, Crosby and a sailor were fighting to release the trapped Marcellite and Adele. One of the starboard settees had broken loose and jammed them against the port side of the cabin. Eventually the rescuers managed to heave it off and push it through one of the skylights, thanks to the quick-wittedness of the bosun who had smashed it open with an axe. Garner was pulling desperately on his wife's right arm, and Crosby tugged at Adele Hunter, but it was no use; the women were still being held down by something they could not see. A number of 150-pound lead ingots, carried as ballast, had smashed through the deck and slid down the port side on top of them. Garner attempted to pull his wife out, but it was useless. The dislocated ballast made it impossible for the yacht to right herself.

Crosby felt Adele's hand slip out of his, and he lost his footing and was sucked under water. By the time he had struggled up, she was entirely submerged and had ceased the fight. He then tried to help Garner rescue Marcellite, but they were unable to free her. By now they were the only people alive below, and with the water level rapidly rising, it was time to save themselves. Garner steadfastly refused to leave his wife. While they were arguing, the *Mohawk* gave another sudden huge lurch, and all four of them were engulfed.

Some of the crew who had been balanced along the mast, as it lay at right-angles to the water, were thrown or jumped off into the sea and had to swim for their lives. Rowland lost his hold on the wheel and dropped between the mainsheet and the boom. Edith, who had been lying down clinging to the planking, was caught between the companionway and the furniture from the cabin, only a free arm preventing her being sucked back into the depths. Montant, submersed up to his neck, found that she was beneath him and managed to pull her out, lost hold of her again, but eventually succeeded in getting her to the surface. They trod water, supporting her between them, till the first of the small craft arrived.

Even then rescue was not straightforward. Mr Beverly Robinson, in trying to help Edith into the *Phantom's* boat, was dragged overboard himself. Montant had gone under, and when he rose to the surface was nearly hit by the boat from the *Dreadnaught*. Someone seized him by the hair and hauled him aboard. 'Never mind me,' he shouted, 'mind the ladies', but it was already too late.

Down below, Crosby saw a streak of light above him and half crawled, half swam towards it. This was the hatch that had been hacked open, and it saved both his life and that of one of the crew, who struggled through the tiny aperture in front of him.

Crosby struck out for Hunt's boat, but even as he caught hold of it, the vessel capsized, and he was eventually rescued by the crew of the *Dreadnaught*. He had lost half his clothing, and must have been suffering considerable after-effects himself, but with great gallantry his first action was to make sure that the shocked and bruised Edith was put safely into a carriage and taken back to the Garner mansion. He then collected Howland and Montant and set off back on the steam yacht *Ideal* to see what could be done aboard the *Mohawk*. But there was no hope of saving anybody else now, or retrieving the bodies of their friends from the submerged cabin.

The tragedy stunned the whole community. Many onlookers could hardly believe what had happened. The Staten Island Garners, with their magnificent house, huge yacht and warm-hearted generosity, loved and respected by all, in a few short minutes were gone.

A simple joint funeral service for William and Marcellite Garner was held at the mansion. Later, twenty or so carriages were ferried across to the foot of Twenty-fourth Street, Brooklyn, and, swelled by sympathetic on-lookers, the cortege carried on to Greenwood Cemetery, where the remains were interred in the family vault facing Larch Avenue. Florence and her sisters, dressed in black crepe, deposited flowers on the coffins of their beloved mother and father.

The orphaned girls were brought up by their aunt, Frances Lawrence at Bayshore, Long Island. They subsequently moved to Pau in France, where they learned religion and etiquette at a convent school, but little else

Then Florence met Lieutenant Colonel Sir William Gordon-Cumming at the Vernons' house and the die was cast.

Back in London, the effect of the verdict on military circles was sadly predictable. The understanding was that Sir William would be promptly cashiered from the army and just as quickly expelled from the Marlborough Club, Guards Club, Turf Club and any other social organisation to which he belonged. In fact he resigned and faced no military tribunal.

It was probably just as well that the Prince of Wales was not present; there is no doubt he would also have been the object of the crowd's wrath. Indeed, when the news reached Ascot, his carriage was roundly booed by racegoers. It was very apparent that the verdict was thoroughly unpopular. The public were wholeheartedly on Gordon-Cumming's side. 'No dog would be hanged on the evidence that convinced a jury that Sir William Gordon-Cumming had cheated at cards,' said *Truth* magazine.[222] In his reminiscences, Sir Edward Clarke wrote: - 'I think I am able now to form an unbiased opinion, and I think I ought to leave that opinion. I believe the verdict was wrong, and that Sir William Gordon-Cumming was innocent of the offence charged against him.'[223]

The verdict was greeted with varying reactions. The court case had held the population spellbound, both sides of the Atlantic. Americans were fascinated. The whole aristocratic scene of Edwardian society was a complete mystery to most. It was incredibly difficult to understand the reverence in which aristocrats were held; Monarchy could be appreciated but the wealthy bed-hopping, gambling lords and ladies were the stuff of rather bad fairy tales.

The American journalists' views were predictable, 'The anti-baccarat crusade was earnestly begun and will extend rapidly all over the Kingdom. The landlord of the Albert Hotel was arrested and fined £10 yesterday, and his licence revoked for keeping his house open after regulation hours and permitting the obnoxious baccarat to be played therein. Five others who were indulging in this game so much loved by the Prince of Wales were fined £1 each.' [224]

'No Magistrate thinks of arresting him [Prince of Wales] for doing what an ordinary gambler would be sent to prison for doing. When he enters court to give testimony concerning his law breaking, the entire audience rises to receive him, and he is placed on a bench beside the Judge as an honoured guest. And when his gambling losses and his other squanderings bring him into trouble, he asks the bread-earners of Great Britain to pay his debts for him. How long are the 'plain people' of Great Britain going to stand the false system which makes of this gambler, debauchee, and idler, their destined ruler, and exalts him to the headship of both the Church and the State?[225]

Gordon-Cumming's reputation was not the only one shattered by the Tranby Croft affair. It had thrown light on how the upper classes behaved in the privacy of their mansions. This was extremely unattractive not only to the Republicans but ordinary members of the public. Is this how the very privileged behaved behind closed doors? What else might they be doing? Above all, very unpleasant attention was focused on the Prince of Wales and the revelations about his gambling habits. This was just what his courtiers had miserably failed to hide.

There were those who had suspicions that there was something going on that had never been revealed in court. Indeed, the judge had specifically warned the jury to concentrate only on the evidence before them. Even to the most ordinary of mortals, it seemed incomprehensible that Gordon-Cumming would completely ruin his life in this way. The aristocrats pulled up their drawbridges and hoped it would go away and, not unnaturally, particularly those with social aspirations, very much took the Prince's side.

Had the Prince of Wales not been involved, it would probably never have reached the Courts. There would have been no panicky courtiers at Tranby Croft. Gordon-Cumming would have merely brushed aside the accusations from a 'bunch of boys.' Indeed, with the host's distaste for gambling, baccarat would hardly likely to have been played at all.

Why all the outcry against the Prince gambling? No one, except the most puritanical of his subjects, objected to him going racing. What actually was the difference? Gambling was gambling. The Prince himself wrote to the Archbishop of Canterbury, 'Horse-racing may produce gambling, of which I have a horror, or it may not; but I have always looked upon it as a manly sport, which is popular with Englishmen of all classes – and there is no reason why it should be looked upon as a gambling transaction.' The Prince, however, was being a little disingenuous. Racecourses of his day were not the polite, well-disciplined ones of today. They were hotbeds of corruption, violence and crime where the lowest kind of criminal mixed with wealthy upper classes. To a certain extent, therefore, outcry against the Prince's behaviour at Tranby Croft, even from the more moderate and thoughtful critics, has to be put into that sort of context.

While technically illegal, Baccarat was only so in public; what people did behind their closed doors was their affair. In effect, the Prince's courtiers, Lord Coventry and General Owen Williams were frightened into making a major misjudgement. They, and the Prince, had no evidence of Gordon-Cumming's cheating apart from what they had been told. Blackmailed by the fairly hollow threat from Lycett Green that he would expose Gordon-Cumming publicly at the races, they were driven to an unseemly protection scheme for the Prince by bullying Gordon-Cumming into signing the document, which he, in his turn, made the misjudgement of agreeing to do so. They thought that, by this, they were establishing a watertight cover for their royal master. More rational thought would have persuaded them that a secret of this sort was unlikely to remain so for long and that there were alternatives to dealing with the problem.

If indeed the verdict was wrong, how did it go wrong? Much of the blame can be laid against the Lord Chief Justice. He allowed his court to become a society spectacle; women attended in fashionable clothes, gossip abounded and people actually brought sandwiches into the courtroom. Lord Coleridge even distributed admission tickets to his friends. More importantly, though, criticism has been made of his summing-up. There is no doubt that it was blatantly biased in favour of the defendants. However, not everyone thought so. The Master of Balliol College, Oxford, Mr B Jowett, wrote to Lord Coleridge, 'May I tell you that I read your charge on the Baccarat Case? I thought it thoroughly right and sound. Everywhere the matter is being discussed; the more fashionable part of the world being in favour of Sir W. G. Cumming, and the common sense of the middle classes against him. Ever yours affectionately, B. Jowett.'[226]

It is doubtful whether the Master of Balliol College was a true judge of what had been going on. He certainly wasn't in court. In fact, he probably had it the wrong way round.

If someone wanted to cheat by adding or withdrawing his stake, the last thing he is going to do is to put his counters where everyone can see them on a white sheet of paper. Surely he would conceal his actions by moving them surreptitiously on the patterned cloth? Even the dullest juryman must have seen that. The only real evidence of cheating was Jack's on the first night and it is more than possible that he was mistaken. Likewise, Berkeley Levett's evidence relates only to the first night's play. The evidence of all the other witnesses relied on what they expected to see or what they had been told they would see. [Expectations make people see fallacies that are not there. Decades of research have proved that expectation is a powerful force. Not only do we tend to see what we expect to see, we also tend to experience what we expect to experience.[227] Mrs Wilson's evidence was a classic case of this. She forgot what she wanted to forget and she saw what she expected to see, having been told what she would see. Others, with the same view of events, did not see what she saw. The conclusion is that, nice though they were, she, Jack and Mrs Lycett Green were deluding themselves. Having made their accusations, there was no going back. It would have spelt immediate social ruin. Mr Lycett Green, not the sharpest of individuals, had to rely on a total loss of memory when being cross-examined, despite being advised what to say and rehearsed by the redoubtable solicitor, Mr George Lewis.

Lycett Green was the danger man as far as the courtiers were concerned. He was unintelligent enough to carry out his threat of disclosure and the only way they could be sure he would not, was to dream up the document scheme. Having reached that decision, they stumbled on. Clearly Lycett Green had some fundamental dislike of Gordon-Cumming. It may have been simple jealousy in that Gordon-Cumming was many things he was not and to which he might have aspired, without hope. Or he was nervous about Gordon-Cumming's well-known seductive charms in relation to his lovely young wife. Clarke

185

could not insinuate this without lowering his client's reputation in the eyes of the jury and Russell, similarly, could not suggest this without querying his clients' motives.

By allowing the question to the Prince of Wales from a member of the jury, did Coleridge prejudice anything? Possibly not, as the Prince had already said, in evidence, that the three of them (he, Lord Coventry and General Owen Williams) believed Gordon-Cumming guilty. Nevertheless, the juryman should have been kept quiet and the doubt had been sown in the jury's minds.

What were the jury to do? For four hours, the judge had battered them with a biased interpretation of the facts to underline Gordon-Cumming's guilt and, what is more, he told them, the Prince of Wales himself believed him guilty. So it must be true. The jury were not stupid but they had been worn out by the onslaught of legal broadside. In thirteen minutes did they really balance the facts, weigh up the various elements of the case, and argue amongst themselves the doubts and probabilities? Not a hope; they delivered their verdict and escaped. How could they really have believed that Gordon-Cumming, a man of impeccable standing and personal honour, against whom there had never been a suspicion of cheating, would lower himself to some cheap trick to gain a few pounds he did not need and to dishonour his Prince whose friendship and good will he so valued?

In *Truth,* Henry Labouchère[228] wrote, 'I have known many charges of cheating, and charges proved on far more substantial grounds than this one. Yet I never knew of one in which the guilty person signed his own condemnation. The more hardened the cheat, the stronger the evidence against him, the more did they deny the charge. And why did the old friends give him this strange counsel? Why did they urge him to sign the document? Lord Coventry tells us. It stands recorded in his diary: - 'To keep the name of the Prince of Wales out of it, and in consideration of their host and hostess who were suffering from domestic affliction.'

Newspapers on both sides of the Atlantic reacted strongly; mostly thoroughly anti the Prince of Wales and the Monarchy. *The Spectator*, a rather more pompous journal than it is today, issued a thunderous 2,000 word editorial on 13 June.

'The intellectual interest of the Baccarat Case, the interest which will attract historians, consists in this, that a majority of those within the

Court, and probably a majority outside it, wished the result to be favourable to Sir William Gordon-Cumming. ….. There was doubt at the beginning of the case, it is true, and it was reasonable, because, though it seemed improbable that a bold man like Sir William would, if innocent, sign a letter which he himself described as an acknowledgment of guilt..... Men do lose their heads very often under ruinous charges, and it was at least as probable that Sir William Gordon-Cumming had lost his, as that he had cheated anybody at cards...... The Wilson household mismanaged their trying affair most grievously, but they did nothing wrong. Their clear course, if they suspected foul play, was to inform the head of the house of the facts, and leave it to him either to stop the play peremptorily, assigning no reason, except privately to the Prince of Wales, who by the etiquette of Courts would have been entitled to "an explanation", or to warn Sir William Gordon-Cumming that he was suspected, and request his departure. The public wanted a verdict for the prosecutor, or, when that was seen to be impossible, a disagreement among the jury, because they wanted a sharp rebuke to be given to "the gambling lot of rich folks" who, with the heir to the Throne in the midst of them, could find no better way of passing the time than playing every night a game for which poor folks are punished every week.'

Representing the pro-Prince of Wales's faction was *The Pall Mall Gazette*, in reality the platform for George Lewis, the defendants' solicitor.

'Is it so very 'scandalous' if a British Prince should gamble at baccarat? If he were judged by the ordinary standard, certainly not. But then, as we have shown, he is not so judged. Royalty is placed in a category by itself. Hence the Prince cannot join in a game of cards without causing all the flutter and excitement which we see today. That is one of the drawbacks to 'exalted rank.' Let us hope, in common charity, that there are compensating advantages.'[229]

The Press Association interviewed one of the jurymen immediately he left the court. He stated that there was no doubt from the first moment the jury entered the private room how the verdict would go. As each juryman was asked whether he was for the plaintiff or the defendants the reply was unhesitatingly given, 'For the defendants.' One of the jury, who sympathised with the plaintiff was struck by the unanimity which prevailed, and although he would have liked to have found for the plaintiff, he could not conscientiously do so in the face of the evidence. It appeared to him that the jury had made up their minds before the summing up of the Lord Chief Justice.'[230] Was this really true? The reality was that the jury were confused by the technical aspects of Gordon-Cumming's method of playing, tried to follow the judge's summing up and were completely mesmerised by a lifestyle of the Tranby Croft houseparty of which they knew absolutely nothing.

One of the more interesting newspapermen was W T Stead who, at the time, edited *The Review of Reviews*. His sheer energy helped to revolutionise the often stuffy world of Victorian journalism, while his blend of sensationalism and indignation set the tone for British tabloids for more than a century. Like many journalists, he was a curious mixture of conviction, opportunism and sheer humbug. He died on the *Titanic*.

'Despite being the subject of 'one thousand millions of prayers' every day, Prince Edwardhas become embroiled in the 'Baccarat Scandal of Tranby Croft'. Observes that 'As a prayer gauge on the principle suggested by Professor Tyndall, His Royal Highness, who in course of time may become Defensor Fidei, can hardly be said, as Heir-Apparent, to have contributed much to strengthen the faith of the modern world in the efficacy of prayer'. Adds that the Prince suffers from that 'fatty degeneration of the moral sense which often sets in after prolonged self-indulgence'.'

French newspapers, Figaro and Gaulois carried rumours of abdication of the Prince rather than the Queen. After all, he had a son who was perfectly able to assume the throne and, of course, did so in 1910 as George V.

Many years later, the debate was still current in the Press.

'The verdict against him has not gone unquestioned: many times since has the issue been debated; did Sir William Gordon-Cumming cheat at cards or no? What is the true answer I would not care to affirm. But I do affirm that the foolish measures taken on the spot unfairly and fundamentally pre-judged this issue, which could never henceforth be satisfactorily tried.'[231]

But what about the Prince? What was his reaction to all this? On 10 June he wrote to Prince George, 'Thank God! - the Army and Society are now well rid of such a damned blackguard. The crowning part of his infamy is that he this morning married an American young lady, Miss Garner (sister to Mme de Breteuil), with money!'[232]

Queen Victoria's views were very clear. She suggested the Prince write a letter to the Archbishop of Canterbury, deploring gambling, which could then be published. The Prince rejected this on the basis that it could be seen by his detractors as hypocritical. He was supported in this decision by Lord Salisbury, the Prime Minister. In the event, the Prince did write, privately to the Archbishop.

On 11 September 1930, E F Benson, the Archbishop's son, published his memoirs, 'As We Were.'[233] He relates the main facts which are generally known, and goes on to give in detail a conversation between his father – Archbishop Benson – and the Prince, and the subsequent letter which the Prince sent to his father on the subject. The Prince desired to see Archbishop Benson on the matter, and the Archbishop called on the Prince at Marlborough House. The Prince without any ado stated his business. He had seen that the whole of the religious and church press was condemning him "as a gambler and worse," and he believed that the Archbishop Benson had been instigating this campaign.

'How the Prince had got hold of the notion that he had been doing anything of the sort,' says the author, 'is quite unexplained, and my father had no curiosity to inquire into that, but contented himself with telling the Prince that there was no truth of any sort or kind in the accusation.'

The Prince strongly affirmed that he was no gambler, and that gambling as he understood the word was hateful to him, but that playing cards for small sums was no such thing. But he would never try to put down betting. 'There was a national instinct for betting, and every small boy in a grocer's shop put his sixpence on the Derby.'

'Very bad developments that leads to,' said my father.

'Certainly it does,' said the Prince, but there's no harm in playing cards for money in itself – and one of the first men I ever played cards with was Bishop Wilberforce.'

The Prince then spoke of certain points in these attacks which had been made on him, which he particularly resented. The Press howled with horror at the idea of counters belonging to him being used at this game of baccarat.

'They say that I carry counters as a Turk carries his prayer carpet,' he said, 'but the reason I carry counters is to check high play. High sums are easily named but these counters range from five shillings to five pounds [sic – there was actually a £10 counter] and that can hurt nobody.'

The Prince certainly learned his lesson and there is no evidence that he ever played baccarat again but his personal life hardly improved with the almost immediate involvement with the Beresford family quarrels. He was never to be entirely free of criticism until he became King. He became a highly conscientious sovereign who made pleasure his servant and not his master after his accession to the throne. The dignity of his public life, his immense popularity and charm, and the zest, punctuality and panache with which he performed his duty forcefully and faithfully until the day on which he died, enhanced the prestige of the monarchy.[234] But it was a close run thing. At the time of the scandal he could have been heading for the tumbrils.

The anti-gambling brigade was vitriolic. At the Wesleyan Methodist Conference, the Venerable Dr Douglass asserted, 'Another year has brought sadness and sorrow to the bosom of our gracious Queen and a diminished spirit to meet the responsibilities of her high position, while over the throne the black shadow of a ghastly spectre has fallen. Among us has risen a second George IV in the heir to the throne of this vast Empire. He has been convicted of being concerned, in an infamous abomination, and the awful spectacle is presented of the heir to the throne publicly acknowledging complicity in gambling transactions.'[235]

The Primitive Methodist Connexion passed a resolution to be sent direct to the Prince of Wales that 'it was not in favour of such a man ruling over us unless he gives up such a practice.' The General Baptist Churches of Lancashire and Yorkshire urged the Prince of Wales to decline to practise or countenance gambling. They were joined by the Congregationalists of Glamorganshire, the Birmingham Church Council and the Bishop of Durham. The Govan Liberal and Radical Association condemned the Prince of Wales in connection with the Baccarat scandal and called on him to resign from the Army.[236] The Royal Archives contain a bundle of letters, 'addresses' and 'resolutions', in varying quality and vehemence, from Non-Conformist clergy taking the Prince to task for his wicked ways. They really believed it and genuinely wanted to see the back of Royalty when the Queen died.

Even the sanctimonious *Own Correspondent* of the *The Times* in Vienna joined in,

'Sir William Gordon-Cumming's action has been watched with the keenest interest in all the military circles of this country. The Prince of Wales, besides being a Field-Marshal in the British Army, is the Colonel-Proprietor of an Austrian regiment, and it was only natural in the circumstances that the Austrian and Hungarian officers should be intensely curious to note whether His Royal Highness's ideas of military duty tallied with those which are held in the Emperor of Austria's army.

'An Englishman must acknowledge with some mortification that the opinions expressed on this baccarat case are not agreeable to hear. In the first place, it is thought most strange that a Field-Marshal and a General in the British Army should condone an act of cheating on the part of a Colonel in the Queen's Guards, and should make themselves privy to a commitment by which this officer was to retain his commission and his membership of various respected clubs. Leaving the Prince of Wales altogether out of the matter, and referring only to General Owen Williams, it must be said that if any Austrian General could have acted as this General has done, he would have found himself embroiled in a deadly quarrel not only with the regiment but with all the clubs to which the offending officer belonged, and he would have had to throw up his commission to avoid a Court-martial.

This, however, is not the only point. If the Prince of Wales had indulged his fondness for baccarat in the company of men of about his own age and near to him in rank, no foreign officer would have found anything to say, but that His Royal Highness should have sat down to gamble with youngsters, one of whom was a mere lieutenant in the army, seems most surprising. According to all the Continental codes of military etiquette, senior officers are bound to discountenance gambling among subalterns, and it is simply unimaginable that a German, Austrian, or French Field-Marshal should sit down to win money from or lose money to a mere lieutenant, who, if he gambles, must be paying away his father's money or prematurely squandering his inheritance. These are the things which, with others, are being said here, and it is a duty to report them, for the echoes of military opinion will be ringing but too loudly over the whole Continent tomorrow.'[237]

It is not easy today, when there are completely different sets of morals, to realise the impact of this scandal on late Victorian society. The Prince of Wales was exposed as good-for-nothing, happily overeating and drinking far too much, sleeping with other men's wives and, technically illegally, gambling for stakes often unaffordable by some of the other players. Did the population really want this man as King? The Queen was absolutely right; at the time the Monarchy really was in danger. If Prince Charles behaved this way today, would we want him as King? It is a sobering thought and one which should be applied to 1890 to realise the immense impact of the scandal.

What happened to the loser?

CHAPTER 15 – Aftermath

For Gordon-Cumming there now followed a bleak desert of social ostracism and exile to his Scottish estates. The one joy in his life, however, was his immediate marriage to Florence who had stood by him throughout his ordeal, much to the dissatisfaction of the remainder of her family. They were married in a simple ceremony, by special licence, the morning after the end of the trial. The Reverend Ralph Walker, senior curate, officiated at the Holy Trinity Church, South Chelsea. It was a strictly private occasion, witnessed by no more than a score of people. Gordon-Cumming arrived first with his best man, Major Vesey Dawson, Coldstream Guards. The bride, in a simple travelling dress, arrived shortly afterwards, accompanied by Lord and Lady Middleton, Gordon-Cumming's sister. There were no bridesmaids and the bride was given away by Lord Thurlow. There were no decorations in the church as carpenters were installing a new organ. The Register was signed by the bride and groom, Lord Thurlow, Lord and Lady Middleton, Lady Elma Thurlow, Major Vesey Dawson and Mr Ernest Willoughby. The wedding breakfast was held at Middleton House in London. That afternoon the bride and groom left for Wollaton Hall, the Middleton seat in Northamptonshire. The following day they travelled to Altyre.

As far as Gordon-Cumming's military career went, the Army wasted no time. This terse entry was made in the London Gazette on 12 June:-

Scots Guards, Major and Lieutenant Colonel Sir William G Gordon-Cumming, Bart., is removed from the Army, Her Majesty having no further occasion for his services. Dated 10th June 1891.[238]

While his normal Record of Service can be found in Regimental Headquarters Scots Guards, no personal file exists.

However, although his military life was now over, there were a number of officers in the Scots Guards who held him in high regard and while not overly popular, he was well respected for his campaign record and leadership. He was also an amusing and agreeable companion, not only in the officers' mess, but also in difficult and dangerous situations. He therefore had a number of colleagues who believed he had been badly treated, to the extent that, in Regimental folklore, it was suggested that he had covered up for the Prince of Wales, although the detail was vague. To express their feelings too loudly, though, would have been met, unsurprisingly, with official disapproval from the Regimental Lieutenant Colonel, Colonel Stracey.

An exact contemporary of Berkeley Levett's was Captain William Arnold Webster Lawson. The Prince of Wales was a good friend of his father, Edward Lawson, 1st Baron Burnham, and a regular guest at his house, Hall Barn, Beaconsfield.[239] The Lawsons owned the *Daily Telegraph.* Clearly young Lawson was one of those who made his supporting views too obvious and, with two other officers was expelled ('rifted' in modern soldier parlance) from the 1st Battalion and posted to the 2nd Scots Guards. To mark this event and a clear snub to authority, Lawson designed a tie, based on the dicing worn round the forage cap of the guardsmen, and presented it to his two fellow officers and, in time, any who agreed with his views.[240] Indeed, it was always referred to as the Lawson tie by the family and the Regiment. The tradition was carried on by his son, Edward and, in turn, his son, Bill Lawson.[241] Many years later, it was adopted as the tie of the Third Guards Club, the regimental officers' dining club.

On 16 June, *The Times* reported proceedings of the House of Commons for the previous day:

'Mr SUMMERS asked the Secretary State for War whether he had taken, or intended to take, any action with regard to the person or persons who in the case of "Sir William Gc v. Wilson and others" were alleged to have broken, or to have been parties to the breach of the Regulation of her Majesty's Army, which provided that "every commissioned officer of her Majesty's service whose character or conduct as an officer and gentleman has been publicly impugned must submit the case within a reasonable time to his commanding officer, or other competent military authority, for investigation."

Mr. STANHOPE. – Any hon. Member who examines the regulation in question will, I think, see that the person who chiefly broke it was Sir William Gordon-Cumming, who failed to submit his case to his commanding officer. Any offence committed by any other officers could only have consisted in advising or pressing him to take any other course. Of the three officers connected with this case, one, General Owen

Williams, has retired from the Army, and is no longer subject to the Queen's Regulations. The other two are undoubtedly so subject. The regulation in question, No. 41, had never been specially brought to the notice of his Royal Highness the Prince of Wales, but now that his attention has been called to it, and that he has also looked back upon all the circumstances of the case, his Royal Highness authorises me to say on his behalf that he sees that an error of judgment was committed in not requiring Sir William Gordon-Cumming at once to submit his case to his commanding officer in accordance with the Queen's Regulations. In this view of the case I certainly concur, but I should like to add the expression of my personal opinion that, if any one of us had unfortunately and suddenly heard that a close friend of our own – who, moreover, had gained distinction by his services to his country – had been accused of dishonourable conduct, we should naturally have hesitated before taking any course which would bring immediate and irretrievable ruin upon his whole future career. Mr. Berkeley Levett, who is in the same position, has addressed a letter to his superior officer expressing in very proper terms his great regret at not having acted in strict accordance with regulations. It is not proposed to take any further action in this matter. (Cheers.)'

Stanhope had written to the Prince of Wales, 'Your Royal Highness sees that an error of judgement was committed in not requiring Gordon-Cumming to submit his case to his Commanding Officer. But I should add that it was quite natural for anyone, when he heard that a friend of his own, distinguished for his services in the Army, was accused of cheating, to hesitate before taking any step which would irretrievably ruin him and his future life.'[242] It is an interesting point that if the Prince had been aware of these regulations at the time, whether it would have made any difference. Instead of the cover-up, would General Owen have reminded the Prince of Wales, as a serving officer, however presentational, of his responsibilities under Queen's Regulations, and advised him to report the matter, formally, to Gordon-Cumming's commanding officer? How the whole scene might have changed. However, given the paranoia of the courtiers, it is doubtful whether that would have been initiated.

On 15 June, the bride and groom arrived to an ecstatic welcome at Forres, the nearest railway station to Altyre. An eyewitness recorded the scene. 'Amid scenes of great enthusiasm Sir William Gordon-Cumming and his bride arrived at Forres Station with the morning mail on Saturday. Decorations in the form of arches, flags and bunting were pushed on rapidly, and willing hands worked all night in order to have everything complete. The weather was dull, but this in no way affected the enthusiasm of the citizens, who crowded the usually quiet station. The council met at half-past 9 o'clock, and, each of the members having signed the address, they marched to the station, Provost Watson wearing his gold chain and robes of office. As the train steamed into the station a cheer was sent up, and no sooner than it was drawn up than a rush was made for the saloon in which Sir William and his bride and Lord and Lady Middleton were seated. Having alighted, they were cordially greeted by Colonel Mackenzie and Mr Pullar, agent, after which a large number crowded round and insisted on shaking hands with Sir William and his bride. The council were drawn up in the open square at the north end of the platform. The Provost in a few words extended a welcome on behalf of the community. The clerk then read an address congratulating Sir William Gordon-Cumming on his marriage, referring to the services rendered to the country by him and by his ancestors, and recognising the readiness with which he had always assisted in the promotion of public and philanthropic movements in the district. Sir William, in reply, said he could not tell them how strongly he felt the kind and cordial welcome extended to him by his fellow-Scotchmen. Cheers were then given, and after the party had taken their seats in an open landau the horses were unyoked and the carriage was dragged for half a mile the town band playing in front. At St. Catherine's the horses were yoked and the party drove on. Sir William and Lady Gordon-Cumming, accompanied by Lady Middleton, attended morning service in St. John's Church yesterday. There was a large congregation. A crowd of several hundred was in waiting as the party came out, and respectful salutations were accorded to them.'[243]

There was no doubt where their loyalties lay.

With Gordon-Cumming on an annual income of £80,000 [£7,682,000] and his fiancée with some $60,000 – $100,000 [$1,580,000 – $2,640,000] there was not, as yet, a financial problem.

On 23 June 1891, a letter arrived from Edward Clarke, 'It is very kind of you and Lady Gordon-Cumming to offer me rest and retirement at

Forres and I should greatly enjoy a visit to your Scottish home, but I am back here and at the Courts and concluding work and it will be some time before I can give myself a holiday. I was somewhat exhausted at the end of your case as much by the disappointment of the verdict, as much by the exertion and anxiety of the previous days. A few days put me right again, and I hope you also have recovered from the strain and have found the pleasanter [ ] for the gross injustice with which you were treated. Convey my thanks and compliments to your wife, ete etc.'

Shane Leslie[244] in letters of December 1958 to Cecily, Gordon-Cumming's youngest daughter wrote, 'Sir Edward Clarke states his opinion of the Tranby Croft case very clearly. For a lawyer of his integrity he must have known more than the Trial divulged.... [His] book convinces me that he realised what lay behind the scene of the Trial. I think that the position was that the officer has to be sacrificed to the Lord's anointed in all countries whether in a love affair or a cardplaying dispute. Your father was mercilessly treated compared to Ld de Ros in 1830.[245] The whole Trial became a conspiracy to save the Prince socially which it failed to do. I think we could annotate the Trial in your father's favour. The evidence was paltry against him and insured the Prince in his statement – neither were properly cross-examined.'

*

On the surface, exile in Scotland did not appear to have had much effect on the Gordon-Cummings. He continued to enjoy hunting, golf, travelling and politics but from a distance. On the death of King Edward VII, Gordon-Cumming wrote to Sir Edward Clarke to ask if it was worth resurrecting the case? But Clarke replied on 24 May 1910 advising silence on the case after the King's death. He was probably right. It is unlikely that anything was going to change and all it would do would be to raise skeletons which a number of people, on both sides, would prefer left in their cupboards.

Families, such as the Gordon-Cummings, whose lineage stretched far back, were bound to have the odd black sheep, and they were no exception.

William's uncle, Roualeyn the lion-hunter, never married but had two illegitimate daughters, Alice and Eleanora. When Roualeyn died in

March 1866, he left a Will in which his brothers William and Henry were Trustees. Eleanora, now Mrs Michel Naake Nakeska, had been married twice, the first in 1876, five weeks after she came of age. In 1907 she took proceedings against William, the surviving Trustee. She claimed her father left his estate to his two daughters, and she, as one of them, claimed one half of the £6,000. The accounts showed a balance of £1,084, and she said the Trustees failed to realise and account for a South African museum containing many valuable trophies and curios, and a museum and property at Fort Augustus. The defence was that the estate had been realised and accounted for. Eleanora said she lived with her father at Fort Augustus as a girl, and remembered the sale of his pots and pans. He valued his collection with the love of a naturalist, and used to say to her "These are thy father's gods, Nell." In 1866 she made a list of the collections from memory, and there was a great deal in the collection that was magnificent. There was in the Will, a clause, 'unless disposed of by private bargain', and she assumed that it might have been put in because some of the magnificent trophies had been appropriated. If that was done, the money was not handed over. She spoke of payments made to her by the executor, and said she had been horribly bamboozled about them. In the Opinion of Lord Ardwall in November 1908, he reached the conclusion that the contents were properly sold despite her father saying the contents were worth £10,000. Ardwall said collectors often overvalue their museum. Despite having attained her majority 32 years ago, she had all the information but had not raised the point until now. She had raised no claim with either of her husbands. It was unfortunate that she had allowed herself to cherish unfounded suspicions against the Trustees. She seemed to have thought that her father's relatives had an ill will to her and treated her very badly. Her claim was dismissed.[246]

The second black sheep was Walter P Gordon-Cumming, the son of Francis, the 3rd baronet's brother, therefore William's first cousin. On 5 January 1907, he wrote to William threatening that unless he was given £200 by 16 January, 'he'll be bankrupt and will take steps which the family will regret.' Gordon-Cumming then wrote to solicitors on 10 January from Bridge House, Dawlish, enclosing the blackmailing letter, and saying, 'Walter is the son of my uncle Frank. He had written some years ago to members of the family accusing my cousin Henry O Grant [married to Eleanora, William's aunt] of unnatural practices. I have little doubt he has been put up to it by Nakeska.' There are further threatening letters in the file which were ignored. An Injunction was taken out against Walter in 1913 after he smashed 34 squares of glass in windows of Altyre House. In August of that year, he wrote an insulting letter to Florence which, again, was ignored.[247]

Florence threw herself into creating a life at Gordonstoun and Altyre. There were about thirty indoor servants at Gordonstoun. The estate was a self-contained community. Florence had a church and school built. She knew everyone on the estate by name and had hovels replaced by modern cottages. It was, though, a benevolent dictatorship. Employees had to go to church, marry their mistresses and keep sober. When they were ill, they received soup and blankets.[248] Gordon-Cumming failed, though, to change habits of a lifetime. He was rude, self-opinionated, chased women and was intolerant but much loved by the people on the estate. He longed for the life from which he was now excluded and the Regiment from which he had been dismissed. He had no purpose in life and the wrong done to him festered in his soul. He clung to the hope that one day he might be able to clear his name.

The Garner fortune dissipated under bad management and the Gordon-Cumming income was reduced to £10,000 [£5,494,000].[249] Altyre and Gordonstoun were closed and a house rented in Devon. Florence and William spent more and more time in different houses with a separate circle of friends. Florence became fat and drank too much. Her mind wandered and she died in 1922, a sad old lady of 53. William lived on to 1930. He died aged 82 and is buried in the Michael Kirk at Gordonstoun.

His third son, Michael, has given his own view on the affair: 'So ended a story of which the main problem was never solved. No one will ever know the truth about the Baccarat Case, whether my father did or did not cheat at cards while playing at Tranby Croft. By the time it was all over, did anyone – outside two families and a few counsel - care? The original issue had been obscured by Royal displeasure, international scandal and the outcries of the Nonconformist Press. In the Daily Mail, on the day after Papa died, there was written: 'The tenantry of Altyre are convinced that his death will be followed by the public vindication of his honour, but so far no documents or messages have been found which in any way throw light on the unhappy incident.' Fact is not tidy, like fiction. Real mysteries remain unsolved.'[250]

CHAPTER 16 - The Final Analysis

The question, as put by the defendants' counsel, Sir Charles Russell, was quite simple. Did Gordon-Cumming cheat or not? The jury thought he did but many others thought he did not. To this day there is no absolute proof either way. No new evidence has come to light. If there is something tucked away in the Royal Archives or family papers of the participants in the saga, it is likely it would have surfaced by now or is being deliberately kept secret. After Queen Victoria's death, her youngest daughter, Princess Beatrice, destroyed a quantity of her mother's voluminous writing if she thought it improper or too revealing. Are there people, even today, who would prefer to leave the stone unturned?

If you accept that the evidence in the trial was flawless, the witnesses unimpeachable, the judge's summing up exemplary and the jury's decision fairly considered, then you will be clear that he did cheat. However, we know that this was not quite the case. If, then, you think that Gordon-Cumming was pressurised into signing the incriminating document to keep the Prince out of the limelight and was persuaded that the secret would be kept, enabling him to retain his position in Society, albeit without playing cards, then you must believe that he did not cheat.

A way to analyse this is to take both sides of the argument, the cheating and the non-cheating, ask questions and look for reasons to support either, then reach a conclusion.

Gordon-Cumming the Innocent. Let us, first, take the proposition that he did not cheat. If he did not cheat why was he accused of doing so? The accusers could have been mistaken. What they saw was not actually cheating but cards being played by a very experienced old hand at the game who knew the 'gamesmanship' of Baccarat. The *coup de trois* – the 'doubling up of an existing stake – was a well-known, and legitimate, ploy. It was not so well known to the inexperienced eye. There was also the power of auto-suggestion; you see what you expect to see.

If one or two of the accusers were not mistaken, did they have ulterior motives for doing so? The key figure here was undoubtedly Lycett

Green. He clearly disliked Gordon-Cumming for a number of reasons. He was jealous of him and could easily detect the cold sneer from Gordon-Cumming with regard to Lycett Green's playboy life of having done very little and whose biggest source of pride and achievement was being a Master of Foxhounds. This compared badly with Gordon-Cumming's dashing good looks, war record and lieutenant colonelcy of the Foot Guards; things which Lycett Green could never hope to achieve. Gordon-Cumming had also stayed earlier at Tranby Croft before Ethel had married Lycett Green. While, in accordance with the conventions of the time, unmarried ladies were, generally, not subject to flirtatious advances (presumably due to the risk of unwanted pregnancy), that would have been no deterrent to Gordon-Cumming. He would have most certainly have flirted with her but did that lead to anything more? Whether it did or didn't, Lycett Green might well have suspected that it did. Later, after they had married, the Lycett Greens had Gordon-Cumming to dinner at their house. There is no evidence that he stayed with them but was there an opportunity to rekindle his flirtation? Lycett Green would have been very alert to this happening. On the other hand, what if Ethel had spurned Gordon-Cumming? It probably would have made little difference to Gordon-Cumming, there were plenty of others around. However, Ethel may have disliked him for it and made her feelings known to her husband thus fuelling his own dislike. Indeed, there was a rumour that it was actually Ethel who revealed the secret.[251] The Lycett Greens had plenty of reasons for bringing Gordon-Cumming down.

Others who might have had motives included Jack Wilson. Again, he was in the same rather useless playboy mould as Lycett Green; withdrawn by his father from university, briefly employed in the family firm but not really up to much. He would certainly have been jealous of Gordon-Cumming for the same reasons as Lycett Green and would have been highly sensitive to Gordon-Cumming's ridicule. Jack was also a close friend of Eddy, the Prince's son, when he was stationed with the 10th Hussars in York. There were rumours that Eddy was homosexual and involved in the Cleveland Street scandal. Was this a secret that Jack desperately wanted to keep and might well have had suspicions that Gordon-Cumming knew? If true, it would certainly have been known by the Secret Service and Gordon-Cumming had possible links to that organisation. Was there a suspicion that Gordon-Cumming had some sort of hold over, not only the Wilson family, but also the Prince himself because of this? Arthur Wilson was elected to the Marlborough Club, the Prince's exclusive 'set', in February 1891, therefore well before the court case.[252] One would have thought that the Prince would have wanted to distance himself from the Wilson family. Was this some sort of *quid pro quo* for something we don't know about?

Gordon-Cumming did antagonise people and while popular with a number of his fellows in the Regiment, there were, undoubtedly, others who disliked him. Was there some slight he perpetrated? Berkeley Levett was a loyal junior officer and did not relish his part in the affair. This was certainly the role he was expected to play but was it a charade? He failed to get Mrs Wilson to withdraw the accusation and, had that happened, the rest would have tumbled. How hard did he try? Was there something in the past between Berkeley Levett and Gordon-Cumming? Had Levett perhaps been reprimanded by Gordon-Cumming for some military misdemeanour and continued to resent it? There were more shadowy figures like Christopher Sykes, the court jester, and Count Lutzow,[253] the 'diplomat'. Neither of them would, on the surface, have been great supporters of Gordon-Cumming. It is not difficult to imagine Gordon-Cumming's opinion of these two and they probably knew it. They were not players and, ostensibly, were not involved – certainly not signatories to the infamous document – but they were bound to have known about it. Did either of them have opportunity to gossip about the events and spill the beans?

The three major players, the Prince of Wales, Lord Coventry and General Owen Williams never saw him cheat at all, yet they had all been present for the whole of both evenings. Why not? They were experienced players, perhaps Lord Coventry less so, but it is mystifying that they completely failed to notice anything untoward. The Prince would have played cards in many places, with all sorts of people and would have been highly attuned to someone not playing the game. How could Gordon-Cumming think he could have got away with it under that sort of scrutiny? Even Reuben Sassoon, who was the 'accountant' and not therefore playing, failed to spot anything.

Why wasn't Arthur Wilson, the host, brought into it? After all, it took place at home, with the Prince of Wales as one of his guests. He was responsible for what went on in his house and had an enormous amount to lose in prestige. He couldn't prevent Baccarat being played, despite his abhorrence of the game, but he could have taken an interest instead of sloping his shoulders and retiring to bed early. When he was eventually told by his wife, he could have approached the Prince and persuaded him to quash the accusations at once. Perhaps he didn't actually believe that Gordon-Cumming had cheated and merely hoped the whole thing would evaporate. Curiously, he was one of the signatories to the infamous document although he had had nothing to do with it.

One of the most difficult aspects of the case to understand is the alacrity with which Lord Coventry and General Owen Williams reached the decision that Gordon-Cumming had cheated, and having done so, gave such bad advice to the Prince. They completely failed to carry out even the most rudimentary investigation or confront Gordon-Cumming with his accusers. They panicked when Lycett Green threatened to expose the scandal at the races the next day and were prepared do anything to stop him. Not for one moment did they consider how Lycett Green was going to do this. Was he going to circulate round all his friends at the race-meeting and tell them? Was he going to announce it at, say, lunch? Was he going to persuade a commentator, if there was one, to make a public announcement? No, even with the most cursory thought it simply didn't hold water. Their motivation was entirely geared to keeping the Prince out of trouble and, worse, the courts. They were highly conscious of the Prince's role in the Mordaunt affair and were terrified of some sort of repeat performance. They concocted the thoroughly inept document tactic without thinking it through properly and realising that this sort of secret was bound to be revealed sooner rather than later.

However, the more fundamental question is did they really believe Gordon-Cumming had cheated? Whether they did or not, at the time, was irrelevant since, at all costs, they had to protect the Prince so everything fell under that. Given the drafting of the document and the secrecy, they were, on the face of it, quite happy to see Gordon-Cumming retaining his rank and position in the Army and continuing membership of his, and their, Clubs and walking around in Society as if nothing had happened. They were both men of stature and personal integrity, how could they possibly face a man on social occasions knowing him to be a cheat and a liar? This was just not believable. Despite what they had to say in court, in their hearts they cannot really have believed it. If they had, they would have hounded Gordon-Cumming from the start and, with the power and influence of the Private Secretaries, Knollys and Ponsonby, kept the Prince well away from it. However, did Owen Williams's conscience prick him to the extent that he had to justify his stance? He must have still felt the embarrassment from his outburst in court. In a letter from the Turf Club of 16 June[254] to Lycett Green he wrote, 'It was as clear as anything could possibly be that Cumming had cheated in a barefaced and systematic manner, and this being the fact, his offence could not be condoned and we were as lenient as possible under the circumstances. If the man had not the hide of a rhinoceros he would have taken advantage of his respite to leave the army and travel to the ends of the earth. The truth is he is a real bad one, and he instanced the old adage of the pitcher too often to the well. Now that his crime has been found out, there are 50 people to give instances of his cheating elsewhere.' Interestingly, not one of these 50 is named or, indeed, ever subsequently surfaced.

Much was made in court of Gordon-Cumming's signing of the document on the premise that no innocent man would have done so. The fact is, the opposite is true. No guilty man would have done so; he would have bluffed his way out of it and robustly challenged his accusers. Gordon-Cumming was bullied and put under enormous pressure to sign to protect the Prince, his old friend and future monarch. He claims to have lost his head in doing so. Russell ridiculed this by suggesting that men of Gordon-Cumming's experience in battle would not lose their head over a matter such as this. However, just because he was gallant in combat did not mean that, when under completely different kind of pressure, he did not wither under extreme duress. In a letter to Colonel Wynne Finch, a Regimental contemporary of Gordon-Cumming's, Lady Middleton wrote, 'My poor brother was always weak in his own affairs – always took wrong advice – always lacked moral courage (lots of physical!) This is a characteristic of our race – the women have the moral, the men the physical pluck.'[255]

One of the most important questions was whether the Prince really believed Gordon-Cumming had cheated. He merely based his decision on what he had been told and that there were five against one. While he was sufficiently protected by the system at Court not to have to bump into Gordon-Cumming too often and therefore be embarrassed by a known (secretly to him) cheat walking round in Society circles, there would have been times when he would not have been able to avoid him. To be seen to 'cut' his old friend in public would have raised suspicions. Why didn't he immediately dismiss the whole thing? He could easily have said to everybody they must have been mistaken; the Colonel was a very old friend of his and couldn't possibly have cheated. The young, inexperienced players would not have been up to the nuances and gamesmanship of the play which he, the Prince, being highly knowledgeable of card playing at this level, would be delighted to explain to them. He knew what trouble he was going to be in if this got out; apart from the Queen's severe displeasure and appearance in court, there would be the howling of the anti-monarchists. With this so apparent to him, he must have realised there was a better option, even if he had an uneasy feeling that Gordon-Cumming might have cheated. Was there, therefore, another reason for his lack of support for his old friend? There were rumours, not the least in Scots Guards regimental folk-lore, that Gordon-Cumming had covered up for the Prince's cheating. There is absolutely no evidence for this and it is very unlikely. The Prince, of course, liked to win but had no real incentive to cheat. Anyway, he was the banker on both nights and therefore not in a position to do so. Some say that because he didn't like losing, he failed to support Gordon-Cumming because he had lost to him. The sums were so paltry by the Prince's standards that, again, that is unlikely. Psychologically, though, he may have just simply hated losing.

What is much more significant is the relationship with Daisy Brooke. She was the Prince's favourite lady at the time and he was very frustrated that she couldn't attend the house party as she had to travel north for her step-father's funeral. What was much worse, however, was his surprise arrival two days before, on 6 September, at Gordon-Cumming's London house in Harriet Street to find Daisy, perhaps not actually *in flagrante delicto*, but certainly in a compromising situation with Gordon-Cumming. The Prince was expecting to meet her there but not with Gordon-Cumming present. There is no record of what was said between them but the conversations must have been stilted to say the least. What an opportunity for the Prince to revenge himself on his rival in love and, effectively, see him out of the game, exiled to darkest Morayshire.

Was there undue influence on the Lord Chief Justice? While Coleridge had been a close friend of Gladstone, and, therefore, that might have been the case, the current Prime Minister, Lord Salisbury, was not a particular acquaintance. Nevertheless, many people saw the trial as Gordon-Cumming v. the Monarchy and a Lord Chief Justice was not going to allow the Monarchy to lose. There is no evidence, though, that he was pressurised. The vital legal point, so clearly identified by Havers, was the weight of the burden of proof. Cheating was an indictable offence, needing a standard of proof *beyond reasonable doubt* to convict. Albeit the case was a civil one of slander where proof *on the balance of probabilities* was not so high, nevertheless, for the defendants to win they had to prove cheating to the higher level. The judge never pointed this out and made no mention of it in his opening remarks or summing-up. Given the evidence, it is unlikely it would have reached the required high level of proof. The judge was legally at fault let alone indulging in a biased summing-up. In a letter of 19 November 1955, Shane Leslie wrote to Cecily, Gordon-Cumming's youngest daughter, 'The Judge was hostile as well as sleepy. The witnesses worked as one man as though they had been coached what to say. All that was considered at stake was how to shield the Prince. The Jury saw to that as soon as the Judge served them their verdict. Your father was utterly bewildered realising he was in a trap. His thought moved slowly rather than in a panic. His great mistake was not throwing back the cheque which Reuben Sassoon wrote to him. He should have torn it up in his face. That was the disaster as he cashed and receipted his supposed cheating. That is where they caught him and an innocent man can often be caught.'

The social exile and ostracism was too high a price to pay to protect the good name of the Prince if Gordon-Cumming hadn't cheated. He must have thought, therefore, that the secret would be kept or that the Prince would protect him. He was probably too realistic to think that the secret could really be kept for long, so he would have to rely on the Prince himself to persuade the defendants personally to withdraw or the Palace officials, paranoid about another appearance in court, force the issue to avoid it.

If Gordon-Cumming did cheat why did he do so? The risk of detection was very real. Why take that risk? He had an enormous amount to lose. If detected, disgrace was inevitable, as we have seen. He had no need of the money; he was wealthy, even by standards of the time, and was engaged to an American heiress. He had no need to belittle the Prince of Wales by winning money off him. Indeed, he valued the Prince's friendship enormously and wouldn't have jeopardised that, even as a joke. He also had some ground to make up with the Prince for being discovered with Daisy. He would have regarded it well below his dignity to win against the callow youths who were playing the game with him and had no need to show how clever he was; they knew that. If he really cheated, why did he push his luck by continuing to do so the next night on a rather more efficiently set up table, where detection was even more likely?

*

Gordon-Cumming the Guilty. Gordon-Cumming was, by nature, a gambler. He liked to win whether it was for pennies or hundreds of pounds. Despite the fact he was wealthy enough not to worry about a few hundred pounds, he had no compunction about pocketing his winnings even after being accused of cheating.

There is a theory in the gambling world that some people, however wealthy, are born cheats. That is what they like doing, not just playing cards for the game's sake. There is no evidence that Gordon-Cumming had cheated previously although, once the news was out, there were always people, it was rumoured, who said that he did. But they remain unnamed.

Did Gordon-Cumming want to humiliate some the others, the self-made Wilsons, the shallow Lycett Green and the idle Jack? Did he need to show off, particularly to Ethel Lycett Green, whom he had taught to play the game?

With the Daisy affair on his mind, did he want to get one over the Prince by winning which he knew the Prince would not like? More fancifully, did he intend to trap the Prince into playing an illegal game?

Gordon-Cumming was an arrogant man. Did the rule of law not apply to him? Was he above it? Even today there have been politicians who thought that about themselves and ended up in prison.

Did he get an adrenaline rush by doing so? Here was a man who had experienced the height of excitement in big game hunting and military action. Was life now too boring and he needed the thrill of doing something illegal and cheating filled that need?

He really did sign the document, knowing he was guilty, as a way of evading retribution. Did he accept he had been found out and wanted to escape with the minimum personal damage? Would Berkeley Levett, a loyal junior officer in his Regiment, have testified against him if he thought the accusation to be untrue?

Finally, Lord Derby said at the time that everyone cheated when playing cards with the Prince of Wales because they didn't like being forced to play for the high stakes that the Prince insisted upon, which they could not afford. Was Gordon-Cumming seeking revenge for all those?

What are we left with? Present descendants fall, predictably, into two camps. Rupert Lycett Green, a former world class gambler and grandson of Edward, maintains that Gordon-Cumming did cheat. His experience tells him that, however rich, gamblers of a certain type, enjoyed cheating. In his view, Gordon-Cumming was such a one. 'With Gordon-Cumming's system of pushing chips forward and back (doubling after a win or after a loss) it was hard to tell if he was loading winnings or reducing losses after the result was known, but I suspect that what happened was this. At some point on a much earlier night, Gordon-Cumming pushed chips out late, on a genuine bet for the next hand, and though technically he should NOT have been paid out, he was. He then tried it again, earlier, knowing the result and got away with it. After that, on the slippery slope, he had two things in his favour. At least he thought so! The first is that all eyes were on the Prince of Wales and the card(s) as the Prince turned them over. Gordon-Cumming would sit down late and therefore as far away from the action as possible, so that no-one playing would be watching what he was doing with his pencil. Of course this made it easier for young Wilson, and then Lycett Green to watch Gordon-Cumming's actions (cheating or not) from the blind side of Gordon-Cumming. Secondly, Gordon-Cumming's failsafe, as he thought, was his association with the Prince of Wales. However this did not work, for two reasons. Firstly, Lycett Green should have kept his trap shut as the prevailing social mores indicated. Jealous maybe, but Lycett was also stubborn and very determined when his mind was made up and he maintained all his life, with support from other country house owners where Gordon-Cumming had been a guest, that he had been observed cheating. The Prince of Wales was well capable of dumping friends if it suited him (see Christopher Sykes) and at this point (re Babbling Brooke) it certainly did that.'[256]

*

Simon, Earl of Woolton, great-grandson of Gordon-Cumming, does not believe he cheated. He reckoned he played very close to the wind and indulged in fairly sharp practice but not sufficient to constitute cheating. It was more a matter of gamesmanship than anything else.[257]

Jane Gordon-Cumming, a granddaughter of Gordon-Cumming, had the benefit of reading her father, Michael's, account of his life with Sir William and produced a proposal for a book on the lives of her grandparents. In her view, 'My own conclusion is that William didn't cheat. Florence and the rest of the family were utterly convinced of his innocence, and although he didn't discuss it, I feel she must have known. And why would he? He wasn't short of money. He'd been playing with the Prince and his set for years. He had no motive to suddenly start cheating his friends. On the other hand I don't really think it was a put up job by enemies of his or the Prince. Those people genuinely thought they saw him cheating, and were surprised and shocked. William was put in the unenviable position of trying to save Bertie from embarrassment without compromising his own good name. Victoria seems to have used him as a scapegoat for her disapproval of her son's way of life, so that the court case became 'William G-C v. Royalty', rather than trying to get at the truth of what happened, so judge and jury felt compelled to find against him, whatever the facts. A muddle rather than conspiracy, I suspect.'[258]

We will never know, unless new evidence comes to light, whether Gordon-Cumming cheated or not. It remains and will probably continue to do, as one of those mysteries which line up alongside the *Mary Celeste*. While Gordon-Cumming lost his case, there remain too many unanswered questions; too many faults of law and too many curiously differing accounts and views to persuade anyone that he did.

On the balance of probabilities however, on which he should have been judged, he cannot have cheated.

EPILOGUE

CHEATING POKER STAR
LOSES £7.8 M WINNINGS

One of the [world's] most successful poker players has lost a claim for £7.8 million of winnings from Britain's oldest casino after a judge ruled he cheated.[259]

Phil Ivey argued that he was using a legitimate technique, called edge sorting (taking advantage of a minor imperfection on the edge of the pattern on the back of the card which turned a 1% advantage to the dealer to a 6.5% advantage to the player), while playing punto banco, a form of baccarat at Crockfords casino in Mayfair, London, in August 2012.

Mr Ivey who has won ten bracelets at the World Series of Poker championships, had told the High Court: "If I am labelled a cheat, that's death."

He is currently being sued in the United States for $9.6 million (£5.9 million) in winnings, after he used the same technique in games of baccarat at the Borgata casino in Atlantic City.

Mr Justice Mitting said yesterday that Mr Ivey was a "truthful witness", but dismissed his claim to recover his disputed winnings. He ruled that the player's actions amounted to "cheating for the purposes of civil law".

The judge said he had "given himself an advantage" by tricking a croupier. "The fact that Mr Ivey was genuinely convinced that he did not cheat, and the practice commanded considerable support from others, was not determinative of the question of whether it amounted to cheating."

Mr Ivey said outside court: "I am obviously disappointed. As I said in court, it is not my nature to cheat and I would never do anything to risk my reputation."

ACKNOWLEDGEMENTS

It is a rare privilege to be allowed to examine papers in the Royal Archives and I am most grateful to Her Majesty Queen Elizabeth II for giving me permission to do so and to the Senior Archivist, Miss Pamela Clark, for handling my research at Windsor Castle.

Jane Ridley, Professor of History at Buckingham University and author of *Bertie: A Life of Edward VII*, gave me enormous encouragement and kindly read through an early draft, giving me helpful direction and suggestions.

I am eternally in debt to Magnus Linklater CBE, formerly Editor of *The Scotsman* and Scottish Editor of *The Times*. Magnus took up a great deal of time ploughing through my drafts and editing gently but firmly throughout. It was an honour for me to have him take such care over my clumsy production.

It is a great pleasure to have the Foreword written by Joshua Rozenberg. He and I are old sparring partners when he was the legal correspondent of *The Daily Telegraph* and I was the Complaints Commissioner of the Bar. I am extremely grateful.

Of the families involved in this saga, I very much appreciated the wholehearted cooperation of Jane Gordon-Cumming, Rupert Lycett Green, Simon, Earl of Woolton and Clive Wilson. Sadly, the present Baronet, Sir Alastair Gordon-Cumming, felt unable to do so since his terrible accident with poisonous mushrooms.

Always helpful and supportive, albeit necessarily from the touch line, were Philip Bambury in Germany and William Mader in America.

Understandably, I was a frequent visitor to Regimental Headquarters, Scots Guards, and am most grateful for the help I was given.

BIBLIOGRAPHY

THE ROYAL ARCHIVES
Windsor Castle
(All references are preceded by **RA**)

VIC/MAIN/L/3/59
VIC/MAIN/Y/182
VIC/MAIN/Z/50/22, 45, 47
VIC/MAIN/Z/199/74-75
VIC/MAIN/Z/475/15
VIC/ADDA4/26, 31-33
VIC/ADDC7/1: 1891 bundle re: Tranby Croft
VIC/ADDA12/1749-1750, 1752, 1755, 1771-1772, 1774, 1788-1790, 1792
VIC/ADDA15/5710
VIC/ADDU32: 18, 21, 24 Feb 1891, 8, 9, 12, 16 Jun 1891
VIC/ADDC2/48
GV/PRIV/AA18/28-29, 55
GV/PRIV/AA19/10-11
GV/PRIV/AA31/17-18
VIC/ADDC39/26-33

MAIN SOURCES
Published
Attwood, Gertrude M., *The Wilsons of Tranby Croft,* (Beverley: Hutton Press Ltd, 1988)
British Library, Newspaper Room for contemporary newspapers
Chronicling America for contemporary United States newspapers
Gleichen, Major General Lord Edward, *With the Camel Corps up the Nile,* (London: Chapman & Hall, 1888)
Goldsworthy, Adrian, *In the Name of Rome,* (London: Weidenfeld & Nicolson, 2003)

Gordon-Cumming, Roualeyn, *Five Years of a Hunter's Life in the Far Interior of South Africa,* (London: John Murray, 1850)

Hattersley, Roy, *The Edwardians,* (London: Little Brown, 2004)

Havers, Michael, the Rt. Hon., Grayson, Edward, Shankland, Peter, *The Royal Baccarat Scandal* (London: Souvenir Press, 1988)

Journal of the Household Brigade

Legge, Edward, *King Edward in his True Colours,* (London: Eveliegh Nash, 1912)

Magnus, Philip, *King Edward the Seventh,* (London: John Murray, 1964)

Matthew, H. C. G., *Edward VII (1841–1910),* Oxford Dictionary of National Biography, Oxford University Press, online edition, May 2007.

Maurice, General Sir F, *History of the Scots Guards Volume 2,* (London: Chatto & Windus, 1934)

Napier, Elma, *Winter is in July,* (London: Jonathan Cape, 1949)

Napier, Elma, *Youth is a Blunder,* (London: Jonathan Cape, 1948)

Ponsonby, Arthur, *Henry Ponsonby, Queen Victoria's Private Secretary,* (London: Macmillan & Co Ltd, 1942)

Purcell, Mark, *Making History: The Library at Wallington,* (National Trust Historic Houses and Collections Annual 2014)

Ridley, Jane, *Bertie – A Life of Edward VII* (London: Chatto & Windus, 2012)

Roby, Kinley, *The King, the Press and the People, a study of Edward VII,* (London: Barrie & Jenkins, 1975)

St Aubyn, Giles, *Edward VII Prince and King,* (London: Collins, 1979)

Teignmouth Shore, W., *The Baccarat Case.* (London: Read Books, William Hodge & Co, 1932)

Tomes, J., *Cumming, Sir William Gordon Gordon-, fourth baronet (1848–1930),* Oxford Dictionary of National Biography, Oxford University Press, September 2007.

Tulloch, Major General Sir Alexander Bruce KCB CMG, *Recollections of Forty Years' Service,* (Edinburgh & London: William Blackwood & Sons, 1903)

Wolseley, Major General Sir Garnet, *The Soldier's Pocket-book for Field Service,* (London: Macmillan & Co, 1874)

Unpublished

Archives, Regimental Headquarters Scots Guards

Gordon-Cumming, Jane, Proposal for *The American Heiress and the Scottish Rake - The True Story of the Royal Baccarat Scandal.*

National Library of Scotland Inventory, Dep.175, Gordon-Cumming of Altyre & Gordonstoun

The Scots Guards in Egypt, 1882, The Letters of Lieutenant C B Balfour, Edited by S G P Ward, MA, B.Litt. Scots Guards Regimental Archives.

ENDNOTES

A NOTE ON MONEY

[1] See Lawrence H. Officer & Samuel H. Williamson, "Measures of Worth," MeasuringWorth, 2012.
www.measuringworth.com/worthmeasures.php

CHAPTER 1 - The Cheat

[2] RA VIC/MAIN/Y/182.7

CHAPTER 2 - The Guards

[3] Napier, Elma, *Youth is a Blunder,* (London: Jonathan Cape, 1948) – afterwards 'Napier'

[4] After Sir William Gordon-Cumming's death in 1930, Gordonstoun was obtained by Kurt Hahn to be run as a school. The buildings were in need of much repair and at the start of the first academic year there were only two pupils. During the 1960s, Prince Charles attended the school at the instigation of his father, the Duke of Edinburgh, who had been one of the first pupils, having previously been educated at Salem in Germany. Prince Charles did not enjoy the regime, which he later called 'Colditz in kilts.' Princes Andrew and Edward followed in their father's and elder brother's footsteps.

[5] Enlarged in 1931, the original house was demolished in 1962.

[6] Gordon-Cumming, Roualeyn, *Five Years of a Hunter's Life in the Far Interior of South Africa,* (London: John Murray, 1850). It was rumoured that he was one of the models for Rider Haggard's *Allan Quartermain* novels.

[7] James Gordon Bennett Jr, owner of the *New York Herald,* was the third richest man in America, after the Astors and the Vanderbilts. He believed in not just reporting news but creating it. As such, in 1870 he sent Henry Stanley to find Dr Livingstone. The fact that Livingstone had not needed

finding was irrelevant; it caused an international sensation and unforgettable words.

[8] Memories of an Old Etonian 1860-1912, George Greville, Hutchinson & Co, London, 1919.

[9] In modern medical terms, he was suffering from *essential tremor*. It is labelled *essential* as there is no associated disease that causes it. It runs in families and consists of uncontrolled shaking movements of hands. It is exacerbated by stress, tiredness, and emotions such as anger or too much adrenaline. There is no cure but can be reduced by drinking alcohol! [The author suffers from it].

[10] Miss Eleanor Cracknell, Eton College Archivist, in correspondence with the author.

[11] Gordon-Cumming, Jane, Proposal for *The American Heiress and the Scottish Rake - The True Story of the Royal Baccarat Scandal.*

[12] Chris Potter, Wellington College Archivist, in correspondence with the author.

[13] In 1877, Queen Victoria restored the previous title of Scots Guards

[14] The Cardwell Reforms were a series of reorganisations of the British Army undertaken by Secretary of State for War, Edward Cardwell, between 1868 and 1874 with Gladstone's support. The Reforms were not that radical but the aim was to centralise the power of the War Office, abolish purchase of officers' commissions, prohibit some of the harsher punishments such as branding and flogging, and create reserve forces stationed in Britain by establishing short terms of service for soldiers.

[15] *Journal of The Household Brigade*, Brigade Miscellany p.272.

[16] The title 'Guardsman' was not introduced until November 1918.

[17] The old symbol for £.

[18] Campaign medals of his grandfather and great uncle are in the possession of the author.

[19] *The Military Career of General Sir Henry Brackenbury 1856-1904: The Thinking Man's Soldier*, PhD Thesis, Christopher Michael Brice, De Montford University, April 2009.

[20] Dr Anthony Morton, Curator, Sandhurst Collection, in correspondence with the author.

[21] *Journal of The Household Brigade*, 1867, p.70.

[22] *Journal of The Household Brigade*, 1867, p.69.

[23] Incorrect. Bamford, the Guards Club barber, was not around until the 1950s-60s.

[24] Gleichen, Major General Lord Edward, *A Guardsman's Memories,* (Edinburgh & London: William Blackwood & Sons, 1932)

[25] National Library of Scotland, Inventory Dep.175 Gordon-Cumming of Altyre & Gordonstoun 177.

[26] *Journal of the Household Brigade* 1877, Notes of a Sporting Tour of India p. 244-249.

[27] A deer with three-pointed antlers.

[28] The Proclamation took place at Delhi on New Year's Day. The Viceroy, Lord Lytton, processed through the city, seated in a gilded howdah on a massive elephant. He was attended by all the Governors, Lieutenant-Governors, Chief Commissioners, and Governor-Generals' Agents throughout India, and some 15,000 troops.

[29] A water-course, very often dried up. In Arabic, a wadi.

[30] The name originates with a rifle built by James Purdey in 1856 and named the *Express Train*, a marketing phrase intended to denote the considerable velocity of the bullet it fired. It was not the first rifle or cartridge of this type but it was Purdey's name *Express* that stuck.

[31] A senior and experienced Indian hunting guide.

[32] He is coy about naming his fellow shots; maybe security or simply that they might have been on some illegal leave!

[33] Ramachandra Pandurang Tope (1814–1859), better known as Tatya Tope was a Maratha leader in the Indian Mutiny and one of its more renowned generals. He was defeated by General Napier's British Indian troops at Ranod and after a further defeat at Sikar abandoned the campaign. Finally he was betrayed by his trusted friend Man Singh. He was executed by the British Government at Shivpuri on 18 April 1859.

CHAPTER 3 – Zulus

[34] *The Times*, 28 Feb 1879 reporting the departure in the early hours of the following day.

[35] *The Journal of The Household Brigade 1879*. MISCELLANEOUS pages 238-243

[36] *The Times*, 28 Feb 1879; the number includes officers and men.

[37] The Gatling gun is one of the best-known early rapid-fire weapons and a forerunner of the modern machine gun. Invented by Richard Gatling, it was used by the Union forces during the American Civil War, which was the first time it was employed in action. Although the first Gatling gun was capable of firing continuously, it required a person to crank it; therefore it was not a true automatic weapon. Nonetheless, the Gatling gun represented a huge leap in firearm technology.

[38] *The Western Daily Press*, Bristol, 28 February 1879 and *Aberdeen Evening Express*, 1 May 1879.

[39] 38 degrees 40' 25.48"S / 19 degrees 25' 39.50"E. Now an official dive site but not popular owing to the large number of great white sharks in the area.

[40] For Captain Carey's later involvement in the death of the Prince Imperial, see the author's book Scapegoats – Thirteen Victims of Military Injustice (London: Elliott & Thompson, 2013)

[41] On 26 February 1852, while transporting troops to Algoa Bay, the *Birkenhead* was wrecked at Danger Point, near Gansbaai, 88 miles from Cape Town. There were not enough serviceable lifeboats for all the passengers, and the soldiers famously stood firm, thereby allowing the women and children to board the boats safely. Only 193 of the 643 people on board survived, and the soldiers' chivalry gave rise to the "women and children first" protocol when abandoning ship.

[42] Nowadays, a bronze oak leaf is worn on the relevant medal ribbon.

[43] National Library of Scotland Inventory, Dep.175, Gordon-Cumming of Altyre & Gordonstoun,
Gordon-Cumming's 1879 diary.

[44] See *Scapegoats*

[45] Colenso, F.E., *History of the Zulu War and Its Origin*, (London, 1880)

[46] Gordon-Cumming returned on the Indian troopship Euphrates which left Durban on 16 August and arrived at Portsmouth on 18 September – The Times 20 Sept 1879.

[47] *London Gazette*, 21 August 1879. Issue 24754, page 5106.

[48] National Library of Scotland Inventory, Dep.175, Gordon-Cumming of Altyre & Gordonstoun,
Gordon-Cumming diary 1881.

CHAPTER 4 - Egypt

[49] Maurice, General Sir F, *History of the Scots Guards Volume 2,* (London: Chatto & Windus, 1934)

[50] The present (14th) Earl fought as a platoon commander in the 2nd Battalion's assault on Tumbledown Mountain in the Falklands Conflict 1982.

[51] *The Scots Guards in Egypt, 1882,* The Letters of Lieutenant C B Balfour, Edited by S G P Ward, MA, B.Litt. Scots Guards Regimental Archives.

[52] National Library of Scotland Inventory, Dep.175, Gordon-Cumming of Altyre & Gordonstoun

Gordon-Cumming diary 1884. *– Afterwards 'Gordon-Cumming diary'.*

[53] Gleichen, Major General Lord Edward, *With the Camel Corps up the Nile,* (London: Chapman & Hall, 1888)

[54] Gordon-Cumming diary 19 November.

[55] Burnaby was commissioned into the Royal Horse Guards in 1859. A born adventurer he took part in balloon ascents and travelled through Spain and Russia. In the summer of 1874 he accompanied the Carlist forces in Spain as correspondent of *The Times,* but before the end of the war he was transferred to Africa to report on Gordon's expedition to the Sudan. Returning to England in March 1875, he penetrated the Khanate of Khiva in Russian Asia, which had just been closed to travellers. His then travelled on horseback, through Asia Minor, from Scutari to Erzerum. In 1882 he crossed the English Channel in a hot air balloon. Having been disappointed to miss the Egyptian Campaign of 1882, he participated in the Suakin campaign of 1884 without official leave, and was wounded at El Teb when acting as an intelligence officer before being killed at Abu Klea.

[56] Lucy H.W., *Cornhill Times* quoted in *North Otago Times* 6 March 1909.

CHAPTER 5 - Agents of the Crown

[57] Tulloch, Major General Sir Alexander Bruce KCB CMG, *Recollections of Forty Years' Service,* (Edinburgh & London: William Blackwood & Sons, 1903) – *afterwards 'Tulloch.'*

[58] Tulloch p.177

[59] Tulloch p.208

[60] Wolseley, Major General Sir Garnet, *The Soldier's Pocket-book for Field Service,* (London: Macmillan & Co, 1874)

[61] Tulloch p.213

[62] Exelby, James, History Today Volume 56, Issue 11 2006

[63] Tulloch p.245

[64] Tulloch p.248 (in French)

[65] Gordon-Cumming diary 1884.

[66] Tulloch p.213

[67] Tulloch p.168

[68] Attwood p.88.

[69] Havers, Michael, the Rt. Hon., Grayson, Edward, Shankland, Peter, *The Royal Baccarat Scandal* (London: Souvenir Press, 1988) – *afterwards 'Havers'.*

[70] Jason Tomes

[71] Havers p.24

[72] Melba was born Helen Mitchell. For her stage name she adopted part of the name of her home town, Melbourne. *Peach Melba* was the dessert created for her by Escoffier when she was staying at the Savoy in 1892.

[73] Napier, Elma, *Winter is in July,* (London: Jonathan Cape, 1949) p.74.

CHAPTER 6 - The Prince

[74] 'My principal occupation is to combat ignorance and prejudice ... to enlighten minds, cultivate morality, and to make people as happy as it suits human nature, and as the means at my disposal permit.' Frederick the Great (1712–86)

[75] St Aubyn, Giles, *Edward VII Prince and King,* (London: Collins, 1979) p.17. – *Afterwards 'St Aubyn.'*

[76] Stockmar was, originally, the personal physician and adviser to Prince Leopold of Saxe-Coburg-Gotha at the time of Leopold's marriage to Charlotte Princess of Wales. He is alleged to have played a significant role in the arrangement of the marriage between Queen Victoria and Prince Albert in 1840, after which he became their unofficial counsellor. A true *eminence grise*, his prominence in political circles and influence with the Royal Family led to resentment at what was seen to be German interference in English affairs. Dying in 1863, he is buried at Frogmore, the Royal cemetery

[77] Ridley, Jane, *Bertie – A Life of Edward VII* (London: Chatto & Windus, 2012) p.26. – *Afterwards 'Ridley.'*

[78] St Aubyn p.24

[79] St Aubyn p.37

[80] Ridley p.35

[81] Ridley p.36

[82] St Aubyn p.39

[83] St Aubyn p.41

[84] Ridley p.44

[85] St Aubyn p.45

[86] Ridley p.48

[87] *Evening Star,* Washington, DC, 12 July1860

[88] St Aubyn p.48

[89] Ridley p.51

[90] Ridley p.63

[91] Roby p.88

[92] EDWARDIAN PROMENADE *Edwardians Unbuttoned*, Evangeline Holland 2008.

[93] Ridley p.233

[94] Ridley p.270

[95] St Aubyn p.139

[96] Ridley p.113

[97] Ridley p.145

[98] Ridley p.58

[99] St Aubyn p.151

[100] http://decadenthandbook.wordpress.com/2009/11/24/the-great-courtesans.

[101] The Prince of Wales attended Kanne's funeral at Brompton Cemetery on 29 April 1888.

[102] Ridley p.135

[103] Purcell, Mark, *Making History: The Library at Wallington,* (National Trust Historic Houses and Collections Annual 2014)

[104] Ridley p.143

[105] St Aubyn p.84

[106] Ridley p.137

[107] Roby p.171

[108] St Aubyn p.161

[109] *Leeds Mercury,* 22 February 1870 for example

[110] *The South-western,* Shreveport, Louisiana, 16 March 1870

[111] Ridley p.166

[112] Ridley p.171 footnote

[113] Ridley in conversation with the author

[114] Ridley p.272

[115] Ridley p.273

[116] Newton himself was later convicted of obstruction of justice for helping his clients escape abroad, and was sentenced to six weeks in prison.

[117] Ridley p.273

[118] Ridley p.263

CHAPTER 7 - The Shipping Magnate

[119] Attwood, Gertrude M., *The Wilsons of Tranby Croft,* (Beverley: Hutton Press Ltd, 1988) – *afterwards 'Attwood'*

[120] Sykes was a close friend of the Prince of Wales. He entertained in great splendour at Brantingham Thorpe, his country house in Yorkshire, during the Doncaster Races, and at his London home in Berkeley Square. The Prince exploited his friend and often humiliated him, for example, on one occasion, pouring a decanter of brandy over his head and having him locked out of his house when wearing fancy dress. However, Sykes's lavish entertainment soon put a strain on his finances and he nearly went bankrupt in 1890, forcing him to sell his houses. At a general election two years later, he lost his parliamentary seat. Despite this, the Prince of

Wales never forgot his devoted friend, and after Sykes's death in 1898, he installed a tablet to his memory at Westminster Abbey.

[121] He was High Sheriff of Yorkshire 1891-92 and elected to the Marlborough Club in February 1891, having been proposed in March 1889 – Legge, Edward, *King Edward in his True Colours,* (London: Eveliegh Nash, 1912) p.130. – *Afterwards 'Legge'.* There was a sarcastic report of this in the New York Times of 26 March 1891 - Roby, Kinley, *The King, the Press and the People, a study of Edward VII,* (London: Barrie & Jenkins, 1975) p.244. – *afterwards 'Roby'*

CHAPTER 8 - A Game of Baccarat

[122] Attwood p86

[123] Havers p.23

[124] Teignmouth Shore, W., *The Baccarat Case.* (London: Read Books, William Hodge & Co, 1932) p.26. – *Afterwards 'Shore'.*

[125] Ridley p. 281

[126] Regina v Richard Dodge The National Archives HO 45/9965/X19516

[127] Another friend of the Prince's was Count Karl Kinsky, sometime Austro-Hungarian Ambassador to London, who won the Grand National in 1883. Was there a connection with Lutzow?

[128] *The Times*, 5 June 1891 p.12 issue 33343

[129] Attwood

[130] Strictly speaking the *cinq à sept* was the time when Frenchmen left their offices and visited their mistresses before returning home to their wives.

[131] Magnus, Philip, *King Edward the Seventh,* (London: John Murray, 1964) p.223 (Hardinge Papers). – *Afterwards 'Magnus.'*

[132] Napier, *Youth...* p.138

[133] Ridley p. 283, Attwood p. 89

[134] Attwood p. 90

[135] Attwood p. 92

[136] Queen's Regulations for the Army 1890, paragraph 41

[137] RA VIC/MAIN/Y/182/7

[138] Roby p. 236

[139] This letter, allegedly in the possession of Lewis's descendants in

America, was sold at auction on 11 Dec 2015 by Dreweatts & Bloomsbury. Photograph of it is held by the author.

[140] Magnus p. 224 and RA GV/PRIV/AA18/29

CHAPTER 9 - The Gathering Storm

[141] RA/GV/PRIV/AA 18/28-29

[142] A copy, made by Lewis in his Instructions to Counsel is in RA/VIC/MAIN/Y/182/27. The original, allegedly in the possession of Lewis's descendants in America, was sold at auction on 11 Dec 2015 by Dreweatts & Bloomsbury. Photograph of it is held by the author.

[143] RA VIC/ADDC39/26

[144] Most likely to be Gordon-Cumming's letter to Williams of 10 September.

[145] RA VIC/ADDC39/27

[146] RA VIC/ADDC39/28

[147] RA VIC/ADDC/39/30

[148] The address of one of Gordon-Cumming's clubs.

[149] Havers p.41

[150] Legge p.138

[151] RA VIC/ADDC39/31

[152] RA/VIC/MAIN/Y/182/28 pages 15 & 16

[153] Sir Francis Knollys, was Private Secretary to the Prince of Wales 1870-1901. He then became Private Secretary to the King on his accession.

[154] Sir Henry Ponsonby was Queen Victoria's Private Secretary 1870–1895.

[155] Having telegraphed the Prince on 24 January, Gordon-Cumming wrote a letter on the same day, asking for an interview, the original of which was sold by Dreweatts & Bloomsbury on 11 December 2015.

[156] RA VIC/ADDC39/32

[157] RA/VIC/MAIN/Y/182/27

[158] RA/VIC/MAIN/Y/182/5

[159] Havers p.50 quoting RA Y/182/28

[160] Known in the Regiment as the Duke of Canute.

[161] RA/VIC/MAIN/Y/182/11

[162] Magnus p.226 and RA/VIC/ADDA 12/1752
[163] Havers p.61 quoting RA/ADD/MSS A/12
[164] *Wichita Daily Eagle*, Kansas, 17 March, and *The Record-Union*, Sacramento, 6 March, quoting the English newspapers *Daily News* and *Echo* which were later forced into a retraction.
[165] RA/VIC/ADDA12/1750
[166] Section 17 of the Gaming Act 1845. It still is.
[167] Havers p.50 quoting RA Y/182/27
[168] Havers p.53
[169] RA/VIC/MAIN/Y/182/27 p.6
[170] Havers p.48 quoting RA Y/182/27
[171] RA/VIC/MAIN/Y/182/5
[172] RA/VIC/ADDA12/1752
[173] RA/VIC/MAIN/Y/182/10
[174] Knollys's father, Sir William 1797-1883, served in the 3rd Guards (afterwards Scots Guards) in the Peninsular Campaign and was Comptroller of the Household to the Prince of Wales 1862-77. He was also Colonel of the Scots Guards. Clearly, this did not affect his son's proper loyalty to his master. A number of the Knollys family later served in the Regiment.
[175] RA/VIC/ADDU32:24 Feb 91
[176] Clarke, Sir Edward QC, *The Story of My Life*, (London: John Murray,1918) p.295
[177] Fordham, Edward Wilfrid, *Notable Cross-Examinations*, (London: Constable & Co Ltd, 1951), quoting Sir Edward Clarke, p.194
[178] Summerscale, Kate, *The Suspicions of Mr Whicher*, (London: Bloomsbury, 2008)
[179] Havers p.71
[180] Havers p.64
[181] Havers p.65

CHAPTER 10 - The Case for the Plaintiff

[182] Teignmouth Shore, W., *The Baccarat Case*. (London: Read Books, William Hodge & Co, 1932). This book, of 294 pages is, in effect, a transcript of the trial and is heavily drawn on in these chapters, without

further reference.

[183] Clarke, Sir Edward QC, *The Story of My Life*, (London: John Murray,1918), p.296

[184] Conversation author and the present Lord Coleridge 11 October 2014.

[185] Pall Mall Gazette, 1 June 1891, issue 8173.

[186] The Wheeling Daily Intelligencer, Wheeling, West Virginia, USA, 2 June 1891.

[187] It was said, no doubt with exaggeration, that the Prince struck Chief Justice Gascoigne for sitting in judgment on one of his debauched companions in 1411. The Prince was, allegedly, sent to jail for contempt.

[188] *Manchester Guardian*, 1 June 1891, p.4

[189] Havers p.70, quoting *Star*.

[190] Havers p.70, quoting *Pall Mall Gazette*.

[191] *St Paul Daily Globe*, St Paul, Minnesota, USA, 2 June 1891

[192] Havers p.84

[193] *Pall Mall Gazette* 2 June 1891 issue 8174

[194] *Los Angeles Herald*, Los Angeles, California, 3 June 1891.

[195] *The Pall Mall Gazette* did some investigation into the intrepid juryman and discovered he was a Mr Goddard Clarke from Camberwell and a worthy of local society being a member of the London Chamber of Commerce and a Liveryman of the Cooper's Company, who gave much time to religious work, Havers p.108.

[196] Yet, on the second night, the Prince of Wales told Gordon-Cumming, 'to take his hands off the table or move his hands further back, because he could not see what the stake was.' So, he was sufficiently aware of the player's handling of stakes but not enough to detect anything untoward in connection with altering those stakes. Why not?

[197] Levett was not there. This was corrected later.

[198] RA VIC/ADDC39/33

CHAPTER 11 - The Defence

[199] The *Pittsburg Dispatch,* 4 June 1891

[200] *The Times*, Richmond, Virginia, 5 June 1891

[201] RA/VIC/MAIN/Y/182/27 page 2

[202] *The Los Angeles Herald,* 4 June 1891

[203] *St Paul Daily Globe*, St Paul, Minnesota, USA, 4 June 1891

[204] *The Evening Herald*, Shenandoah, Pennsylvania, 4 June 1891

[205] *Pall Mall Gazette*, 4 June 1891, Issue 8176

[206] Contained in Instructions to Counsel RA/VIC/MAIN/Y/182/27

[207] Havers p.143

[208] RA VIC/MAIN/Y/182/28 page 6

[209] Havers p.147

[210] Havers p.152

CHAPTER 12 - Closing Stages

[211] RA/VIC/ADDU32 9 June 1891

[212] RA/VIC/ADDU32 12 June 1891

[213] Of course, there were no ladies on juries in those days.

[214] *Los Angeles Herald*, California, 9 June 1891

[215] Stevens & Haynes, Law Publishers, Bell Yard, Temple Bar, London

[216] *The Sun*, New York, 9 June 1891

[217] *Pittsburg Daily Dispatch*, Pittsburg, Pennsylvania 9 June 1891

[218] *The Morning Call*, San Francisco, California 9 June 1891

CHAPTER 14 – Verdict

[219] *Salt Lake City Herald*, Utah, 10 June 1891

[220] Sources for this chapter are, Gordon-Cumming, Jane, *Proposal for The American Heiress and the Scottish Rake - The True Story of the Royal Baccarat Scandal* - Chapter 1; *New York Times,* 21 July 1876; *New York Tribune,* 22 July 1876; *Evening Star*, Washington 22 July 1876; *The Sun*, New York 22 July 1876; *The Worthington Advance*, Minnesota 22 July 1876; *The Wheeling Daily Intelligencer, 2*2 July 1876; *Yachting World Newsletter,* Yachting Club of America.

[221] The town house has gone, but the Garner Mansion still stands in Castleton Street, New Brighton, now part of the Richmond University Medical Centre.

[222] *Truth* 18 June 1891.

[223] Clarke, Sir Edward QC, *The Story of My Life*, (London: John Murray, 1918)

[224] *The Morning Call*, San Francisco, 12 June 1891.

[225] *New York World*, 21 June 1891

[226] Coleridge, Ernest Hartley, *Life and Correspondence of John Duke, Lord Coleridge*, (London: William Heinemann, 1904) Volume 2, p.30, letter 17 June 1891.

[227] *The Hidden Power of Self-deception*, Joseph T. Hallinan

[228] Henry Du Pré Labouchère (1831–1912) was an English politician, writer, publisher and theatre owner. He was a junior member of the British diplomatic service, a Member of Parliament in the 1860s and again from 1880 to 1906, and edited and funded his own magazine, *Truth*.

[229] *Pall Mall Gazette*, 2 June 1891, Issue 8174

[230] *The Pall Mall Gazette*, 10 June 1891, Issue 8181

[231] Lustgarten, Edgar, *Honour at Stake*, Aberdeen Evening Express, 4 June 1954.

[232] RA GV/PRIV/AA19/10.

[233] *Western Daily Press*, 11 September 1930, CARD PARTY SCANDAL, New Light on the Tranby Croft Affair.

[234] Magnus p.457

[235] *The Times,* 15 June 1891

[236] *The Times,* 11 June 1891

[237] *The Times*, 10 June 1891

CHAPTER 15 – Aftermath

[238] *London Gazette*, 12 June 1891, Issue 26171, p. 3118

[239] Author in conversation with Lawson's great grandson, Harry, 7th Lord Burnham.

[240] Lawson later had an outstanding military career in the Boer War, being awarded the DSO.

[241] The author's first Commanding Officer 1st Battalion Scots Guards 1960.

[242] RA VIC/ADDC7/1: bundle of letters re Tranby Croft.

[243] *The Times*, 15 June 1891

[244] Sir John Randolph Leslie, 3rd Baronet (24 September 1885 – 14 August 1971), was an Irish-born diplomat and writer. He was a first cousin of Sir Winston Churchill.

[245] Henry William FitzGerald de Ros, 22nd Baron de Ros (1793 – 1839) was involved in a gambling scandal in 1836. He was accused of cheating at Graham's Club by marking the cards with his thumbnail. He sued his accusers for libel, but lost the case.

[246] National Library of Scotland Inventory, Dep.175, Gordon-Cumming of Altyre & Gordonstoun102, 1-3.

[247] Inventory Dep. 175 102, 4.

[248] Napier, 'Youth...p.87

[249] All her present day descendants own a share of land in Texas but, sadly, no oil – so far. Author in conversation with Simon, Earl of Woolton.

[250] Napier, 'Youth....p.237

CHAPTER 16 - The Final Analysis

[251] *Pittsburgh Dispatch*, 4 February 1891.

[252] *The Pall Mall Gazette* actually published on Monday 8 June that Arthur Stanley Wilson had been elected member of the Marlborough Club on Thursday 4 June. It was incorrect.

[253] *The Manchester Courier and Lancashire General Advertiser* reported that a duel had been fought in Vienna on 28 December 1890 between Count von Deym, Austrian Ambassador in London, and Count von Lutzow, his Secretary at the Embassy. It was unclear whether the weapons were pistols or swords but neither party was harmed which says little for the martial abilities of Austrian diplomats. It was apparently a row over the precedence of their wives on official occasions in London.

[254] *Sunday Times Magazine* 2 March 1969. Shown to the newspaper for first time by Sir Stephen Lycett Green, his grandson.

[255] 17 May 1893 in possession of Simon, Earl of Woolton.

[256] Author in conversation with Rupert Lycett Green, grandson of Edward Lycett Green, 24 February 2015.

[257] Author in conversation with the Earl of Woolton, great grandson of Gordon-Cumming.

[258] Author in conversation with Jane Gordon-Cumming, granddaughter of Gordon-Cumming, 6 March 2014.

EPILOGUE

259 David Brown, *The Times*, 9 October 2014

26788385R00134

Printed in Great Britain
by Amazon